NEW JERSEY PETITIONS 1740, 1745 THROUGH 1754

(Petitions 1740 begin on page 8)

(Petitions 1745-1754 begin on page 17)

Copyright 18 March 2021
Stemmons Publishing
1078 Shields Lane
South Jordan, Utah 84095

INTRODUCTION

1006-NEW JERSEY PETITIONS 1740, 1745 THROUGH 1754 It contains 740 entries for a period of time in New Jersey when records are sparse. It includes but is not limit to petitions regarding:

- Issues regarding exports and imports.
- Issues regarding devaluation of currency, money supply, etc.
- Issues regarding local agencies, boundary changes, etc.
- Seeking new legislation.
- Issues about military and government officers.
- Seeking resolution of land problems, etc.
- Protesting against the great number of taverns.
- Resolution of tax issues.
- Issues about crimes, pardon, amnesty, etc.

While that may not seem like very many names, it was during the time when the population was small, and the residence of people was sometimes hard to track. Even though a small percent of the heads of household of New Jersey during this period is listed in **NEW JERSEY PETITIONS 1740, 1745 THROUGH 1754**, this book can be very helpful, nonetheless.

In looking through these petitions, it appears that the people of this era had basically the same concerns we have. One can see the forces of democracy beginning to stir that were to result in independence from Great Britain just a short three decades away.

While not a comprehensive list of the inhabitants of the Province of New Jersey, the names in **NEW JERSEY PETITIONS 1740, 1745 THROUGH 1754** represent a beginning; a foundation upon which to build that will someday produce a valuable census of the population.

It is suggested that those using this book read through the section "List of Petitions" to obtain a flavor of the personal concerns of these people and what was important to them in this exciting historical time. Even at this time of great distress and hardship life had to go on. These petitions are almost like an open window into the lives of these people. Sometimes additional information on individual petitions will be included in this section. For information on how to obtain this book search by the title or "Books by John Stemmons" at Amazon.com. This comes automatically with a paperback binding.

Also helpful are the "Value of Petitions/Memorials (Signature Lists)" and "Guidelines for Entry of Names" sections.

The names are broken up into two parts, 1740, and 1745 through 1754. Within each part, the names are listed alphabetically.

Appreciation is extended to the New Jersey State Archives for their kind assistance in obtaining copies of these petitions. We hope that **NEW JERSEY PETITIONS 1740, 1745 THROUGH 1754** will be a helpful and productive addition to New Jersey research.

INDEXES

Indexes are expensive to compile.

Which is why many books do not have them. Most that do just have a simple name index. A noteworthy exception is the *Territorial Papers of the United States* which gives some limited context as explained below.

Indexes are expensive but using modern technology we at Stemmons Publishing have included nearly all the context you may need. 100% context is probably not possible such as in a census that lists multiple neighbors. Search for entries of the same page in our book(s) or the original document if you require more information.

PUBLICATIONS FROM STEMMONS PUBLISHING

These following publications are not just traditional alphabetical lists of names, they include the context of information with each name!!

Why is that so important? Because many of the names in our books were obtained from various sources including South Carolina jury lists, the *Territorial Papers of the United States* (28 volumes each with its own index), petitions, tax lists, etc., and like most books with indexes common names require a lot of time to check each entry in the index. Can you imagine how many Smiths you would have to go through page-by-page for a compilation the size of *Territorial Papers of the United States*? Their indexes provide some context such as signing a petition. No explanation is given of what, when, or why the petition was made. Because we have included the context with each name, you can easily search all the Smiths, Taylors, Browns, Williams, etc., without all the drudgery! And since most of us have common surnames, we may need some help. Now, the originals of the South Carolina jury lists are housed in the South Carolina Department of Archives and History. Therefore, you may not have access to the originals. The way we index names means it is almost as good as being at the Archives yourself and doubly so since these documents are loose papers and do not have an original index. Our books provide an enhanced way of using *Territorial Papers of the United States* that the original compilers did not envision. So, if you have this collection, your obtaining our books compiled from those volumes will help your access to *Territorial Papers of the United States* even if you are not interested in our books about South Carolina jury lists. Now, that's what I call achieving the potential of a real index! It takes the bare skeleton of a name on a list and covers it with the flesh, hair, eyes, etc., of a human body. The names are more able to stand alone by themselves than is the case with a traditional index. We did not index subjects. *Territorial Papers of the United States* did.

Checking a name from our books and going to the page in *Territorial Papers of the United States* will show the list of names. Those listed next to the person of interest may be neighbors and relatives.

List of Petitions

Petitions with 10 names or less without a date and locality were usually not included in this publication. Although we tried to copy all of those that were available, there may be some that we missed. Because the information for each petition below is a summary, the text of the original petition may contain additional details not provided in this list.

The pages may not be in the same order as found in the folder, but they are usually in the order that they were copied. Since most of the petitions do not have page numbers, they were supplied by the compiler. Because there were no page numbers on these documents, you may need to search one or more pages in order to find the name if you use the originals. You may not agree with our interpretation of the name. Often there was more than one column of names on each page. We extracted the beginning column first and then others in sequence. If a sheet of paper was affixed (with glue, etc.) to a page it was counted as one whole page. Some of the columns therefore could be quite long.

1. Petition, 11 Jun 1740, to the House of Representatives of New Jersey Province from "Freeholders Inhabitants of the County of Middlesex" seeking for a duty to be assessed upon any commodities imported into or exported from the province. New Jersey State Archives, *Manuscript Collection, 1680s-1970s, Legislative Records, 1724-1755, Box 1-12, Folder 13*. Three pages.

2. Petition, 12 Mar 1745/6, to the House of Representatives from freeholders of Cape May County complaining of the devaluation of their paper money [likely due in part to the present war] and asking for creation of a fund, apparently to stabilize it. New Jersey State Archives, *Manuscript Collection, 1680s-1970s, Legislative Records, 1724-1755*, Box 1-12, Folder 22. One page.

3. Petition, 10 Apr 1746, to the General Assembly from freeholders and inhabitants of Essex County seeking a repeal of acts for the preserving of timber and a duty on imported strong liquors. They cannot build ships because of the present war with France and Spain. New Jersey State Archives, *Manuscript Collection, 1680s-1970s, Legislative Records, 1724-1755*, Box 1-12, Folder 25. Two pages.

4. Petition, 12 Jan 1747/8, to Jonathan Belcher, Governor, from inhabitants of Bethlehem in Hunterdon County seeking to have the southerly part of Bethlehem Township made into a new township. New Jersey State Archives, *Legislature,-Petitions and Other Papers . . . Estab. of Municipal Boundaries*, Box 1, Folder 1. One page.

5. Petition, 18 Nov 1748, to the House of Representatives from inhabitants of Nottingham, Burlington County complaining of those hunting out of season who have killed their hogs and cattle. Sometimes people are in danger of being shot. New Jersey State Archives, *Manuscript Collection, 1680s-1970s, Legislative Records, 1724-1755*, Box 1-12, Folder 46. One page.

6. Petition, 1 Mar 1748/9, to the governor, etc., seeking passage of a law forbidding the killing of deer by dogs because the meat and hides are mostly worthless. New Jersey State Archives, *Manuscript Collection, 1680s-1970s, Governors' Papers, 1749-1785*, Box 1-1, Folder 4. One page.

7. Petition, 1748/9, to the House of Representatives from inhabitants freeholders of Hunterdon and Burlington Counties seeking for a law requiring every person to record their "Mortgage Deeds" to ensure validity of titles to land. New Jersey State Archives, *Manuscript Collection, 1680s-1970s, Oversized Legislative Papers (items #1-25)*, Box 1-43, Folder 2. One page.

8. Petition, 1750/1, the House of Representatives from inhabitants of the province protesting against the great number of taverns in the province. New Jersey State Archives, *Manuscript Collection, 1680s-1970s, Legislative Records, 1724-1755*, Box 1-12, Folder 59. One page.

9. Petition, 6 Oct 1751, to Governor Jonathan Belcher from owners of "Bloomaries" in Morris County seeking removal of a tax on their iron works (Bloomeries). Many make 5-6 tons or less a year. They seek instead for a bounty on all they produce. New Jersey State Archives, *Manuscript Collection, 1680s-1970s, State Library MSS Coll., #1-100,* Box 5-1, Folder 28. Two pages.
10. Petition, 30 May 1753, to the House of Representatives from inhabitants in and about Northampton who are requesting an increase in the amount of currency which is scarce. Gold and silver are chiefly transported elsewhere and are scarce also. New Jersey State Archives, *Manuscript Collection, 1680s-1970s, Legislative Records, 1724-1755,* Box 1-12, Folder 65. One page.
11. Petition, 24 Sep? 1753, to the House of Representatives from inhabitants of the province expressing distress because of a lack of currency as a medium of trade. They present various arguments for the value of a paper currency. New Jersey State Archives, *Manuscript Collection, 1680s-1970s, Oversized Legislative Papers (items #1-25),* Box 1-43, Folder 4. One page.
12. Petition, 1754, to the House of Representatives from freeholders of the province opposing the election of Samuel Nevell as a judge of the Supreme Court. New Jersey State Archives, *Manuscript Collection, 1680s-1970s, Legislative Records, 1724-1755,* Box 1-12, Folder 66. Four pages. [Page 2 is from Middlesex County.]
13. Petition, 1754, to the General Assembly from freeholders/inhabitants of Perth Amboy Township in Middlesex County opposing the election of Samuel Nevill as a judge of the Supreme Court. New Jersey State Archives, *Manuscript Collection, 1680s-1970s, Oversized Legislative Papers,* (Items #1-25), Box 1-43, Folder 2. One page.

Value of Petitions/Memorials (Signature Lists)

Among the most important information petitions and name lists (including censuses) can provide is the location of residence of individuals. Once the location of a person has been determined, a researcher can then study available records for that locality to find out more information about ancestors. But, in addition to residence, many other things can be learned.
1. Much information about an individual can be obtained from the signature such as:
    a. A wavy signature may be a sign of old age or potential health problems such as palsy.
    b. A signature with spelling or syntax problems (such as not capitalizing the beginning letter) may indicate the level of education of a person.
    c. Signatures that show skill in handwriting may indicate a higher level of education and social status.
    d. A slow deliberate writing may indicate age, health problems, and/or limited education.
    e. The spelling of the name may provide a clue on how the name was pronounced. Sometimes the pronunciation will indicate an accent that could suggest a country of origin. Using the Gothic script when signing one's name suggests the person was from one of the European countries such as Germany.
    f. Using an "x" or other character by the name sometimes with "his mark" or "her mark" usually indicates the person is illiterate. This information can be useful when trying to decide between individuals of the same name.

g. Sometimes additional information is given with the signature perhaps as a means of identifying persons of the same name. Occasionally the occupation, military rank, civic office, name of father, marital status of female signers, etc., may be identified.

h. Comparing the handwriting of a signature on a petition with signatures in other localities can identify individuals because their handwriting is similar. This is especially helpful when common names are involved.

i. Using handwriting analysis (Graphology) one may be able to determine some personality traits of an individual.

2. The text of the petition may provide details about the person(s) that signed it such as:

a. Persons with the same surname in close proximity on the petition may be related.

b. Insights into personal feelings, cultural settings, literacy, hardships, and historical details about an individual.

c. Information about individuals who lived in the area prior to its becoming a part of the United States.

d. Family history details may be include such as the following quote from an actual petition dated 10 Nov 1773: ". . . for in ancient times when our Ancestors Settled the Town of Bergen they was under the Necessity of Settling Together on account of the Natives of the Country and their Lands laid out in Such Narrow Lotts in general from fourteen to Eighteen Dutch Rods in width In all running about A Northwest Course So that a road as aforesaid would Cut those Narrow Lotts Cattecorners and make A vast many of So little value to their Proper owners that it would be hardly worth their while to keep them in fence" . (New Jersey State Archives, *R. Group: Legislature, Series: Petitions re Bridges, Canals, Dams, Ferries and Roads, 1765-1835, Loose Papers Relating to Roads,* Box 4, Folder 3.) Not only does this statement provide historical details about the challenges experienced by the first settlers of Bergen, New Jersey, it also indicates that those who signed the petition descended from those early pioneers implying that they and their ancestors have lived in the area from the beginning. Thus one may not need to find a place of origin for many that signed the petition because it should be the area in and around Bergen.

e. By tracking names in petitions over a period of time one may be able to determine migration patterns of family members especially if an individual shows up on an earlier petition in one area, and somewhere else on a later petition.

f. Petitions may also be available to help replace records destroyed in courthouse fires, etc.

Please note:

It is important to realize that the variety of spellings for names from signature lists is unusually large. Often these people who signed the petition were so creative in spelling their name that one may miss important entries when relying on traditional ways of alphabetizing. To correct this weakness, sometimes it is necessary to go through every entry.

Guidelines for Entry of Names

Many times, names have been difficult to decipher. Other times, the document itself has been damaged in various ways that impacted our ability to read the information. Several methods have been employed to indicate to the reader when we had difficulty. They are as follows:

1. When a surname has been difficult to determine and could be read alternately, we have indicated this by using two and sometimes three possibilities. For example, Rud or Ried. For your convenience we have made separate entries for each possibility: Rud or Ried and Ried or Rud. We encourage individuals to go to the original source and make a determination for themselves if the name is important for their research. For given names, we will also indicate more than one possibility, but will not make separate entries for each one.

2. When an undetermined number of letters were unreadable, we used the ellipsis ". . ." in place of the letters we could not decipher, while we included those characters we could read. For example: Cr . . . [surname] and . . . seph [given name]. It would be difficult to determine the surname with confidence, but the given name is most likely "Joseph".

3. When a known number of characters could not be read, an asterisk "*" was used in place of each letter we could not decipher. Often the name can be determined based on where the asterisk is placed. For example, with Brow* one can readily determine the name is most likely Brown. However, when one or more asterisks are placed at the beginning of a name, the possibilities become more numerous and therefore difficult to determine.

4. When we were unsure about the reading, we would include a question mark "?" after the name.

5. Sometimes we could not read the name because the writing was too faint, it was covered with ink blotches, portions of the document was damaged/missing, or for many other reasons. We tried to indicate this when we felt a name was there by using "[Unreadable]", "[Missing]", "[Illegible]", "[Name crossed out]", etc., in place of the name. In some cases, a name might be read by examining carefully the original document.

6. When the first letter was obviously wrong and would interfere in a researcher's ability to readily see the name, we have placed in brackets what we thought the name should be along with the spelling of the name in the original. One can use the search feature on the Internet to find these names. An example is Knewkurk [Newkirk], Richard. A researcher might never know to look under the spelling Knewkurk and therefore miss potentially vital information. By searching for the name Newkirk, one would find this entry.

7. Sometimes it is difficult to tell which is the given name and which is the surname. When there has been doubt about the proper order of given name/surname, we have made an entry such as: Everet or Jones, [surname], and Jones or Everet [given name]. Then we have made another entry with the names reversed such as Jones or Everet [surname], and Everet or Jones [given name].

When deciphering entries, we have always tried to err on the side of reasonable, known, practical, and possible names rather than unreasonable, impossible, or impractical spellings.

There are 97 entries.

ALLWARD, James, Middlesex County, - Name on petition, 11 Jun 1740, to the House of Representatives of New Jersey Province from "Freeholders Inhabitants of the County of Middlesex" seeking for a duty to be assessed upon any commodities imported into or exported from the province.- *Manuscript Collection-Legislative Records [New Jersey State Archives],* Box 1-12, Folder 13, pg. 2.

Allward, James, Male -He signed his name with an "x".

ALLWARD, John, Middlesex County, - Name on petition, 11 Jun 1740, to the House of Representatives of New Jersey Province from "Freeholders Inhabitants of the County of Middlesex" seeking for a duty to be assessed upon any commodities imported into or exported from the province.- *Manuscript Collection-Legislative Records [New Jersey State Archives],* Box 1-12, Folder 13, pg. 2.

Allward, John, Male

BARLOW, Thos, Middlesex County, - Name on petition, 11 Jun 1740, to the House of Representatives of New Jersey Province from "Freeholders Inhabitants of the County of Middlesex" seeking for a duty to be assessed upon any commodities imported into or exported from the province.- *Manuscript Collection-Legislative Records [New Jersey State Archives],* Box 1-12, Folder 13, pg. 2.

Barlow, Thos, Male

BEVERADGE, John, Middlesex County, - Name on petition, 11 Jun 1740, to the House of Representatives of New Jersey Province from "Freeholders Inhabitants of the County of Middlesex" seeking for a duty to be assessed upon any commodities imported into or exported from the province.- *Manuscript Collection-Legislative Records [New Jersey State Archives],* Box 1-12, Folder 13, pg. 3.

Beveradge, John, Male

BISHOP, Richard, Middlesex County, - Name on petition, 11 Jun 1740, to the House of Representatives of New Jersey Province from "Freeholders Inhabitants of the County of Middlesex" seeking for a duty to be assessed upon any commodities imported into or exported from the province.- *Manuscript Collection-Legislative Records [New Jersey State Archives],* Box 1-12, Folder 13, pg. 3.

Bishop, Richard, Male

BONHAM, Zachariah, Middlesex County, - Name on petition, 11 Jun 1740, to the House of Representatives of New Jersey Province from "Freeholders Inhabitants of the County of Middlesex" seeking for a duty to be assessed upon any commodities imported into or exported from the province.- *Manuscript Collection-Legislative Records [New Jersey State Archives],* Box 1-12, Folder 13, pg. 3.

Bonham, Zachariah, Male

BREES?, Cornelius, Middlesex County, - Name on petition, 11 Jun 1740, to the House of Representatives of New Jersey Province from "Freeholders Inhabitants of the County of Middlesex" seeking for a duty to be assessed upon any commodities imported into or exported from the province.- *Manuscript Collection-Legislative Records [New Jersey State Archives],* Box 1-12, Folder 13, pg. 2.

Brees?, Cornelius, Male

BURNET, Will:, Middlesex County, - Name on petition, 11 Jun 1740, to the House of Representatives of New Jersey Province from "Freeholders Inhabitants of the County of Middlesex" seeking for a duty to be assessed upon any commodities imported into or exported from the province.- *Manuscript Collection-Legislative Records [New Jersey State Archives],* Box 1-12, Folder 13, pg. 2.

Burnet, Will:, Male

CAMEL, James, Middlesex County, - Name on petition, 11 Jun 1740, to the House of Representatives of New Jersey Province from "Freeholders Inhabitants of the County of Middlesex" seeking for a duty to be assessed upon any commodities imported into or exported from the province.- *Manuscript Collection-Legislative Records [New Jersey State Archives],* Box 1-12, Folder 13, pg. 3.

Camel, James, Male

CARMAN, Richard, Middlesex County, - Name on petition, 11 Jun 1740, to the House of Representatives of New Jersey Province from "Freeholders Inhabitants of the County of Middlesex" seeking for a duty to be assessed upon any commodities imported into or exported from the province.- *Manuscript Collection-Legislative Records [New Jersey State Archives],* Box 1-12, Folder 13, pg. 2.

Carman, Richard, Male

CAWOOD, Thomas, Middlesex County, - Name on petition, 11 Jun 1740, to the House of Representatives of New Jersey Province from "Freeholders Inhabitants of the County of Middlesex" seeking for a duty to be assessed upon any commodities imported into or exported from the province.- *Manuscript Collection-Legislative Records [New Jersey State Archives],* Box 1-12, Folder 13, pg. 2.

Cawood, Thomas, Male

CLARKSON, James, Middlesex County, - Name on petition, 11 Jun 1740, to the House of Representatives of New Jersey Province from "Freeholders Inhabitants of the County of Middlesex" seeking for a duty to be assessed upon any commodities imported into or exported from the province.- *Manuscript Collection-Legislative Records [New Jersey State Archives],* Box 1-12, Folder 13, pg. 3.

Clarkson, James, Male

CLARKSON, John, Middlesex County, - Name on petition, 11 Jun 1740, to the House of Representatives of New Jersey Province from "Freeholders Inhabitants of the County of Middlesex" seeking for a duty to be assessed upon any commodities imported into or exported from the province.- *Manuscript Collection-Legislative Records [New Jersey State Archives],* Box 1-12, Folder 13, pg. 3.

Clarkson, John, Male

CLOSSON, John, jun, Middlesex County, - Name on petition, 11 Jun 1740, to the House of Representatives of New Jersey Province from "Freeholders Inhabitants of the County of Middlesex" seeking for a duty to be assessed upon any commodities imported into or exported from the province.- *Manuscript Collection-Legislative Records [New Jersey State Archives],* Box 1-12, Folder 13, pg. 2.

Closson, John, jun, Male -He signed his name with an "x".

CLOSSON, John, sen, Middlesex County, - Name on petition, 11 Jun 1740, to the House of Representatives of New Jersey Province from "Freeholders Inhabitants of the County of Middlesex" seeking for a duty to be assessed upon any commodities imported into or exported from the province.- *Manuscript Collection-Legislative Records [New Jersey State Archives],* Box 1-12, Folder 13, pg. 2.

Closson, John, sen, Male -He signed his name with an "o".

COLLENS, Benjamin, Middlesex County, - Name on petition, 11 Jun 1740, to the House of Representatives of New Jersey Province from "Freeholders Inhabitants of the County of Middlesex" seeking for a duty to be assessed upon any commodities imported into or exported from the province.- *Manuscript Collection-Legislative Records [New Jersey State Archives],* Box 1-12, Folder 13, pg. 2.

Collens, Benjamin, Male

CRAWFORD, Andrew, Middlesex County, - Name on petition, 11 Jun 1740, to the House of Representatives of New Jersey Province from "Freeholders Inhabitants of the County of Middlesex" seeking for a duty to be assessed upon any commodities imported into or exported from the province.- *Manuscript Collection-Legislative Records [New Jersey State Archives],* Box 1-12, Folder 13, pg. 2.

Crawford, Andrew, Male

CUTLER OR CUTTER, Richd, Middlesex County, - Name on petition, 11 Jun 1740, to the House of Representatives of New Jersey Province from "Freeholders Inhabitants of the County of Middlesex" seeking for a duty to be assessed upon any commodities imported into or exported from the province.- *Manuscript Collection-Legislative Records [New Jersey State Archives],* Box 1-12, Folder 13, pg. 3.

Cutler or Cutter, Richd, Male

CUTTER OR CUTLER, Richd, Middlesex County, - Name on petition, 11 Jun 1740, to the House of Representatives of New Jersey Province from "Freeholders Inhabitants of the County of Middlesex" seeking for a duty to be assessed upon any commodities imported into or exported from the province.- *Manuscript Collection-Legislative Records [New Jersey State Archives],* Box 1-12, Folder 13, pg. 3.

Cutter or Cutler, Richd, Male

DE GRAIT?, johannes, Middlesex County, - Name on petition, 11 Jun 1740, to the House of Representatives of New Jersey Province from "Freeholders Inhabitants of the County of Middlesex" seeking for a duty to be assessed upon any commodities imported into or exported from the province.- *Manuscript Collection-Legislative Records [New Jersey State Archives],* Box 1-12, Folder 13, pg. 3.

De Grait?, johannes, Male

DICKY?, Jacob, Middlesex County, - Name on petition, 11 Jun 1740, to the House of Representatives of New Jersey Province from "Freeholders Inhabitants of the County of Middlesex" seeking for a duty to be assessed upon any commodities imported into or exported from the province.- *Manuscript Collection-Legislative Records [New Jersey State Archives],* Box 1-12, Folder 13, pg. 3.

dicky?, Jacob, Male

DRAKE, Abraham, jun., Middlesex County, - Name on petition, 11 Jun 1740, to the House of Representatives of New Jersey Province from "Freeholders Inhabitants of the County of Middlesex" seeking for a duty to be assessed upon any commodities imported into or exported from the province.- *Manuscript Collection-Legislative Records [New Jersey State Archives],* Box 1-12, Folder 13, pg. 3.

Drake, Abraham, jun., Male

DRAKE, Abraham, Sen, Middlesex County, - Name on petition, 11 Jun 1740, to the House of Representatives of New Jersey Province from "Freeholders Inhabitants of the County of Middlesex" seeking for a duty to be assessed upon any commodities imported into or exported from the province.- *Manuscript Collection-Legislative Records [New Jersey State Archives],* Box 1-12, Folder 13, pg. 3.

Drake, Abraham, Sen, Male

DRAKE, Andreu, Middlesex County, - Name on petition, 11 Jun 1740, to the House of Representatives of New Jersey Province from "Freeholders Inhabitants of the County of Middlesex" seeking for a duty to be assessed upon any commodities imported into or exported from the province.- *Manuscript Collection-Legislative Records [New Jersey State Archives],* Box 1-12, Folder 13, pg. 3.

Drake, Andreu, Male

DRAKE, Daniel, Middlesex County, - Name on petition, 11 Jun 1740, to the House of Representatives of New Jersey Province from "Freeholders Inhabitants of the County of Middlesex" seeking for a duty to be assessed upon any commodities imported into or exported from the province.- *Manuscript Collection-Legislative Records [New Jersey State Archives],* Box 1-12, Folder 13, pg. 3.

Drake, Daniel, Male

DRAKE, Ebenezer, Middlesex County, - Name on petition, 11 Jun 1740, to the House of Representatives of New Jersey Province from "Freeholders Inhabitants of the County of Middlesex" seeking for a duty to be assessed upon any commodities imported into or exported from the province.- *Manuscript Collection-Legislative Records [New Jersey State Archives],* Box 1-12, Folder 13, pg. 3.

Drake, Ebenezer, Male

DRAKE, Jeremiah, Middlesex County, - Name on petition, 11 Jun 1740, to the House of Representatives of New Jersey Province from "Freeholders Inhabitants of the County of Middlesex" seeking for a duty to be assessed upon any commodities imported into or exported from the province.- *Manuscript Collection-Legislative Records [New Jersey State Archives],* Box 1-12, Folder 13, pg. 3.

Drake, Jeremiah, Male

DUNHAM, Edmund, Middlesex County, - Name on petition, 11 Jun 1740, to the House of Representatives of New Jersey Province from "Freeholders Inhabitants of the County of Middlesex" seeking for a duty to be assessed upon any commodities imported into or exported from the province.- *Manuscript Collection-Legislative Records [New Jersey State Archives],* Box 1-12, Folder 13, pg. 3.

Dunham, Edmund, Male

DUNN?, Phineas, Middlesex County, - Name on petition, 11 Jun 1740, to the House of Representatives of New Jersey Province from "Freeholders Inhabitants of the County of Middlesex" seeking for a duty to be assessed upon any commodities imported into or exported from the province.- *Manuscript Collection-Legislative Records [New Jersey State Archives],* Box 1-12, Folder 13, pg. 3.

dunn?, Phineas, Male

DUNSTUR?, Dal Dom, Middlesex County, - Name on petition, 11 Jun 1740, to the House of Representatives of New Jersey Province from "Freeholders Inhabitants of the County of Middlesex" seeking for a duty to be assessed upon any commodities imported into or exported from the province.- *Manuscript Collection-Legislative Records [New Jersey State Archives],* Box 1-12, Folder 13, pg. 3.

Dunstur?, Dal Dom, Male

FITCH RANDOLPH, moses, Middlesex County, - Name on petition, 11 Jun 1740, to the House of Representatives of New Jersey Province from "Freeholders Inhabitants of the County of Middlesex" seeking for a duty to be assessed upon any commodities imported into or exported from the province.- *Manuscript Collection-Legislative Records [New Jersey State Archives],* Box 1-12, Folder 13, pg. 3.

fitch randolph, moses, Male

FITZRANDOLPH, Jonathan, Middlesex County, - Name on petition, 11 Jun 1740, to the House of Representatives of New Jersey Province from "Freeholders Inhabitants of the County of Middlesex" seeking for a duty to be assessed upon any commodities imported into or exported from the province.- *Manuscript Collection-Legislative Records [New Jersey State Archives],* Box 1-12, Folder 13, pg. 3.

Fitzrandolph, Jonathan, Male

FITZRANDOLPH, Joseph, Middlesex County, - Name on petition, 11 Jun 1740, to the House of Representatives of New Jersey Province from "Freeholders Inhabitants of the County of Middlesex" seeking for a duty to be assessed upon any commodities imported into or exported from the province.- *Manuscript Collection-Legislative Records [New Jersey State Archives],* Box 1-12, Folder 13, pg. 3.

Fitzrandolph, Joseph, Male

GEDDER?, John, Middlesex County, - Name on petition, 11 Jun 1740, to the House of Representatives of New Jersey Province from "Freeholders Inhabitants of the County of Middlesex" seeking for a duty to be assessed upon any commodities imported into or exported from the province.- *Manuscript Collection-Legislative Records [New Jersey State Archives],* Box 1-12, Folder 13, pg. 2.

Gedder?, John, Male

GOOD?, Samll, Middlesex County, - Name on petition, 11 Jun 1740, to the House of Representatives of New Jersey Province from "Freeholders Inhabitants of the County of Middlesex" seeking for a duty to be assessed upon any commodities imported into or exported from the province.- *Manuscript Collection-Legislative Records [New Jersey State Archives],* Box 1-12, Folder 13, pg. 2.

Good?, Samll, Male

GOODFELLOW, Timothy, Middlesex County, - Name on petition, 11 Jun 1740, to the House of Representatives of New Jersey Province from "Freeholders Inhabitants of the County of Middlesex" seeking for a duty to be assessed upon any commodities imported into or exported from the province.- *Manuscript Collection-Legislative Records [New Jersey State Archives],* Box 1-12, Folder 13, pg. 2.

Goodfellow, Timothy, Male

GROSMAN?, Henry, Middlesex County, - Name on petition, 11 Jun 1740, to the House of Representatives of New Jersey Province from "Freeholders Inhabitants of the County of Middlesex" seeking for a duty to be assessed upon any commodities imported into or exported from the province.- *Manuscript Collection-Legislative Records [New Jersey State Archives],* Box 1-12, Folder 13, pg. 3.

grosman?, Henry, Male

HARPER?, Jerimiah, Middlesex County, - Name on petition, 11 Jun 1740, to the House of Representatives of New Jersey Province from "Freeholders Inhabitants of the County of Middlesex" seeking for a duty to be assessed upon any commodities imported into or exported from the province.- *Manuscript Collection-Legislative Records [New Jersey State Archives],* Box 1-12, Folder 13, pg. 2.

Harper?, Jerimiah, Male

HARTWICK, Lowrance, Middlesex County, - Name on petition, 11 Jun 1740, to the House of Representatives of New Jersey Province from "Freeholders Inhabitants of the County of Middlesex" seeking for a duty to be assessed upon any commodities imported into or exported from the province.- *Manuscript Collection-Legislative Records [New Jersey State Archives],* Box 1-12, Folder 13, pg. 3.

Hartwick, Lowrance, Male

HAYWOOD, James, Middlesex County, - Name on petition, 11 Jun 1740, to the House of Representatives of New Jersey Province from "Freeholders Inhabitants of the County of Middlesex" seeking for a duty to be assessed upon any commodities imported into or exported from the province.- *Manuscript Collection-Legislative Records [New Jersey State Archives],* Box 1-12, Folder 13, pg. 3.

Haywood, James, Male

HERBURN, John, Middlesex County, - Name on petition, 11 Jun 1740, to the House of Representatives of New Jersey Province from "Freeholders Inhabitants of the County of Middlesex" seeking for a duty to be assessed upon any commodities imported into or exported from the province.- *Manuscript Collection-Legislative Records [New Jersey State Archives],* Box 1-12, Folder 13, pg. 3.

herburn, John, Male

HICKSTUN?, Jonathan, Middlesex County, - Name on petition, 11 Jun 1740, to the House of Representatives of New Jersey Province from "Freeholders Inhabitants of the County of Middlesex" seeking for a duty to be assessed upon any commodities imported into or exported from the province.- *Manuscript Collection-Legislative Records [New Jersey State Archives],* Box 1-12, Folder 13, pg. 3.

Hickstun?, Jonathan, Male

HIGGINS, Jediah, Middlesex County, - Name on petition, 11 Jun 1740, to the House of Representatives of New Jersey Province from "Freeholders Inhabitants of the County of Middlesex" seeking for a duty to be assessed upon any commodities imported into or exported from the province.- *Manuscript Collection-Legislative Records [New Jersey State Archives],* Box 1-12, Folder 13, pg. 2.

Higgins, Jediah, Male

HOOPER, James, Middlesex County, - Name on petition, 11 Jun 1740, to the House of Representatives of New Jersey Province from "Freeholders Inhabitants of the County of Middlesex" seeking for a duty to be assessed upon any commodities imported into or exported from the province.- *Manuscript Collection-Legislative Records [New Jersey State Archives],* Box 1-12, Folder 13, pg. 3.

Hooper, James, Male

HOWLL?, Ben, Middlesex County, - Name on petition, 11 Jun 1740, to the House of Representatives of New Jersey Province from "Freeholders Inhabitants of the County of Middlesex" seeking for a duty to be assessed upon any commodities imported into or exported from the province.- *Manuscript Collection-Legislative Records [New Jersey State Archives],* Box 1-12, Folder 13, pg. 2.

Howll?, Ben, Male

INSLEE, Jonathan, Middlesex County, - Name on petition, 11 Jun 1740, to the House of Representatives of New Jersey Province from "Freeholders Inhabitants of the County of Middlesex" seeking for a duty to be assessed upon any commodities imported into or exported from the province.- *Manuscript Collection-Legislative Records [New Jersey State Archives],* Box 1-12, Folder 13, pg. 3.

Inslee, Jonathan, Male

JENNINGS, John, Middlesex County, - Name on petition, 11 Jun 1740, to the House of Representatives of New Jersey Province from "Freeholders Inhabitants of the County of Middlesex" seeking for a duty to be assessed upon any commodities imported into or exported from the province.- *Manuscript Collection-Legislative Records [New Jersey State Archives],* Box 1-12, Folder 13, pg. 3.

Jennings, John, Male

JOHNSON, Joseph, Middlesex County, - Name on petition, 11 Jun 1740, to the House of Representatives of New Jersey Province from "Freeholders Inhabitants of the County of Middlesex" seeking for a duty to be assessed upon any commodities imported into or exported from the province.- *Manuscript Collection-Legislative Records [New Jersey State Archives],* Box 1-12, Folder 13, pg. 2.

Johnson, Joseph, Male

KENT, David, Ju, Middlesex County, - Name on petition, 11 Jun 1740, to the House of Representatives of New Jersey Province from "Freeholders Inhabitants of the County of Middlesex" seeking for a duty to be assessed upon any commodities imported into or exported from the province.- *Manuscript Collection-Legislative Records [New Jersey State Archives],* Box 1-12, Folder 13, pg. 3.

Kent, David, Ju, Male

KENT, David, Senr, Middlesex County, - Name on petition, 11 Jun 1740, to the House of Representatives of New Jersey Province from "Freeholders Inhabitants of the County of Middlesex" seeking for a duty to be assessed upon any commodities imported into or exported from the province.- *Manuscript Collection-Legislative Records [New Jersey State Archives],* Box 1-12, Folder 13, pg. 2.

Kent, David, Senr, Male

KENT, William, Middlesex County, - Name on petition, 11 Jun 1740, to the House of Representatives of New Jersey Province from "Freeholders Inhabitants of the County of Middlesex" seeking for a duty to be assessed upon any commodities imported into or exported from the province.- *Manuscript Collection-Legislative Records [New Jersey State Archives],* Box 1-12, Folder 13, pg. 2.

Kent, William, Male

LESTER?, Gerit, Middlesex County, - Name on petition, 11 Jun 1740, to the House of Representatives of New Jersey Province from "Freeholders Inhabitants of the County of Middlesex" seeking for a duty to be assessed upon any commodities imported into or exported from the province.- *Manuscript Collection-Legislative Records [New Jersey State Archives],* Box 1-12, Folder 13, pg. 3.

Lester?, Gerit, Male

LOOSSBOURROW, Nathan, Middlesex County, - Name on petition, 11 Jun 1740, to the House of Representatives of New Jersey Province from "Freeholders Inhabitants of the County of Middlesex" seeking for a duty to be assessed upon any commodities imported into or exported from the province.- *Manuscript Collection-Legislative Records [New Jersey State Archives],* Box 1-12, Folder 13, pg. 3.

loossbourrow, Nathan, Male

MANNING, Isaac?, Middlesex County, - Name on petition, 11 Jun 1740, to the House of Representatives of New Jersey Province from "Freeholders Inhabitants of the County of Middlesex" seeking for a duty to be assessed upon any commodities imported into or exported from the province.- *Manuscript Collection-Legislative Records [New Jersey State Archives],* Box 1-12, Folder 13, pg. 3.

manning, Isaac?, Male

MANNING, James, Middlesex County, - Name on petition, 11 Jun 1740, to the House of Representatives of New Jersey Province from "Freeholders Inhabitants of the County of Middlesex" seeking for a duty to be assessed upon any commodities imported into or exported from the province.- *Manuscript Collection-Legislative Records [New Jersey State Archives],* Box 1-12, Folder 13, pg. 3.

Manning, James, Male

MANNING, Jethro, Middlesex County, - Name on petition, 11 Jun 1740, to the House of Representatives of New Jersey Province from "Freeholders Inhabitants of the County of Middlesex" seeking for a duty to be assessed upon any commodities imported into or exported from the province.- *Manuscript Collection-Legislative Records [New Jersey State Archives],* Box 1-12, Folder 13, pg. 3.

Manning, Jethro, Male

MANNING, Trisstmom?, Middlesex County, - Name on petition, 11 Jun 1740, to the House of Representatives of New Jersey Province from "Freeholders Inhabitants of the County of Middlesex" seeking for a duty to be assessed upon any commodities imported into or exported from the province.- *Manuscript Collection-Legislative Records [New Jersey State Archives],* Box 1-12, Folder 13, pg. 3.

Manning, Trisstmom?, Male

MARSH, Joseph, Middlesex County, - Name on petition, 11 Jun 1740, to the House of Representatives of New Jersey Province from "Freeholders Inhabitants of the County of Middlesex" seeking for a duty to be assessed upon any commodities imported into or exported from the province.- *Manuscript Collection-Legislative Records [New Jersey State Archives],* Box 1-12, Folder 13, pg. 3.

Marsh, Joseph, Male

MARTIN, Benjamin, Middlesex County, - Name on petition, 11 Jun 1740, to the House of Representatives of New Jersey Province from "Freeholders Inhabitants of the County of Middlesex" seeking for a duty to be assessed upon any commodities imported into or exported from the province.- *Manuscript Collection-Legislative Records [New Jersey State Archives],* Box 1-12, Folder 13, pg. 3.
  Martin, Benjamin, Male

MARTIN, Jonthan, Middlesex County, - Name on petition, 11 Jun 1740, to the House of Representatives of New Jersey Province from "Freeholders Inhabitants of the County of Middlesex" seeking for a duty to be assessed upon any commodities imported into or exported from the province.- *Manuscript Collection-Legislative Records [New Jersey State Archives],* Box 1-12, Folder 13, pg. 2.
  Martin, Jonthan, Male

MARTIN, Moses, Middlesex County, - Name on petition, 11 Jun 1740, to the House of Representatives of New Jersey Province from "Freeholders Inhabitants of the County of Middlesex" seeking for a duty to be assessed upon any commodities imported into or exported from the province.- *Manuscript Collection-Legislative Records [New Jersey State Archives],* Box 1-12, Folder 13, pg. 3.
  Martin, Moses, Male

MOORES, Samll, Middlesex County, - Name on petition, 11 Jun 1740, to the House of Representatives of New Jersey Province from "Freeholders Inhabitants of the County of Middlesex" seeking for a duty to be assessed upon any commodities imported into or exported from the province.- *Manuscript Collection-Legislative Records [New Jersey State Archives],* Box 1-12, Folder 13, pg. 3.
  Moores, Samll, Male

MOORES, Thomas, Middlesex County, - Name on petition, 11 Jun 1740, to the House of Representatives of New Jersey Province from "Freeholders Inhabitants of the County of Middlesex" seeking for a duty to be assessed upon any commodities imported into or exported from the province.- *Manuscript Collection-Legislative Records [New Jersey State Archives],* Box 1-12, Folder 13, pg. 3.
  moores, Thomas, Male

MUNDY, John, Middlesex County, - Name on petition, 11 Jun 1740, to the House of Representatives of New Jersey Province from "Freeholders Inhabitants of the County of Middlesex" seeking for a duty to be assessed upon any commodities imported into or exported from the province.- *Manuscript Collection-Legislative Records [New Jersey State Archives],* Box 1-12, Folder 13, pg. 3.
  Mundy, John, Male

MUNDY, Thomas, Middlesex County, - Name on petition, 11 Jun 1740, to the House of Representatives of New Jersey Province from "Freeholders Inhabitants of the County of Middlesex" seeking for a duty to be assessed upon any commodities imported into or exported from the province.- *Manuscript Collection-Legislative Records [New Jersey State Archives],* Box 1-12, Folder 13, pg. 3.
  Mundy, Thomas, Male

NEVILL, John, Middlesex County, - Name on petition, 11 Jun 1740, to the House of Representatives of New Jersey Province from "Freeholders Inhabitants of the County of Middlesex" seeking for a duty to be assessed upon any commodities imported into or exported from the province.- *Manuscript Collection-Legislative Records [New Jersey State Archives],* Box 1-12, Folder 13, pg. 3.
  Nevill, John, Male

NEVILL, Samuel, Middlesex County, - Name on petition, 11 Jun 1740, to the House of Representatives of New Jersey Province from "Freeholders Inhabitants of the County of Middlesex" seeking for a duty to be assessed upon any commodities imported into or exported from the province.- *Manuscript Collection-Legislative Records [New Jersey State Archives],* Box 1-12, Folder 13, pg. 2.
  Nevill, Samuel, Male

OAKE?, Wm, Middlesex County, - Name on petition, 11 Jun 1740, to the House of Representatives of New Jersey Province from "Freeholders Inhabitants of the County of Middlesex" seeking for a duty to be assessed upon any commodities imported into or exported from the province.- *Manuscript Collection-Legislative Records [New Jersey State Archives],* Box 1-12, Folder 13, pg. 2.
  Oake?, Wm, Male

PACK?, Thomas, Middlesex County, - Name on petition, 11 Jun 1740, to the House of Representatives of New Jersey Province from "Freeholders Inhabitants of the County of Middlesex" seeking for a duty to be assessed upon any commodities imported into or exported from the province.- *Manuscript Collection-Legislative Records [New Jersey State Archives],* Box 1-12, Folder 13, pg. 3.

Pack?, Thomas, Male

PATTON?, Henry, Middlesex County, - Name on petition, 11 Jun 1740, to the House of Representatives of New Jersey Province from "Freeholders Inhabitants of the County of Middlesex" seeking for a duty to be assessed upon any commodities imported into or exported from the province.- *Manuscript Collection-Legislative Records [New Jersey State Archives],* Box 1-12, Folder 13, pg. 2.

patton?, Henry, Male

POTTEN?, Phinehas, Middlesex County, - Name on petition, 11 Jun 1740, to the House of Representatives of New Jersey Province from "Freeholders Inhabitants of the County of Middlesex" seeking for a duty to be assessed upon any commodities imported into or exported from the province.- *Manuscript Collection-Legislative Records [New Jersey State Archives],* Box 1-12, Folder 13, pg. 3.

Potten?, Phinehas, Male

RUCKALOO, Peter, Middlesex County, - Name on petition, 11 Jun 1740, to the House of Representatives of New Jersey Province from "Freeholders Inhabitants of the County of Middlesex" seeking for a duty to be assessed upon any commodities imported into or exported from the province.- *Manuscript Collection-Legislative Records [New Jersey State Archives],* Box 1-12, Folder 13, pg. 3.

Ruckaloo, Peter, Male

RUNION, Peter, Middlesex County, - Name on petition, 11 Jun 1740, to the House of Representatives of New Jersey Province from "Freeholders Inhabitants of the County of Middlesex" seeking for a duty to be assessed upon any commodities imported into or exported from the province.- *Manuscript Collection-Legislative Records [New Jersey State Archives],* Box 1-12, Folder 13, pg. 3.

Runion, Peter, Male

SALTAR?, Ebenezar, Middlesex County, - Name on petition, 11 Jun 1740, to the House of Representatives of New Jersey Province from "Freeholders Inhabitants of the County of Middlesex" seeking for a duty to be assessed upon any commodities imported into or exported from the province.- *Manuscript Collection-Legislative Records [New Jersey State Archives],* Box 1-12, Folder 13, pg. 2.

Saltar?, Ebenezar, Male

SCHUYLER, Dh?, Middlesex County, - Name on petition, 11 Jun 1740, to the House of Representatives of New Jersey Province from "Freeholders Inhabitants of the County of Middlesex" seeking for a duty to be assessed upon any commodities imported into or exported from the province.- *Manuscript Collection-Legislative Records [New Jersey State Archives],* Box 1-12, Folder 13, pg. 3.

Schuyler, Dh?, Male

SHIPPY, Ishmael, Middlesex County, - Name on petition, 11 Jun 1740, to the House of Representatives of New Jersey Province from "Freeholders Inhabitants of the County of Middlesex" seeking for a duty to be assessed upon any commodities imported into or exported from the province.- *Manuscript Collection-Legislative Records [New Jersey State Archives],* Box 1-12, Folder 13, pg. 2.

Shippy, Ishmael, Male

SHOTWELL, John, Middlesex County, - Name on petition, 11 Jun 1740, to the House of Representatives of New Jersey Province from "Freeholders Inhabitants of the County of Middlesex" seeking for a duty to be assessed upon any commodities imported into or exported from the province.- *Manuscript Collection-Legislative Records [New Jersey State Archives],* Box 1-12, Folder 13, pg. 3.

Shotwell, John, Male

SMALLEY, Elisha, Middlesex County, - Name on petition, 11 Jun 1740, to the House of Representatives of New Jersey Province from "Freeholders Inhabitants of the County of Middlesex" seeking for a duty to be assessed upon any commodities imported into or exported from the province.- *Manuscript Collection-Legislative Records [New Jersey State Archives],* Box 1-12, Folder 13, pg. 2.

Smalley, Elisha, Male

SMATHRS?, Robert?, Middlesex County, - Name on petition, 11 Jun 1740, to the House of Representatives of New Jersey Province from "Freeholders Inhabitants of the County of Middlesex" seeking for a duty to be assessed upon any commodities imported into or exported from the province.- *Manuscript Collection-Legislative Records [New Jersey State Archives],* Box 1-12, Folder 13, pg. 3.

Smathrs?, Robert?, Male

STANFORD, John, Middlesex County, - Name on petition, 11 Jun 1740, to the House of Representatives of New Jersey Province from "Freeholders Inhabitants of the County of Middlesex" seeking for a duty to be assessed upon any commodities imported into or exported from the province.- *Manuscript Collection-Legislative Records [New Jersey State Archives],* Box 1-12, Folder 13, pg. 3.

Stanford, John, Male

STOLLE?, Benjn:, Middlesex County, - Name on petition, 11 Jun 1740, to the House of Representatives of New Jersey Province from "Freeholders Inhabitants of the County of Middlesex" seeking for a duty to be assessed upon any commodities imported into or exported from the province.- *Manuscript Collection-Legislative Records [New Jersey State Archives],* Box 1-12, Folder 13, pg. 3.

Stolle?, Benjn:, Male

STOORD?, Oswald, Middlesex County, - Name on petition, 11 Jun 1740, to the House of Representatives of New Jersey Province from "Freeholders Inhabitants of the County of Middlesex" seeking for a duty to be assessed upon any commodities imported into or exported from the province.- *Manuscript Collection-Legislative Records [New Jersey State Archives],* Box 1-12, Folder 13, pg. 3.

Stoord?, Oswald, Male

THORP, Benjamin, Middlesex County, - Name on petition, 11 Jun 1740, to the House of Representatives of New Jersey Province from "Freeholders Inhabitants of the County of Middlesex" seeking for a duty to be assessed upon any commodities imported into or exported from the province.- *Manuscript Collection-Legislative Records [New Jersey State Archives],* Box 1-12, Folder 13, pg. 2.

Thorp, Benjamin, Male

THORP, Norris, Middlesex County, - Name on petition, 11 Jun 1740, to the House of Representatives of New Jersey Province from "Freeholders Inhabitants of the County of Middlesex" seeking for a duty to be assessed upon any commodities imported into or exported from the province.- *Manuscript Collection-Legislative Records [New Jersey State Archives],* Box 1-12, Folder 13, pg. 3.

Thorp, Norris, Male

TRUDE?, Ac, Middlesex County, - Name on petition, 11 Jun 1740, to the House of Representatives of New Jersey Province from "Freeholders Inhabitants of the County of Middlesex" seeking for a duty to be assessed upon any commodities imported into or exported from the province.- *Manuscript Collection-Legislative Records [New Jersey State Archives],* Box 1-12, Folder 13, pg. 2.

Trude?, Ac, Male

VAN AUSDALEN, Dirck, Middlesex County, - Name on petition, 11 Jun 1740, to the House of Representatives of New Jersey Province from "Freeholders Inhabitants of the County of Middlesex" seeking for a duty to be assessed upon any commodities imported into or exported from the province.- *Manuscript Collection-Legislative Records [New Jersey State Archives],* Box 1-12, Folder 13, pg. 3.

van ausdalen, Dirck, Male

VAN DURREN, Henry, Middlesex County, - Name on petition, 11 Jun 1740, to the House of Representatives of New Jersey Province from "Freeholders Inhabitants of the County of Middlesex" seeking for a duty to be assessed upon any commodities imported into or exported from the province.- *Manuscript Collection-Legislative Records [New Jersey State Archives],* Box 1-12, Folder 13, pg. 3.

van Durren, Henry, Male

WALKER, Saml, Middlesex County, - Name on petition, 11 Jun 1740, to the House of Representatives of New Jersey Province from "Freeholders Inhabitants of the County of Middlesex" seeking for a duty to be assessed upon any commodities imported into or exported from the province.- *Manuscript Collection-Legislative Records [New Jersey State Archives],* Box 1-12, Folder 13, pg. 2.

Walker, Saml, Male

WALKER, Saml, Junr, Middlesex County, - Name on petition, 11 Jun 1740, to the House of Representatives of New Jersey Province from "Freeholders Inhabitants of the County of Middlesex" seeking for a duty to be assessed upon any commodities imported into or exported from the province.- *Manuscript Collection-Legislative Records [New Jersey State Archives],* Box 1-12, Folder 13, pg. 2.
Walker, Saml, Junr, Male

WALKER, Thos, Middlesex County, - Name on petition, 11 Jun 1740, to the House of Representatives of New Jersey Province from "Freeholders Inhabitants of the County of Middlesex" seeking for a duty to be assessed upon any commodities imported into or exported from the province.- *Manuscript Collection-Legislative Records [New Jersey State Archives],* Box 1-12, Folder 13, pg. 2.
Walker, Thos, Male

WARNE, Samell, Middlesex County, - Name on petition, 11 Jun 1740, to the House of Representatives of New Jersey Province from "Freeholders Inhabitants of the County of Middlesex" seeking for a duty to be assessed upon any commodities imported into or exported from the province.- *Manuscript Collection-Legislative Records [New Jersey State Archives],* Box 1-12, Folder 13, pg. 3.
Warne, Samell, Male

WATSON, John, Middlesex County, - Name on petition, 11 Jun 1740, to the House of Representatives of New Jersey Province from "Freeholders Inhabitants of the County of Middlesex" seeking for a duty to be assessed upon any commodities imported into or exported from the province.- *Manuscript Collection-Legislative Records [New Jersey State Archives],* Box 1-12, Folder 13, pg. 2.
Watson, John, Male

WEBB, G?, Middlesex County, - Name on petition, 11 Jun 1740, to the House of Representatives of New Jersey Province from "Freeholders Inhabitants of the County of Middlesex" seeking for a duty to be assessed upon any commodities imported into or exported from the province.- *Manuscript Collection-Legislative Records [New Jersey State Archives],* Box 1-12, Folder 13, pg. 3.
Webb, G?, Male

WEEKES, Zachars:, Middlesex County, - Name on petition, 11 Jun 1740, to the House of Representatives of New Jersey Province from "Freeholders Inhabitants of the County of Middlesex" seeking for a duty to be assessed upon any commodities imported into or exported from the province.- *Manuscript Collection-Legislative Records [New Jersey State Archives],* Box 1-12, Folder 13, pg. 3.
Weekes, Zachars:, Male

WHITLOCK, John, Middlesex County, - Name on petition, 11 Jun 1740, to the House of Representatives of New Jersey Province from "Freeholders Inhabitants of the County of Middlesex" seeking for a duty to be assessed upon any commodities imported into or exported from the province.- *Manuscript Collection-Legislative Records [New Jersey State Archives],* Box 1-12, Folder 13, pg. 3.
Whitlock, John, Male

WILLIAMS, Joseph, Middlesex County, - Name on petition, 11 Jun 1740, to the House of Representatives of New Jersey Province from "Freeholders Inhabitants of the County of Middlesex" seeking for a duty to be assessed upon any commodities imported into or exported from the province.- *Manuscript Collection-Legislative Records [New Jersey State Archives],* Box 1-12, Folder 13, pg. 3.
Williams, Joseph, Male

WILLIAMSON, Will:, Middlesex County, - Name on petition, 11 Jun 1740, to the House of Representatives of New Jersey Province from "Freeholders Inhabitants of the County of Middlesex" seeking for a duty to be assessed upon any commodities imported into or exported from the province.- *Manuscript Collection-Legislative Records [New Jersey State Archives],* Box 1-12, Folder 13, pg. 3.
Williamson, Will:, Male

NEW JERSEY PETITIONS 1745-1754

There are 643 entries.

ABBOTT, George, - Name on a petition, 24 Sep? 1753, to the House of Representatives from inhabitants of the province expressing distress because of a lack of currency as a medium of trade. They present various arguments for the value of a paper currency.- *Manuscript Collection-Oversized Legislative Papers [New Jersey State Archives],* Box 1-43, Folder 4, pg. 1.
   Abbott, George, Male

ABBOTT, John, Burlington County, Nottingham - Name on a petition, 18 Nov 1748, to the House of Representatives from inhabitants of Nottingham, Burlington County complaining of those hunting out of season who have killed their hogs and cattle. Sometimes people are in danger of being shot.- *Manuscript Collection-Legislative Records [New Jersey State Archives],* Box 1-12, Folder 46, pg. 1.
   Abbott, John, Male

ABBOTT, Timothy, Burlington County, Nottingham - Name on a petition, 18 Nov 1748, to the House of Representatives from inhabitants of Nottingham, Burlington County complaining of those hunting out of season who have killed their hogs and cattle. Sometimes people are in danger of being shot.- *Manuscript Collection-Legislative Records [New Jersey State Archives],* Box 1-12, Folder 46, pg. 1.
   Abbott, Timothy, Male

ALELETON, Jacob, Morris County, - Name on a petition, 6 Oct 1751, to Governor Jonathan Belcher from owners of "Bloomaries" in Morris County seeking removal of a tax on their iron works (Bloomeries). Many make 5-6 tons or less a year. They seek instead for a bounty on all they produce.- *Manuscript Collection-MSS Coll., #1-100 [New Jersey State Archives],* Box 5-1, Folder 28, pg. 2.
   Aleleton, Jacob, Male

ALLEN, James, Hunterdon County, Bethlehem - Name on a petition, 12 Jan 1747/8, to Jonathan Belcher, Governor, from inhabitants of Bethlehem in Hunterdon County seeking to have the southerly part of Bethlehem Township made into a new township.- *Legislature-Petitions re: Municipal Boundaries [New Jersey State Archives],* Box 1, Folder 1, pg. 1.

   allen, James, Male

ALLEN, John, Junr, Burlington & Hunterdon Cos., - Name on a petition, 1748/9, to the House of Representatives from inhabitants freeholders of Hunterdon and Burlington Counties seeking for a law requiring every person to record their "Mortgage Deeds" to ensure validity of titles to land.- *Manuscript Collection-Oversized Legislative Papers [New Jersey State Archives],* Box 1-43, Folder 2, pg. 1.
   Allen, John, Junr, Male

ALLEN, Samuel, Burlington County, Nottingham - Name on a petition, 18 Nov 1748, to the House of Representatives from inhabitants of Nottingham, Burlington County complaining of those hunting out of season who have killed their hogs and cattle. Sometimes people are in danger of being shot.- *Manuscript Collection-Legislative Records [New Jersey State Archives],* Box 1-12, Folder 46, pg. 1.
   allen, Samuel, Male

ALLEN, Willia, Hunterdon County, Bethlehem - Name on a petition, 12 Jan 1747/8, to Jonathan Belcher, Governor, from inhabitants of Bethlehem in Hunterdon County seeking to have the southerly part of Bethlehem Township made into a new township.- *Legislature-Petitions re: Municipal Boundaries [New Jersey State Archives],* Box 1, Folder 1, pg. 1.
   allen, Willia, Male

ALLIN, Ebenezer, Morris County, - Name on a petition, 6 Oct 1751, to Governor Jonathan Belcher from owners of "Bloomaries" in Morris County seeking removal of a tax on their iron works (Bloomeries). Many make 5-6 tons or less a year. They seek instead for a bounty on all they produce.- *Manuscript Collection-MSS Coll., #1-100 [New Jersey State Archives],* Box 5-1, Folder 28, pg. 2.
   Allin, Ebenezer, Male

ALLING, Samuel, Essex County, - Name on petition, 10 Apr 1746, to the General Assembly by freeholders & inhabitants of Essex Co. seeking a repeal of acts for preserving of timber & a duty on imported strong liquors. They cannot build ships because of the present war with France & Spain.- *Manuscript Collection-Legislative Records [New Jersey State Archives]*, Box 1-12, Folder 25, pg. 1.

Alling, Samuel, Male

ALLINSON, Thos, Burlington County, Northampton Township - Name on a petition, 30 May 1753, to the House of Representatives from inhabitants in and about Northampton who are requesting an increase in the amount of currency which is scarce. Gold and silver are chiefly transported elsewhere and are scarce also.- *Manuscript Collection-Legislative Records [New Jersey State Archives]*, Box 1-12, Folder 65, pg. 1.

Allinson, Thos, Male

ANDREWS, Peter, - Name on a petition, 1750/1, the House of Representatives from inhabitants of the province protesting against the great number of taverns in the province.- *Manuscript Collection-Legislative Records [New Jersey State Archives]*, Box 1-12, Folder 59, pg. 1.

Andrews, Peter, Male

ANDREWS, Peter, Burlington County, Northampton Township - Name on a petition, 30 May 1753, to the House of Representatives from inhabitants in and about Northampton who are requesting an increase in the amount of currency which is scarce. Gold and silver are chiefly transported elsewhere and are scarce also.- *Manuscript Collection-Legislative Records [New Jersey State Archives]*, Box 1-12, Folder 65, pg. 1.

Andrews, Peter, Male

ANIN, John, - Name on petition, 1 Mar 1748/9, to the governor, etc., seeking passage of a law forbidding the killing of deer by dogs because the meat and hides are mostly worthless.- *Manuscript Collection-Governors' Papers [New Jersey State Archives]*, Box 1-1, Folder 4, pg. 1.

anin, John, Male

ANIN?, Alexander, - Name on petition, 1 Mar 1748/9, to the governor, etc., seeking passage of a law forbidding the killing of deer by dogs because the meat and hides are mostly worthless.- *Manuscript Collection-Governors' Papers [New Jersey State Archives]*, Box 1-1, Folder 4, pg. 1.

Anin?, Alexander, Male

ANSTON, [Missing], Essex County, - Name on petition, 10 Apr 1746, to the General Assembly by freeholders & inhabitants of Essex Co. seeking a repeal of acts for preserving of timber & a duty on imported strong liquors. They cannot build ships because of the present war with France & Spain.- *Manuscript Collection-Legislative Records [New Jersey State Archives]*, Box 1-12, Folder 25, pg. 1.

anston, [Missing], Male

APELGATE, Beniamin, Middlesex County, Perth Amboy Township - Name on a petition, 1754, to the General Assembly from freeholders/inhabitants of Perth Amboy Township in Middlesex County opposing the election of Samuel Nevill as a judge of the Supreme Court.- *Manuscript Collection-Oversized Legislative Papers [New Jersey State Archives]*, Box 1-43, Folder 2, pg. 1.

Apelgate, Beniamin, Male

APPELGATE, Jacob, Middlesex County, Perth Amboy Township - Name on a petition, 1754, to the General Assembly from freeholders/inhabitants of Perth Amboy Township in Middlesex County opposing the election of Samuel Nevill as a judge of the Supreme Court.- *Manuscript Collection-Oversized Legislative Papers [New Jersey State Archives]*, Box 1-43, Folder 2, pg. 1.

appelgate, Jacob, Male

APPELGATE, Zebulun, Middlesex County, Perth Amboy Township - Name on a petition, 1754, to the General Assembly from freeholders/inhabitants of Perth Amboy Township in Middlesex County opposing the election of Samuel Nevill as a judge of the Supreme Court.- *Manuscript Collection-Oversized Legislative Papers [New Jersey State Archives]*, Box 1-43, Folder 2, pg. 1.

appelgate, Zebulun, Male

ARESON?, Adren, Hunterdon County, Bethlehem - Name on a petition, 12 Jan 1747/8, to Jonathan Belcher, Governor, from inhabitants of Bethlehem in Hunterdon County seeking to have the southerly part of Bethlehem Township made into a new township.- *Legislature-Petitions re: Municipal Boundaries [New Jersey State Archives]*, Box 1, Folder 1, pg. 1.

Areson?, Adren, Male

AREY, Isaac, Middlesex County, - Name on a petition, 1754, to the House of Representatives from freeholders of the province opposing the election of Samuel Nevell as a judge of the Supreme Court.- *Manuscript Collection-Legislative Records [New Jersey State Archives]*, Box 1-12, Folder 66, pg. 2.

Arey, Isaac, Male

ATCHLY, Thomas, - Name on a petition, 1754, to the House of Representatives from freeholders

of the province opposing the election of Samuel Nevell as a judge of the Supreme Court.- *Manuscript Collection-Legislative Records [New Jersey State Archives], Box 1-12, Folder 66, pg. 3.*
  Atchly, Thomas, Male

ATKINSON, John, - Name on a petition, 1750/1, the House of Representatives from inhabitants of the province protesting against the great number of taverns in the province.- *Manuscript Collection-Legislative Records [New Jersey State Archives], Box 1-12, Folder 59, pg. 1.*
  Atkinson, John, Male

ATKINSON, John, - Name on a petition, 24 Sep? 1753, to the House of Representatives from inhabitants of the province expressing distress because of a lack of currency as a medium of trade. They present various arguments for the value of a paper currency.- *Manuscript Collection-Oversized Legislative Papers [New Jersey State Archives], Box 1-43, Folder 4, pg. 1.*
  Atkinson, John, Male

ATKINSON, Samll, Junr, Burlington County, Northampton Township - Name on a petition, 30 May 1753, to the House of Representatives from inhabitants in and about Northampton who are requesting an increase in the amount of currency which is scarce. Gold and silver are chiefly transported elsewhere and are scarce also.- *Manuscript Collection-Legislative Records [New Jersey State Archives], Box 1-12, Folder 65, pg. 1.*
  Atkinson, Samll, Junr, Male

ATKINSON, Thos, Burlington County, Northampton Township - Name on a petition, 30 May 1753, to the House of Representatives from inhabitants in and about Northampton who are requesting an increase in the amount of currency which is scarce. Gold and silver are chiefly transported elsewhere and are scarce also.- *Manuscript Collection-Legislative Records [New Jersey State Archives], Box 1-12, Folder 65, pg. 1.*
  atkinson, Thos, Male

AUS . . ., Charles, Burlington & Hunterdon Cos., - Name on a petition, 1748/9, to the House of Representatives from inhabitants freeholders of Hunterdon and Burlington Counties seeking for a law requiring every person to record their "Mortgage Deeds" to ensure validity of titles to land.- *Manuscript Collection-Oversized Legislative Papers [New Jersey State Archives], Box 1-43, Folder 2, pg. 1.*
  Aus . . ., Charles, Male

AYERS, John, Junr, - Name on petition, 1 Mar 1748/9, to the governor, etc., seeking passage of a law forbidding the killing of deer by dogs because the meat and hides are mostly worthless.- *Manuscript Collection-Governors' Papers [New Jersey State Archives], Box 1-1, Folder 4, pg. 1.*
  Ayers, John, Junr, Male

AYERS, Moses, - Name on petition, 1 Mar 1748/9, to the governor, etc., seeking passage of a law forbidding the killing of deer by dogs because the meat and hides are mostly worthless.- *Manuscript Collection-Governors' Papers [New Jersey State Archives], Box 1-1, Folder 4, pg. 1.*
  Ayers, Moses, Male

AYERS, obediah, - Name on petition, 1 Mar 1748/9, to the governor, etc., seeking passage of a law forbidding the killing of deer by dogs because the meat and hides are mostly worthless.- *Manuscript Collection-Governors' Papers [New Jersey State Archives], Box 1-1, Folder 4, pg. 1.*
  ayers, obediah, Male

BAKER, Daniel, - Name on a petition, 1754, to the House of Representatives from freeholders of the province opposing the election of Samuel Nevell as a judge of the Supreme Court.- *Manuscript Collection-Legislative Records [New Jersey State Archives], Box 1-12, Folder 66, pg. 4.*
  baker, Daniel, Male

BALDWIN, Amos, Essex County, - Name on petition, 10 Apr 1746, to the General Assembly by freeholders & inhabitants of Essex Co. seeking a repeal of acts for preserving of timber & a duty on imported strong liquors. They cannot build ships because of the present war with France & Spain.- *Manuscript Collection-Legislative Records [New Jersey State Archives], Box 1-12, Folder 25, pg. 1.*
  Baldwin, Amos, Male

BALDWIN, Daniel, Junr, Essex County, - Name on petition, 10 Apr 1746, to the General Assembly by freeholders & inhabitants of Essex Co. seeking a repeal of acts for preserving of timber & a duty on imported strong liquors. They cannot build ships because of the present war with France & Spain.- *Manuscript Collection-Legislative Records [New Jersey State Archives], Box 1-12, Folder 25, pg. 2.*
  Baldwin, Daniel, Junr, Male

BALDWIN, Daniel, seinr, Essex County, - Name on petition, 10 Apr 1746, to the General Assembly by freeholders & inhabitants of Essex Co. seeking a repeal of acts for preserving of timber & a duty on imported strong liquors. They cannot build ships because of the present war with France & Spain.- *Manuscript Collection-Legislative Records [New Jersey State Archives], Box 1-12, Folder 25, pg. 2.

Baldwin, Daniel, seinr, Male

BALDWIN, Ezekiel, Essex County, - Name on petition, 10 Apr 1746, to the General Assembly by freeholders & inhabitants of Essex Co. seeking a repeal of acts for preserving of timber & a duty on imported strong liquors. They cannot build ships because of the present war with France & Spain.- *Manuscript Collection-Legislative Records [New Jersey State Archives], Box 1-12, Folder 25, pg. 2.

Baldwin, Ezekiel, Male

BALDWIN, John, Essex County, - Name on petition, 10 Apr 1746, to the General Assembly by freeholders & inhabitants of Essex Co. seeking a repeal of acts for preserving of timber & a duty on imported strong liquors. They cannot build ships because of the present war with France & Spain.- *Manuscript Collection-Legislative Records [New Jersey State Archives], Box 1-12, Folder 25, pg. 1.

Baldwin, John, Male

BALDWIN, John, Essex County, - Name on petition, 10 Apr 1746, to the General Assembly by freeholders & inhabitants of Essex Co. seeking a repeal of acts for preserving of timber & a duty on imported strong liquors. They cannot build ships because of the present war with France & Spain.- *Manuscript Collection-Legislative Records [New Jersey State Archives], Box 1-12, Folder 25, pg. 2.

Baldwin, John, Male

BALDWIN, mosses, Essex County, - Name on petition, 10 Apr 1746, to the General Assembly by freeholders & inhabitants of Essex Co. seeking a repeal of acts for preserving of timber & a duty on imported strong liquors. They cannot build ships because of the present war with France & Spain.- *Manuscript Collection-Legislative Records [New Jersey State Archives], Box 1-12, Folder 25, pg. 2.

Baldwin, mosses, Male

BALDWIN, Nathan, Essex County, - Name on petition, 10 Apr 1746, to the General Assembly by freeholders & inhabitants of Essex Co. seeking a repeal of acts for preserving of timber & a duty on imported strong liquors. They cannot build ships because of the present war with France & Spain.- *Manuscript Collection-Legislative Records [New Jersey State Archives], Box 1-12, Folder 25, pg. 2.

Baldwin, Nathan, Male

BALL, Aaron, Essex County, - Name on petition, 10 Apr 1746, to the General Assembly by freeholders & inhabitants of Essex Co. seeking a repeal of acts for preserving of timber & a duty on imported strong liquors. They cannot build ships because of the present war with France & Spain.- *Manuscript Collection-Legislative Records [New Jersey State Archives], Box 1-12, Folder 25, pg. 2.

Ball, Aaron, Male

BALL, David, Essex County, - Name on petition, 10 Apr 1746, to the General Assembly by freeholders & inhabitants of Essex Co. seeking a repeal of acts for preserving of timber & a duty on imported strong liquors. They cannot build ships because of the present war with France & Spain.- *Manuscript Collection-Legislative Records [New Jersey State Archives], Box 1-12, Folder 25, pg. 2.

Ball, David, Male

BALL, Eezekiel, Essex County, - Name on petition, 10 Apr 1746, to the General Assembly by freeholders & inhabitants of Essex Co. seeking a repeal of acts for preserving of timber & a duty on imported strong liquors. They cannot build ships because of the present war with France & Spain.- *Manuscript Collection-Legislative Records [New Jersey State Archives], Box 1-12, Folder 25, pg. 2.

Ball, Eezekiel, Male

BALL, Isaac, Essex County, - Name on petition, 10 Apr 1746, to the General Assembly by freeholders & inhabitants of Essex Co. seeking a repeal of acts for preserving of timber & a duty on imported strong liquors. They cannot build ships because of the present war with France & Spain.- *Manuscript Collection-Legislative Records [New Jersey State Archives], Box 1-12, Folder 25, pg. 1.

Ball, Isaac, Male

BALL, Jonaes, Essex County, - Name on petition, 10 Apr 1746, to the General Assembly by freeholders & inhabitants of Essex Co. seeking a repeal of acts for preserving of timber & a duty on imported strong liquors. They cannot build ships because of the present war with France & Spain.- *Manuscript Collection-Legislative Records [New Jersey State Archives], Box 1-12, Folder 25, pg. 2.

Ball, Jonaes, Male

BALL, Joseph, Essex County, - Name on petition, 10 Apr 1746, to the General Assembly by freeholders & inhabitants of Essex Co. seeking a repeal of acts for preserving of timber & a duty on imported strong liquors. They cannot build ships because of the present war with France & Spain.-

Manuscript Collection-Legislative Records [New Jersey State Archives], Box 1-12, Folder 25, pg. 1.
  Ball, Joseph, Male
BALL, Nathanael, Essex County, - Name on petition, 10 Apr 1746, to the General Assembly by freeholders & inhabitants of Essex Co. seeking a repeal of acts for preserving of timber & a duty on imported strong liquors. They cannot build ships because of the present war with France & Spain.- *Manuscript Collection-Legislative Records [New Jersey State Archives]*, Box 1-12, Folder 25, pg. 2.
  Ball, Nathanael, Male
BALL, Samuel, Essex County, - Name on petition, 10 Apr 1746, to the General Assembly by freeholders & inhabitants of Essex Co. seeking a repeal of acts for preserving of timber & a duty on imported strong liquors. They cannot build ships because of the present war with France & Spain.- *Manuscript Collection-Legislative Records [New Jersey State Archives]*, Box 1-12, Folder 25, pg. 1.
  Ball, Samuel, Male
BALL, Thomas, Essex County, - Name on petition, 10 Apr 1746, to the General Assembly by freeholders & inhabitants of Essex Co. seeking a repeal of acts for preserving of timber & a duty on imported strong liquors. They cannot build ships because of the present war with France & Spain.- *Manuscript Collection-Legislative Records [New Jersey State Archives]*, Box 1-12, Folder 25, pg. 2.
  Ball, Thomas, Male
BALL, Timothy, Essex County, - Name on petition, 10 Apr 1746, to the General Assembly by freeholders & inhabitants of Essex Co. seeking a repeal of acts for preserving of timber & a duty on imported strong liquors. They cannot build ships because of the present war with France & Spain.- *Manuscript Collection-Legislative Records [New Jersey State Archives]*, Box 1-12, Folder 25, pg. 2.
  Ball, Timothy, Male
BALLDWIN, David, Essex County, - Name on petition, 10 Apr 1746, to the General Assembly by freeholders & inhabitants of Essex Co. seeking a repeal of acts for preserving of timber & a duty on imported strong liquors. They cannot build ships because of the present war with France & Spain.- *Manuscript Collection-Legislative Records [New Jersey State Archives]*, Box 1-12, Folder 25, pg. 1.
  Balldwin, David, Male
BALY, Horris, Essex County, - Name on petition, 10 Apr 1746, to the General Assembly by freeholders & inhabitants of Essex Co. seeking a repeal of acts for preserving of timber & a duty on imported strong liquors. They cannot build ships because of the present war with France & Spain.- *Manuscript Collection-Legislative Records [New Jersey State Archives]*, Box 1-12, Folder 25, pg. 2.
  baly, Horris, Male
BANCRAFT, David, Cape May County, - Name on petition, 12 Mar 1745/6, to the House of Representatives from freeholders of Cape May County complaining of the devaluation of their paper money [likely due in part to the present war] and asking for creation of a fund, apparently to stabilize it.- *Manuscript Collection-Legislative Records [New Jersey State Archives]*, Box 1-12, Folder 22, pg. 1.
  Bancraft, David, Male
BANCRAFT, Samuel, Cape May County, - Name on petition, 12 Mar 1745/6, to the House of Representatives from freeholders of Cape May County complaining of the devaluation of their paper money [likely due in part to the present war] and asking for creation of a fund, apparently to stabilize it.- *Manuscript Collection-Legislative Records [New Jersey State Archives]*, Box 1-12, Folder 22, pg. 1.
  Bancraft, Samuel, Male
BANCRAFT, Thomas, Cape May County, - Name on petition, 12 Mar 1745/6, to the House of Representatives from freeholders of Cape May County complaining of the devaluation of their paper money [likely due in part to the present war] and asking for creation of a fund, apparently to stabilize it.- *Manuscript Collection-Legislative Records [New Jersey State Archives]*, Box 1-12, Folder 22, pg. 1.
  Bancraft, Thomas, Male
BANCROFT, Samuel, Cape May County, - Name on petition, 12 Mar 1745/6, to the House of Representatives from freeholders of Cape May County complaining of the devaluation of their paper money [likely due in part to the present war] and asking for creation of a fund, apparently to stabilize it.- *Manuscript Collection-Legislative Records [New Jersey State Archives]*, Box 1-12, Folder 22, pg. 1.
  Bancroft, Samuel, Male
BANCROFT OR PANCOOST?, Thos, Burlington & Hunterdon Cos., - Name on a petition, 1748/9, to the House of Representatives from inhabitants freeholders of Hunterdon and Burlington Counties seeking for a law requiring

every person to record their "Mortgage Deeds" to ensure validity of titles to land.- *Manuscript Collection-Oversized Legislative Papers [New Jersey State Archives], Box 1-43, Folder 2, pg. 1.*

Bancroft or Pancoost?, Thos, Male

BANKS, James, Essex County, - Name on petition, 10 Apr 1746, to the General Assembly by freeholders & inhabitants of Essex Co. seeking a repeal of acts for preserving of timber & a duty on imported strong liquors. They cannot build ships because of the present war with France & Spain.- *Manuscript Collection-Legislative Records [New Jersey State Archives], Box 1-12, Folder 25, pg. 1.*

Banks, James, Male

BARD, Peter, Burlington County, Northampton Township - Name on a petition, 30 May 1753, to the House of Representatives from inhabitants in and about Northampton who are requesting an increase in the amount of currency which is scarce. Gold and silver are chiefly transported elsewhere and are scarce also.- *Manuscript Collection-Legislative Records [New Jersey State Archives], Box 1-12, Folder 65, pg. 1.*

Bard, Peter, Male

BARKELOO, Jaques, Hunterdon County, Bethlehem - Name on a petition, 12 Jan 1747/8, to Jonathan Belcher, Governor, from inhabitants of Bethlehem in Hunterdon County seeking to have the southerly part of Bethlehem Township made into a new township.- *Legislature-Petitions re: Municipal Boundaries [New Jersey State Archives], Box 1, Folder 1, pg. 1.*

Barkeloo, Jaques, Male

BARLOW, Wm, Cape May County, - Name on petition, 12 Mar 1745/6, to the House of Representatives from freeholders of Cape May County complaining of the devaluation of their paper money [likely due in part to the present war] and asking for creation of a fund, apparently to stabilize it.- *Manuscript Collection-Legislative Records [New Jersey State Archives], Box 1-12, Folder 22, pg. 1.*

Barlow, Wm, Male

BARNS, William, Hunterdon County, Bethlehem - Name on a petition, 12 Jan 1747/8, to Jonathan Belcher, Governor, from inhabitants of Bethlehem in Hunterdon County seeking to have the southerly part of Bethlehem Township made into a new township.- *Legislature-Petitions re: Municipal Boundaries [New Jersey State Archives], Box 1, Folder 1, pg. 1.*

Barns, William, Male

BARTON, John, - Name on a petition, 24 Sep? 1753, to the House of Representatives from inhabitants of the province expressing distress because of a lack of currency as a medium of trade. They present various arguments for the value of a paper currency.- *Manuscript Collection-Oversized Legislative Papers [New Jersey State Archives], Box 1-43, Folder 4, pg. 1.*

Barton, John, Male

BASTEDO, John, - Name on a petition, 1754, to the House of Representatives from freeholders of the province opposing the election of Samuel Nevell as a judge of the Supreme Court.- *Manuscript Collection-Legislative Records [New Jersey State Archives], Box 1-12, Folder 66, pg. 3.*

Bastedo, John, Male

BATES, william, Morris County, - Name on a petition, 6 Oct 1751, to Governor Jonathan Belcher from owners of "Bloomaries" in Morris County seeking removal of a tax on their iron works (Bloomeries). Many make 5-6 tons or less a year. They seek instead for a bounty on all they produce.- *Manuscript Collection-MSS Coll., #1-100 [New Jersey State Archives], Box 5-1, Folder 28, pg. 2.*

Bates, william, Male

BAULDWIN, Joseph, Essex County, - Name on petition, 10 Apr 1746, to the General Assembly by freeholders & inhabitants of Essex Co. seeking a repeal of acts for preserving of timber & a duty on imported strong liquors. They cannot build ships because of the present war with France & Spain.- *Manuscript Collection-Legislative Records [New Jersey State Archives], Box 1-12, Folder 25, pg. 1.*

Bauldwin, Joseph, Male

BAYLES, Daniel, Juner, - Name on a petition, 1754, to the House of Representatives from freeholders of the province opposing the election of Samuel Nevell as a judge of the Supreme Court.- *Manuscript Collection-Legislative Records [New Jersey State Archives], Box 1-12, Folder 66, pg. 3.*

Bayles, Daniel, Juner, Male

BAYLES, John, - Name on a petition, 1754, to the House of Representatives from freeholders of the province opposing the election of Samuel Nevell as a judge of the Supreme Court.- *Manuscript Collection-Legislative Records [New Jersey State Archives], Box 1-12, Folder 66, pg. 3.*

Bayles, John, Male

BAYLES, Samuel, - Name on a petition, 1754, to the House of Representatives from freeholders of the province opposing the election of Samuel Nevell as a judge of the Supreme Court.- *Manuscript Collection-Legislative Records [New Jersey State Archives],* Box 1-12, Folder 66, pg. 3.

Bayles, Samuel, Male

BEACH, Abner, Morris County, - Name on a petition, 6 Oct 1751, to Governor Jonathan Belcher from owners of "Bloomaries" in Morris County seeking removal of a tax on their iron works (Bloomeries). Many make 5-6 tons or less a year. They seek instead for a bounty on all they produce.- *Manuscript Collection-MSS Coll., #1-100 [New Jersey State Archives],* Box 5-1, Folder 28, pg. 2.

Beach, Abner, Male

BEACH, Josiah, Essex County, - Name on petition, 10 Apr 1746, to the General Assembly by freeholders & inhabitants of Essex Co. seeking a repeal of acts for preserving of timber & a duty on imported strong liquors. They cannot build ships because of the present war with France & Spain.- *Manuscript Collection-Legislative Records [New Jersey State Archives],* Box 1-12, Folder 25, pg. 1.

Beach, Josiah, Male

BEACH, Tophan, Essex County, - Name on petition, 10 Apr 1746, to the General Assembly by freeholders & inhabitants of Essex Co. seeking a repeal of acts for preserving of timber & a duty on imported strong liquors. They cannot build ships because of the present war with France & Spain.- *Manuscript Collection-Legislative Records [New Jersey State Archives],* Box 1-12, Folder 25, pg. 1.

Beach, Tophan, Male

BEAKES, Nathan, Burlington & Hunterdon Cos., - Name on a petition, 1748/9, to the House of Representatives from inhabitants freeholders of Hunterdon and Burlington Counties seeking for a law requiring every person to record their "Mortgage Deeds" to ensure validity of titles to land.- *Manuscript Collection-Oversized Legislative Papers [New Jersey State Archives],* Box 1-43, Folder 2, pg. 1.

Beakes, Nathan, Male

BECK, Thomas, Cape May County, - Name on petition, 12 Mar 1745/6, to the House of Representatives from freeholders of Cape May County complaining of the devaluation of their paper money [likely due in part to the present war] and asking for creation of a fund, apparently to stabilize it.- *Manuscript Collection-Legislative Records [New Jersey State Archives],* Box 1-12, Folder 22, pg. 1.

Beck, Thomas, Male

BEDFORD, Stephen, Essex County, - Name on petition, 10 Apr 1746, to the General Assembly by freeholders & inhabitants of Essex Co. seeking a repeal of acts for preserving of timber & a duty on imported strong liquors. They cannot build ships because of the present war with France & Spain.- *Manuscript Collection-Legislative Records [New Jersey State Archives],* Box 1-12, Folder 25, pg. 2.

Bedford, Stephen, Male

BEDFORD, Tophan, Essex County, - Name on petition, 10 Apr 1746, to the General Assembly by freeholders & inhabitants of Essex Co. seeking a repeal of acts for preserving of timber & a duty on imported strong liquors. They cannot build ships because of the present war with France & Spain.- *Manuscript Collection-Legislative Records [New Jersey State Archives],* Box 1-12, Folder 25, pg. 2.

Bedford, Tophan, Male

BEECH, Samuell, Essex County, - Name on petition, 10 Apr 1746, to the General Assembly by freeholders & inhabitants of Essex Co. seeking a repeal of acts for preserving of timber & a duty on imported strong liquors. They cannot build ships because of the present war with France & Spain.- *Manuscript Collection-Legislative Records [New Jersey State Archives],* Box 1-12, Folder 25, pg. 2.

Beech, Samuell, Male

BEEKER, John, - Name on a petition, 24 Sep? 1753, to the House of Representatives from inhabitants of the province expressing distress because of a lack of currency as a medium of trade. They present various arguments for the value of a paper currency.- *Manuscript Collection-Oversized Legislative Papers [New Jersey State Archives],* Box 1-43, Folder 4, pg. 1.

Beeker, John, Male

BEILLIN?, Joseph, Burlington & Hunterdon Cos., - Name on a petition, 1748/9, to the House of Representatives from inhabitants freeholders of Hunterdon and Burlington Counties seeking for a law requiring every person to record their "Mortgage Deeds" to ensure validity of titles to land.- *Manuscript Collection-Oversized Legislative Papers [New Jersey State Archives],* Box 1-43, Folder 2, pg. 1.

Beillin?, Joseph, Male

BENNET, Adriaen, - Name on a petition, 1754, to the House of Representatives from freeholders of the province opposing the election of Samuel Nevell as a judge of the Supreme Court.- *Manuscript Collection-Legislative Records [New Jersey State Archives],* Box 1-12, Folder 66, pg. 3.

Bennet, Adriaen, Male

BENNET, Thomas, - Name on a petition, 1750/1, the House of Representatives from inhabitants of the province protesting against the great number of taverns in the province.- *Manuscript Collection-Legislative Records [New Jersey State Archives],* Box 1-12, Folder 59, pg. 1.

Bennet, Thomas, Male

BICKERDIKE OR RICKERDIKE, Gideon, Burlington & Hunterdon Cos., - Name on a petition, 1748/9, to the House of Representatives from inhabitants freeholders of Hunterdon and Burlington Counties seeking for a law requiring every person to record their "Mortgage Deeds" to ensure validity of titles to land.- *Manuscript Collection-Oversized Legislative Papers [New Jersey State Archives],* Box 1-43, Folder 2, pg. 1.

Bickerdike or Rickerdike, Gideon, Male

BILES, Benja, Burlington & Hunterdon Cos., - Name on a petition, 1748/9, to the House of Representatives from inhabitants freeholders of Hunterdon and Burlington Counties seeking for a law requiring every person to record their "Mortgage Deeds" to ensure validity of titles to land.- *Manuscript Collection-Oversized Legislative Papers [New Jersey State Archives],* Box 1-43, Folder 2, pg. 1.

Biles, Benja, Male

BISPHANE, Benj, Burlington County, Northampton Township - Name on a petition, 30 May 1753, to the House of Representatives from inhabitants in and about Northampton who are requesting an increase in the amount of currency which is scarce. Gold and silver are chiefly transported elsewhere and are scarce also.- *Manuscript Collection-Legislative Records [New Jersey State Archives],* Box 1-12, Folder 65, pg. 1.

Bisphane, Benj, Male

BLAIR?, Hermin, Hunterdon County, Bethlehem - Name on a petition, 12 Jan 1747/8, to Jonathan Belcher, Governor, from inhabitants of Bethlehem in Hunterdon County seeking to have the southerly part of Bethlehem Township made into a new township.- *Legislature-Petitions re: Municipal Boundaries [New Jersey State Archives],* Box 1, Folder 1, pg. 1.

Blair?, Hermin, Male

BO*D*E, Francis, Burlington County, Nottingham - Name on a petition, 18 Nov 1748, to the House of Representatives from inhabitants of Nottingham, Burlington County complaining of those hunting out of season who have killed their hogs and cattle. Sometimes people are in danger of being shot.- *Manuscript Collection-Legislative Records [New Jersey State Archives],* Box 1-12, Folder 46, pg. 1.

Bo*d*e, Francis, Male

BOND, Elijah, Burlington & Hunterdon Cos., - Name on a petition, 1748/9, to the House of Representatives from inhabitants freeholders of Hunterdon and Burlington Counties seeking for a law requiring every person to record their "Mortgage Deeds" to ensure validity of titles to land.- *Manuscript Collection-Oversized Legislative Papers [New Jersey State Archives],* Box 1-43, Folder 2, pg. 1.

Bond, Elijah, Male

BORDEN, Jonathan, - Name on a petition, 1750/1, the House of Representatives from inhabitants of the province protesting against the great number of taverns in the province.- *Manuscript Collection-Legislative Records [New Jersey State Archives],* Box 1-12, Folder 59, pg. 1.

Borden, Jonathan, Male

BORDEN, Jos, Sr, Burlington & Hunterdon Cos., - Name on a petition, 1748/9, to the House of Representatives from inhabitants freeholders of Hunterdon and Burlington Counties seeking for a law requiring every person to record their "Mortgage Deeds" to ensure validity of titles to land.- *Manuscript Collection-Oversized Legislative Papers [New Jersey State Archives],* Box 1-43, Folder 2, pg. 1.

Borden, Jos, Sr, Male

BORDEN, Safty?, Burlington & Hunterdon Cos., - Name on a petition, 1748/9, to the House of Representatives from inhabitants freeholders of Hunterdon and Burlington Counties seeking for a law requiring every person to record their "Mortgage Deeds" to ensure validity of titles to land.- *Manuscript Collection-Oversized Legislative Papers [New Jersey State Archives],* Box 1-43, Folder 2, pg. 1.

Borden, Safty?, Male

BOWS OR ROWS, Thos, Essex County, - Name on petition, 10 Apr 1746, to the General Assembly by freeholders & inhabitants of Essex Co. seeking a repeal of acts for preserving of timber & a duty on imported strong liquors. They cannot build ships because of the present war with France & Spain.- *Manuscript Collection-Legislative Records [New Jersey State Archives],* Box 1-12, Folder 25, pg. 1.

Bows or Rows, Thos, Male

BOYLAN, Aaron, - Name on petition, 1 Mar 1748/9, to the governor, etc., seeking passage of a law forbidding the killing of deer by dogs because the meat and hides are mostly worthless.- *Manuscript Collection-Governors' Papers [New Jersey State Archives],* Box 1-1, Folder 4, pg. 1.

Boylan, Aaron, Male

BOYLAN, James, - Name on petition, 1 Mar 1748/9, to the governor, etc., seeking passage of a law forbidding the killing of deer by dogs because the meat and hides are mostly worthless.- *Manuscript Collection-Governors' Papers [New Jersey State Archives],* Box 1-1, Folder 4, pg. 1.

Boylan, James, Male

BRADOCK, Robert, - Name on a petition, 24 Sep? 1753, to the House of Representatives from inhabitants of the province expressing distress because of a lack of currency as a medium of trade. They present various arguments for the value of a paper currency.- *Manuscript Collection-Oversized Legislative Papers [New Jersey State Archives],* Box 1-43, Folder 4, pg. 1.

Bradock, Robert, Male

BRANIN, mickel, - Name on a petition, 24 Sep? 1753, to the House of Representatives from inhabitants of the province expressing distress because of a lack of currency as a medium of trade. They present various arguments for the value of a paper currency.- *Manuscript Collection-Oversized Legislative Papers [New Jersey State Archives],* Box 1-43, Folder 4, pg. 1.

Branin, mickel, Male

BRAY, James, Hunterdon County, Bethlehem - Name on a petition, 12 Jan 1747/8, to Jonathan Belcher, Governor, from inhabitants of Bethlehem in Hunterdon County seeking to have the southerly part of Bethlehem Township made into a new township.- *Legislature-Petitions re: Municipal Boundaries [New Jersey State Archives],* Box 1, Folder 1, pg. 1.

Bray, James, Male

BRIGGS, Francis, Burlington County, Northampton Township - Name on a petition, 30 May 1753, to the House of Representatives from inhabitants in and about Northampton who are requesting an increase in the amount of currency which is scarce. Gold and silver are chiefly transported elsewhere and are scarce also.- *Manuscript Collection-Legislative Records [New Jersey State Archives],* Box 1-12, Folder 65, pg. 1.

Briggs, Francis, Male

BROCK?, Oddy, - Name on a petition, 1750/1, the House of Representatives from inhabitants of the province protesting against the great number of taverns in the province.- *Manuscript Collection-Legislative Records [New Jersey State Archives],* Box 1-12, Folder 59, pg. 1.

brock?, Oddy, Male

BROWNE, Aaron, Essex County, - Name on petition, 10 Apr 1746, to the General Assembly by freeholders & inhabitants of Essex Co. seeking a repeal of acts for preserving of timber & a duty on imported strong liquors. They cannot build ships because of the present war with France & Spain.- *Manuscript Collection-Legislative Records [New Jersey State Archives],* Box 1-12, Folder 25, pg. 1.

Browne, Aaron, Male

BROWNE, Stephen, Essex County, - Name on petition, 10 Apr 1746, to the General Assembly by freeholders & inhabitants of Essex Co. seeking a repeal of acts for preserving of timber & a duty on imported strong liquors. They cannot build ships because of the present war with France & Spain.- *Manuscript Collection-Legislative Records [New Jersey State Archives],* Box 1-12, Folder 25, pg. 2.

Browne, Stephen, Male

BRUEN, Obadiah, Essex County, - Name on petition, 10 Apr 1746, to the General Assembly by freeholders & inhabitants of Essex Co. seeking a repeal of acts for preserving of timber & a duty on imported strong liquors. They cannot build ships because of the present war with France & Spain.- *Manuscript Collection-Legislative Records [New Jersey State Archives],* Box 1-12, Folder 25, pg. 1.

Bruen, Obadiah, Male

BUCKINGSHIRE, Thos, - Name on a petition, 24 Sep? 1753, to the House of Representatives from inhabitants of the province expressing distress because of a lack of currency as a medium of trade. They present various arguments for the value of a paper currency.- *Manuscript Collection-*

Oversized Legislative Papers [New Jersey State Archives], Box 1-43, Folder 4, pg. 1.
Buckingshire, Thos, Male

BUDD, John P?, Burlington County, Northampton Township - Name on a petition, 30 May 1753, to the House of Representatives from inhabitants in and about Northampton who are requesting an increase in the amount of currency which is scarce. Gold and silver are chiefly transported elsewhere and are scarce also.- *Manuscript Collection-Legislative Records [New Jersey State Archives]*, Box 1-12, Folder 65, pg. 1.
Budd, John P?, Male

BUDD, Thomas, - Name on a petition, 1750/1, the House of Representatives from inhabitants of the province protesting against the great number of taverns in the province.- *Manuscript Collection-Legislative Records [New Jersey State Archives]*, Box 1-12, Folder 59, pg. 1.
Budd, Thomas, Male

BUDD, William, junr, - Name on a petition, 1750/1, the House of Representatives from inhabitants of the province protesting against the great number of taverns in the province.- *Manuscript Collection-Legislative Records [New Jersey State Archives]*, Box 1-12, Folder 59, pg. 1.
Budd, William, junr, Male

BURCHUM, John, Hunterdon County, Bethlehem - Name on a petition, 12 Jan 1747/8, to Jonathan Belcher, Governor, from inhabitants of Bethlehem in Hunterdon County seeking to have the southerly part of Bethlehem Township made into a new township.- *Legislature-Petitions re: Municipal Boundaries [New Jersey State Archives]*, Box 1, Folder 1, pg. 1.
Burchum, John, Male

BURNET, Thomas, Essex County, - Name on petition, 10 Apr 1746, to the General Assembly by freeholders & inhabitants of Essex Co. seeking a repeal of acts for preserving of timber & a duty on imported strong liquors. They cannot build ships because of the present war with France & Spain.- *Manuscript Collection-Legislative Records [New Jersey State Archives]*, Box 1-12, Folder 25, pg. 2.
Burnet, Thomas, Male

BURR, Henry, - Name on a petition, 24 Sep? 1753, to the House of Representatives from inhabitants of the province expressing distress because of a lack of currency as a medium of trade. They present various arguments for the value of a paper currency.- *Manuscript Collection-Oversized Legislative Papers [New Jersey State Archives]*, Box 1-43, Folder 4, pg. 1.
Burr, Henry, Male

BURR, John, Jnr, Burlington County, Northampton Township - Name on a petition, 30 May 1753, to the House of Representatives from inhabitants in and about Northampton who are requesting an increase in the amount of currency which is scarce. Gold and silver are chiefly transported elsewhere and are scarce also.- *Manuscript Collection-Legislative Records [New Jersey State Archives]*, Box 1-12, Folder 65, pg. 1.
Burr, John, Jnr, Male

BURR, Joseph, Burlington County, Northampton Township - Name on a petition, 30 May 1753, to the House of Representatives from inhabitants in and about Northampton who are requesting an increase in the amount of currency which is scarce. Gold and silver are chiefly transported elsewhere and are scarce also.- *Manuscript Collection-Legislative Records [New Jersey State Archives]*, Box 1-12, Folder 65, pg. 1.
Burr, Joseph, Male

BURR, Solomon, Burlington County, Northampton Township - Name on a petition, 30 May 1753, to the House of Representatives from inhabitants in and about Northampton who are requesting an increase in the amount of currency which is scarce. Gold and silver are chiefly transported elsewhere and are scarce also.- *Manuscript Collection-Legislative Records [New Jersey State Archives]*, Box 1-12, Folder 65, pg. 1.
Burr, Solomon, Male

BURR?, Joseph, - Name on a petition, 24 Sep? 1753, to the House of Representatives from inhabitants of the province expressing distress because of a lack of currency as a medium of trade. They present various arguments for the value of a paper currency.- *Manuscript Collection-Oversized Legislative Papers [New Jersey State Archives]*, Box 1-43, Folder 4, pg. 1.
Burr?, Joseph, Male

BURR?, Joseph, - Name on a petition, 1750/1, the House of Representatives from inhabitants of the province protesting against the great number of taverns in the province.- *Manuscript Collection-Legislative Records [New Jersey State Archives]*, Box 1-12, Folder 59, pg. 1.
Burr?, Joseph, Male

CADWALADER, Thos, Burlington & Hunterdon Cos., - Name on a petition, 1748/9, to the House of

Representatives from inhabitants freeholders of Hunterdon and Burlington Counties seeking for a law requiring every person to record their "Mortgage Deeds" to ensure validity of titles to land.- *Manuscript Collection-Oversized Legislative Papers [New Jersey State Archives]*, Box 1-43, Folder 2, pg. 1.

Cadwalader, Thos, Male

CAIN, james, - Name on petition, 1 Mar 1748/9, to the governor, etc., seeking passage of a law forbidding the killing of deer by dogs because the meat and hides are mostly worthless.- *Manuscript Collection-Governors' Papers [New Jersey State Archives]*, Box 1-1, Folder 4, pg. 1.

cain, james, Male

CAMMEL?, Nathaniel, Essex County, - Name on petition, 10 Apr 1746, to the General Assembly by freeholders & inhabitants of Essex Co. seeking a repeal of acts for preserving of timber & a duty on imported strong liquors. They cannot build ships because of the present war with France & Spain.- *Manuscript Collection-Legislative Records [New Jersey State Archives]*, Box 1-12, Folder 25, pg. 2.

Cammel?, Nathaniel, Male

CAMPBEL, Duncan, - Name on a petition, 1754, to the House of Representatives from freeholders of the province opposing the election of Samuel Nevell as a judge of the Supreme Court.- *Manuscript Collection-Legislative Records [New Jersey State Archives]*, Box 1-12, Folder 66, pg. 3.

Campbel, Duncan, Male

CAMPBELL, Samuel, Essex County, - Name on petition, 10 Apr 1746, to the General Assembly by freeholders & inhabitants of Essex Co. seeking a repeal of acts for preserving of timber & a duty on imported strong liquors. They cannot build ships because of the present war with France & Spain.- *Manuscript Collection-Legislative Records [New Jersey State Archives]*, Box 1-12, Folder 25, pg. 2.

campbell, Samuel, Male

CANFIELD, Thomas, Essex County, - Name on petition, 10 Apr 1746, to the General Assembly by freeholders & inhabitants of Essex Co. seeking a repeal of acts for preserving of timber & a duty on imported strong liquors. They cannot build ships because of the present war with France & Spain.- *Manuscript Collection-Legislative Records [New Jersey State Archives]*, Box 1-12, Folder 25, pg. 1.

Canfield, Thomas, Male

CARSON, John, - Name on a petition, 1754, to the House of Representatives from freeholders of the province opposing the election of Samuel Nevell as a judge of the Supreme Court.- *Manuscript Collection-Legislative Records [New Jersey State Archives]*, Box 1-12, Folder 66, pg. 4.

Carson, John, Male

CATENLANDING?, Jonathan, - Name on petition, 1 Mar 1748/9, to the governor, etc., seeking passage of a law forbidding the killing of deer by dogs because the meat and hides are mostly worthless.- *Manuscript Collection-Governors' Papers [New Jersey State Archives]*, Box 1-1, Folder 4, pg. 1.

Catenlanding?, Jonathan, Male

CHAMBERLIN, John, Middlesex County, - Name on a petition, 1754, to the House of Representatives from freeholders of the province opposing the election of Samuel Nevell as a judge of the Supreme Court.- *Manuscript Collection-Legislative Records [New Jersey State Archives]*, Box 1-12, Folder 66, pg. 2.

Chamberlin, John, Male

CHAMBERS, David, - Name on petition, 1 Mar 1748/9, to the governor, etc., seeking passage of a law forbidding the killing of deer by dogs because the meat and hides are mostly worthless.- *Manuscript Collection-Governors' Papers [New Jersey State Archives]*, Box 1-1, Folder 4, pg. 1.

Chambers, David, Male

CHAMBERS, Willam, - Name on petition, 1 Mar 1748/9, to the governor, etc., seeking passage of a law forbidding the killing of deer by dogs because the meat and hides are mostly worthless.- *Manuscript Collection-Governors' Papers [New Jersey State Archives]*, Box 1-1, Folder 4, pg. 1.

Chambers, Willam, Male

CLARK, John, Burlington County, Northampton Township - Name on a petition, 30 May 1753, to the House of Representatives from inhabitants in and about Northampton who are requesting an increase in the amount of currency which is scarce. Gold and silver are chiefly transported elsewhere and are scarce also.- *Manuscript Collection-Legislative Records [New Jersey State Archives]*, Box 1-12, Folder 65, pg. 1.

Clark, John, Male

CLEAYTON, J? M, Burlington & Hunterdon Cos., - Name on a petition, 1748/9, to the House of Representatives from inhabitants freeholders of Hunterdon and Burlington Counties seeking for a law requiring every person to record their "Mortgage Deeds" to ensure validity of titles to land.- *Manuscript Collection-Oversized Legislative Papers [New Jersey State Archives],* Box 1-43, Folder 2, pg. 1.

Cleayton, J? M, Male

CLEAYTON, Jos, Burlington & Hunterdon Cos., - Name on a petition, 1748/9, to the House of Representatives from inhabitants freeholders of Hunterdon and Burlington Counties seeking for a law requiring every person to record their "Mortgage Deeds" to ensure validity of titles to land.- *Manuscript Collection-Oversized Legislative Papers [New Jersey State Archives],* Box 1-43, Folder 2, pg. 1.

Cleayton, Jos, Male

CLYERS, Eisha, - Name on petition, 1 Mar 1748/9, to the governor, etc., seeking passage of a law forbidding the killing of deer by dogs because the meat and hides are mostly worthless.- *Manuscript Collection-Governors' Papers [New Jersey State Archives],* Box 1-1, Folder 4, pg. 1.

Clyers, Eisha, Male

CLYERS, John, - Name on petition, 1 Mar 1748/9, to the governor, etc., seeking passage of a law forbidding the killing of deer by dogs because the meat and hides are mostly worthless.- *Manuscript Collection-Governors' Papers [New Jersey State Archives],* Box 1-1, Folder 4, pg. 1.

Clyers, John, Male

COALE OR COATE, Tho, Hunterdon County, Bethlehem - Name on a petition, 12 Jan 1747/8, to Jonathan Belcher, Governor, from inhabitants of Bethlehem in Hunterdon County seeking to have the southerly part of Bethlehem Township made into a new township.- *Legislature-Petitions re: Municipal Boundaries [New Jersey State Archives],* Box 1, Folder 1, pg. 1.

Coale or Coate, Tho, Male

COATE OR COALE, Tho, Hunterdon County, Bethlehem - Name on a petition, 12 Jan 1747/8, to Jonathan Belcher, Governor, from inhabitants of Bethlehem in Hunterdon County seeking to have the southerly part of Bethlehem Township made into a new township.- *Legislature-Petitions re: Municipal Boundaries [New Jersey State Archives],* Box 1, Folder 1, pg. 1.

Coate or Coale, Tho, Male

COCK, Henry, Hunterdon County, Bethlehem - Name on a petition, 12 Jan 1747/8, to Jonathan Belcher, Governor, from inhabitants of Bethlehem in Hunterdon County seeking to have the southerly part of Bethlehem Township made into a new township.- *Legislature-Petitions re: Municipal Boundaries [New Jersey State Archives],* Box 1, Folder 1, pg. 1.

Cock, Henry, Male

COCK, T S, Hunterdon County, Bethlehem - Name on a petition, 12 Jan 1747/8, to Jonathan Belcher, Governor, from inhabitants of Bethlehem in Hunterdon County seeking to have the southerly part of Bethlehem Township made into a new township.- *Legislature-Petitions re: Municipal Boundaries [New Jersey State Archives],* Box 1, Folder 1, pg. 1.

Cock, T S, Male

COCK, Tho, Hunterdon County, Bethlehem - Name on a petition, 12 Jan 1747/8, to Jonathan Belcher, Governor, from inhabitants of Bethlehem in Hunterdon County seeking to have the southerly part of Bethlehem Township made into a new township.- *Legislature-Petitions re: Municipal Boundaries [New Jersey State Archives],* Box 1, Folder 1, pg. 1.

Cock, Tho, Male

COCKER, Emanuel, Essex County, - Name on petition, 10 Apr 1746, to the General Assembly by freeholders & inhabitants of Essex Co. seeking a repeal of acts for preserving of timber & a duty on imported strong liquors. They cannot build ships because of the present war with France & Spain.- *Manuscript Collection-Legislative Records [New Jersey State Archives],* Box 1-12, Folder 25, pg. 1.

Cocker, Emanuel, Male

COLDWIN, Abraham, Morris County, - Name on a petition, 6 Oct 1751, to Governor Jonathan Belcher from owners of "Bloomaries" in Morris County seeking removal of a tax on their iron works (Bloomeries). Many make 5-6 tons or less a year. They seek instead for a bounty on all they produce.- *Manuscript Collection-MSS Coll., #1-100 [New Jersey State Archives],* Box 5-1, Folder 28, pg. 2.

Coldwin, Abraham, Male

COLLINS, Matthew, - Name on a petition, 1754, to the House of Representatives from freeholders of the province opposing the election of Samuel Nevell as a judge of the Supreme Court.- *Manuscript Collection-Legislative Records [New Jersey State Archives],* Box 1-12, Folder 66, pg. 3.

Collins, Matthew, Male

CONARRO, Thomas, Burlington County, Northampton Township - Name on a petition, 30 May 1753, to the House of Representatives from inhabitants in and about Northampton who are requesting an increase in the amount of currency which is scarce. Gold and silver are chiefly transported elsewhere and are scarce also.- *Manuscript Collection-Legislative Records [New Jersey State Archives]*, Box 1-12, Folder 65, pg. 1.

Conarro, Thomas, Male

COREL?, Abraham, - Name on petition, 1 Mar 1748/9, to the governor, etc., seeking passage of a law forbidding the killing of deer by dogs because the meat and hides are mostly worthless.- *Manuscript Collection-Governors' Papers [New Jersey State Archives]*, Box 1-1, Folder 4, pg. 1.

Corel?, Abraham, Male

CORNFALT?, John H?, Hunterdon County, Bethlehem - Name on a petition, 12 Jan 1747/8, to Jonathan Belcher, Governor, from inhabitants of Bethlehem in Hunterdon County seeking to have the southerly part of Bethlehem Township made into a new township.- *Legislature-Petitions re: Municipal Boundaries [New Jersey State Archives]*, Box 1, Folder 1, pg. 1.

Cornfalt?, John H?, Male

COVENHOVEN, Cornelius, Middlesex County, - Name on a petition, 1754, to the House of Representatives from freeholders of the province opposing the election of Samuel Nevell as a judge of the Supreme Court.- *Manuscript Collection-Legislative Records [New Jersey State Archives]*, Box 1-12, Folder 66, pg. 2.

Covenhoven, Cornelius, Male

COVENHOVEN, Dominicus, Middlesex County, - Name on a petition, 1754, to the House of Representatives from freeholders of the province opposing the election of Samuel Nevell as a judge of the Supreme Court.- *Manuscript Collection-Legislative Records [New Jersey State Archives]*, Box 1-12, Folder 66, pg. 2.

Covenhoven, Dominicus, Male

COVENHOVEN, Jacob, Middlesex County, - Name on a petition, 1754, to the House of Representatives from freeholders of the province opposing the election of Samuel Nevell as a judge of the Supreme Court.- *Manuscript Collection-Legislative Records [New Jersey State Archives]*, Box 1-12, Folder 66, pg. 2.

Covenhoven, Jacob, Male

COVENHOVEN, John, Middlesex County, - Name on a petition, 1754, to the House of Representatives from freeholders of the province opposing the election of Samuel Nevell as a judge of the Supreme Court.- *Manuscript Collection-Legislative Records [New Jersey State Archives]*, Box 1-12, Folder 66, pg. 2.

Covenhoven, John, Male

COVENNHOVEN, Lucke?, Middlesex County, - Name on a petition, 1754, to the House of Representatives from freeholders of the province opposing the election of Samuel Nevell as a judge of the Supreme Court.- *Manuscript Collection-Legislative Records [New Jersey State Archives]*, Box 1-12, Folder 66, pg. 2.

Covennhoven, Lucke?, Male

COVINHOVEN, Wm, Middlesex County, - Name on a petition, 1754, to the House of Representatives from freeholders of the province opposing the election of Samuel Nevell as a judge of the Supreme Court.- *Manuscript Collection-Legislative Records [New Jersey State Archives]*, Box 1-12, Folder 66, pg. 2.

Covinhoven, Wm, Male

COWELL, David, Burlington & Hunterdon Cos., - Name on a petition, 1748/9, to the House of Representatives from inhabitants freeholders of Hunterdon and Burlington Counties seeking for a law requiring every person to record their "Mortgage Deeds" to ensure validity of titles to land.- *Manuscript Collection-Oversized Legislative Papers [New Jersey State Archives]*, Box 1-43, Folder 2, pg. 1.

Cowell, David, Male

CRAIN, Hazariah, Junior, Essex County, - Name on petition, 10 Apr 1746, to the General Assembly by freeholders & inhabitants of Essex Co. seeking a repeal of acts for preserving of timber & a duty on imported strong liquors. They cannot build ships because of the present war with France & Spain.- *Manuscript Collection-Legislative Records [New Jersey State Archives]*, Box 1-12, Folder 25, pg. 1.

Crain, Hazariah, Junior, Male

CRAIN, Job, Essex County, - Name on petition, 10 Apr 1746, to the General Assembly by freeholders & inhabitants of Essex Co. seeking a repeal of acts for preserving of timber & a duty on imported strong liquors. They cannot build ships because of the present war with France & Spain.- *Manuscript Collection-Legislative Records [New Jersey State Archives]*, Box 1-12, Folder 25, pg. 1.

Crain, Job, Male

CRAIN? [NAME MISSING], Hazariah, Senr?, Essex County, - Name on petition, 10 Apr 1746, to the General Assembly by freeholders & inhabitants of Essex Co. seeking a repeal of acts for preserving of timber & a duty on imported strong liquors. They cannot build ships because of the present war with France & Spain.- *Manuscript Collection-Legislative Records [New Jersey State Archives],* Box 1-12, Folder 25, pg. 1.

Crain? [name missing], Hazariah, Senr?, Male - The last name is missing, but there is a Hazariah Crain Junior on the third line below this entry.

CRAN, Willam, Essex County, - Name on petition, 10 Apr 1746, to the General Assembly by freeholders & inhabitants of Essex Co. seeking a repeal of acts for preserving of timber & a duty on imported strong liquors. They cannot build ships because of the present war with France & Spain.- *Manuscript Collection-Legislative Records [New Jersey State Archives],* Box 1-12, Folder 25, pg. 1.

Cran, Willam, Male

CRAN?, Nathaniel, Essex County, - Name on petition, 10 Apr 1746, to the General Assembly by freeholders & inhabitants of Essex Co. seeking a repeal of acts for preserving of timber & a duty on imported strong liquors. They cannot build ships because of the present war with France & Spain.- *Manuscript Collection-Legislative Records [New Jersey State Archives],* Box 1-12, Folder 25, pg. 1.

cran?, Nathaniel, Male

CRANE, David, Essex County, - Name on petition, 10 Apr 1746, to the General Assembly by freeholders & inhabitants of Essex Co. seeking a repeal of acts for preserving of timber & a duty on imported strong liquors. They cannot build ships because of the present war with France & Spain.- *Manuscript Collection-Legislative Records [New Jersey State Archives],* Box 1-12, Folder 25, pg. 1.

Crane, David, Male

CRANE, Elijah, Essex County, - Name on petition, 10 Apr 1746, to the General Assembly by freeholders & inhabitants of Essex Co. seeking a repeal of acts for preserving of timber & a duty on imported strong liquors. They cannot build ships because of the present war with France & Spain.- *Manuscript Collection-Legislative Records [New Jersey State Archives],* Box 1-12, Folder 25, pg. 1.

Crane, Elijah, Male

CRANE, Isaac, Essex County, - Name on petition, 10 Apr 1746, to the General Assembly by freeholders & inhabitants of Essex Co. seeking a repeal of acts for preserving of timber & a duty on imported strong liquors. They cannot build ships because of the present war with France & Spain.- *Manuscript Collection-Legislative Records [New Jersey State Archives],* Box 1-12, Folder 25, pg. 2.

Crane, Isaac, Male

CRANE, John, Essex County, - Name on petition, 10 Apr 1746, to the General Assembly by freeholders & inhabitants of Essex Co. seeking a repeal of acts for preserving of timber & a duty on imported strong liquors. They cannot build ships because of the present war with France & Spain.- *Manuscript Collection-Legislative Records [New Jersey State Archives],* Box 1-12, Folder 25, pg. 1.

Crane, John, Male

CRANE, Jonas, Essex County, - Name on petition, 10 Apr 1746, to the General Assembly by freeholders & inhabitants of Essex Co. seeking a repeal of acts for preserving of timber & a duty on imported strong liquors. They cannot build ships because of the present war with France & Spain.- *Manuscript Collection-Legislative Records [New Jersey State Archives],* Box 1-12, Folder 25, pg. 1.

Crane, Jonas, Male

CRANE, Josiah, Essex County, - Name on petition, 10 Apr 1746, to the General Assembly by freeholders & inhabitants of Essex Co. seeking a repeal of acts for preserving of timber & a duty on imported strong liquors. They cannot build ships because of the present war with France & Spain.- *Manuscript Collection-Legislative Records [New Jersey State Archives],* Box 1-12, Folder 25, pg. 2.

Crane, Josiah, Male

CROSBY?, moses, Cape May County, - Name on petition, 12 Mar 1745/6, to the House of Representatives from freeholders of Cape May County complaining of the devaluation of their paper money [likely due in part to the present war] and asking for creation of a fund, apparently to stabilize it.- *Manuscript Collection-Legislative Records [New Jersey State Archives],* Box 1-12, Folder 22, pg. 1.

Crosby?, moses, Male

CROWELL, Barnabas, Cape May County, - Name on petition, 12 Mar 1745/6, to the House of Representatives from freeholders of Cape May County complaining of the devaluation of their paper money [likely due in part to the present war] and asking for creation of a fund, apparently to stabilize it.- *Manuscript Collection-Legislative Records [New Jersey State Archives],* Box 1-12, Folder 22, pg. 1.

Crowell, Barnabas, Male

CROWELL, Samuel, Essex County, - Name on petition, 10 Apr 1746, to the General Assembly by freeholders & inhabitants of Essex Co. seeking a repeal of acts for preserving of timber & a duty on imported strong liquors. They cannot build ships because of the present war with France & Spain.- *Manuscript Collection-Legislative Records [New Jersey State Archives],* Box 1-12, Folder 25, pg. 2.

Crowell, Samuel, Male

CUBBERLEY, Isaac, Middlesex County, - Name on a petition, 1754, to the House of Representatives from freeholders of the province opposing the election of Samuel Nevell as a judge of the Supreme Court.- *Manuscript Collection-Legislative Records [New Jersey State Archives],* Box 1-12, Folder 66, pg. 2.

Cubberley, Isaac, Male

CUBBERLEY, James, Burlington County, Nottingham - Name on a petition, 18 Nov 1748, to the House of Representatives from inhabitants of Nottingham, Burlington County complaining of those hunting out of season who have killed their hogs and cattle. Sometimes people are in danger of being shot.- *Manuscript Collection-Legislative Records [New Jersey State Archives],* Box 1-12, Folder 46, pg. 1.

Cubberley, James, Male

CUBBERLEY, Thomas, Burlington County, Nottingham - Name on a petition, 18 Nov 1748, to the House of Representatives from inhabitants of Nottingham, Burlington County complaining of those hunting out of season who have killed their hogs and cattle. Sometimes people are in danger of being shot.- *Manuscript Collection-Legislative Records [New Jersey State Archives],* Box 1-12, Folder 46, pg. 1.

Cubberley, Thomas, Male

CUBBERLEY, William, Burlington County, Nottingham - Name on a petition, 18 Nov 1748, to the House of Representatives from inhabitants of Nottingham, Burlington County complaining of those hunting out of season who have killed their hogs and cattle. Sometimes people are in danger of being shot.- *Manuscript Collection-Legislative Records [New Jersey State Archives],* Box 1-12, Folder 46, pg. 1.

Cubberley, William, Male

CUMINS?, James, Burlington & Hunterdon Cos., - Name on a petition, 1748/9, to the House of Representatives from inhabitants freeholders of Hunterdon and Burlington Counties seeking for a law requiring every person to record their "Mortgage Deeds" to ensure validity of titles to land.- *Manuscript Collection-Oversized Legislative Papers [New Jersey State Archives],* Box 1-43, Folder 2, pg. 1.

Cumins?, James, Male

CUNDET, Jotham, Essex County, - Name on petition, 10 Apr 1746, to the General Assembly by freeholders & inhabitants of Essex Co. seeking a repeal of acts for preserving of timber & a duty on imported strong liquors. They cannot build ships because of the present war with France & Spain.- *Manuscript Collection-Legislative Records [New Jersey State Archives],* Box 1-12, Folder 25, pg. 1.

Cundet, Jotham, Male

CUNDICT, John, Essex County, - Name on petition, 10 Apr 1746, to the General Assembly by freeholders & inhabitants of Essex Co. seeking a repeal of acts for preserving of timber & a duty on imported strong liquors. They cannot build ships because of the present war with France & Spain.- *Manuscript Collection-Legislative Records [New Jersey State Archives],* Box 1-12, Folder 25, pg. 1.

Cundict, John, Male

CURDET, Isaac, Essex County, - Name on petition, 10 Apr 1746, to the General Assembly by freeholders & inhabitants of Essex Co. seeking a repeal of acts for preserving of timber & a duty on imported strong liquors. They cannot build ships because of the present war with France & Spain.- *Manuscript Collection-Legislative Records [New Jersey State Archives],* Box 1-12, Folder 25, pg. 1.

Curdet, Isaac, Male

CURDET, Nathaniel, Essex County, - Name on petition, 10 Apr 1746, to the General Assembly by freeholders & inhabitants of Essex Co. seeking a repeal of acts for preserving of timber & a duty on imported strong liquors. They cannot build ships because of the present war with France & Spain.- *Manuscript Collection-Legislative Records [New Jersey State Archives],* Box 1-12, Folder 25, pg. 1.

Curdet, Nathaniel, Male

CURDET?, Samll, Essex County, - Name on petition, 10 Apr 1746, to the General Assembly by freeholders & inhabitants of Essex Co. seeking a repeal of acts for preserving of timber & a duty on imported strong liquors. They cannot build ships because of the present war with France & Spain.- *Manuscript Collection-Legislative Records [New Jersey State Archives],* Box 1-12, Folder 25, pg. 1.

Cordet?, Samll, Male

CURREY, Jeph,** Essex County, - Name on petition, 10 Apr 1746, to the General Assembly by freeholders & inhabitants of Essex Co. seeking a repeal of acts for preserving of timber & a duty on imported strong liquors. They cannot build ships because of the present war with France & Spain.- *Manuscript Collection-Legislative Records [New Jersey State Archives]*, Box 1-12, Folder 25, pg. 1.

Currey, J**eph, Male

CURTIS?, Tho, Hunterdon County, Bethlehem - Name on a petition, 12 Jan 1747/8, to Jonathan Belcher, Governor, from inhabitants of Bethlehem in Hunterdon County seeking to have the southerly part of Bethlehem Township made into a new township.- *Legislature-Petitions re: Municipal Boundaries [New Jersey State Archives]*, Box 1, Folder 1, pg. 1.

Curtis?, Tho, Male

CURVYE?, Jonathan, Hunterdon County, Bethlehem - Name on a petition, 12 Jan 1747/8, to Jonathan Belcher, Governor, from inhabitants of Bethlehem in Hunterdon County seeking to have the southerly part of Bethlehem Township made into a new township.- *Legislature-Petitions re: Municipal Boundaries [New Jersey State Archives]*, Box 1, Folder 1, pg. 1.

Curvye?, Jonathan, Male

DAVIS, Caleb, Essex County, - Name on petition, 10 Apr 1746, to the General Assembly by freeholders & inhabitants of Essex Co. seeking a repeal of acts for preserving of timber & a duty on imported strong liquors. They cannot build ships because of the present war with France & Spain.- *Manuscript Collection-Legislative Records [New Jersey State Archives]*, Box 1-12, Folder 25, pg. 1.

Davis, Caleb, Male

DAVISON, John, Middlesex County, Perth Amboy Township - Name on a petition, 1754, to the General Assembly from freeholders/inhabitants of Perth Amboy Township in Middlesex County opposing the election of Samuel Nevill as a judge of the Supreme Court.- *Manuscript Collection-Oversized Legislative Papers [New Jersey State Archives]*, Box 1-43, Folder 2, pg. 1.

Davison, John, Male

DAVISON, Robert, Middlesex County, Perth Amboy Township - Name on a petition, 1754, to the General Assembly from freeholders/inhabitants of Perth Amboy Township in Middlesex County opposing the election of Samuel Nevill as a judge of the Supreme Court.- *Manuscript Collection-Oversized Legislative Papers [New Jersey State Archives]*, Box 1-43, Folder 2, pg. 1.

Davison, Robert, Male

DAVISON, William, - Name on a petition, 1754, to the House of Representatives from freeholders of the province opposing the election of Samuel Nevell as a judge of the Supreme Court.- *Manuscript Collection-Legislative Records [New Jersey State Archives]*, Box 1-12, Folder 66, pg. 3.

Davison, William, Male

DAY, Jonathan, Essex County, - Name on petition, 10 Apr 1746, to the General Assembly by freeholders & inhabitants of Essex Co. seeking a repeal of acts for preserving of timber & a duty on imported strong liquors. They cannot build ships because of the present war with France & Spain.- *Manuscript Collection-Legislative Records [New Jersey State Archives]*, Box 1-12, Folder 25, pg. 2.

Day, Jonathan, Male

DAY, Joseph, Essex County, - Name on petition, 10 Apr 1746, to the General Assembly by freeholders & inhabitants of Essex Co. seeking a repeal of acts for preserving of timber & a duty on imported strong liquors. They cannot build ships because of the present war with France & Spain.- *Manuscript Collection-Legislative Records [New Jersey State Archives]*, Box 1-12, Folder 25, pg. 2.

Day, Joseph, Male

DEAN, John, Burlington & Hunterdon Cos., - Name on a petition, 1748/9, to the House of Representatives from inhabitants freeholders of Hunterdon and Burlington Counties seeking for a law requiring every person to record their "Mortgage Deeds" to ensure validity of titles to land.- *Manuscript Collection-Oversized Legislative Papers [New Jersey State Archives]*, Box 1-43, Folder 2, pg. 1.

Dean, John, Male

DEAN, Thomas, Essex County, - Name on petition, 10 Apr 1746, to the General Assembly by freeholders & inhabitants of Essex Co. seeking a repeal of acts for preserving of timber & a duty on imported strong liquors. They cannot build ships because of the present war with France & Spain.- *Manuscript Collection-Legislative Records [New Jersey State Archives]*, Box 1-12, Folder 25, pg. 2.

Dean, Thomas, Male

DECONE?, Jos, Burlington & Hunterdon Cos., - Name on a petition, 1748/9, to the House of Representatives from inhabitants freeholders of Hunterdon and Burlington Counties seeking for a law requiring every person to record their "Mortgage Deeds" to ensure validity of titles to land.- *Manuscript Collection-Oversized Legislative Papers [New Jersey State Archives],* Box 1-43, Folder 2, pg. 1.

DeCone?, Jos, Male

DEON, Benjamen, - Name on a petition, 1754, to the House of Representatives from freeholders of the province opposing the election of Samuel Nevell as a judge of the Supreme Court.- *Manuscript Collection-Legislative Records [New Jersey State Archives],* Box 1-12, Folder 66, pg. 3.

Deon, Benjamen, Male

DERKINS, Abraham, Burlington County, Northampton Township - Name on a petition, 30 May 1753, to the House of Representatives from inhabitants in and about Northampton who are requesting an increase in the amount of currency which is scarce. Gold and silver are chiefly transported elsewhere and are scarce also.- *Manuscript Collection-Legislative Records [New Jersey State Archives],* Box 1-12, Folder 65, pg. 1.

Derkins, Abraham, Male

DERUMPLE, Joseph, - Name on petition, 1 Mar 1748/9, to the governor, etc., seeking passage of a law forbidding the killing of deer by dogs because the meat and hides are mostly worthless.- *Manuscript Collection-Governors' Papers [New Jersey State Archives],* Box 1-1, Folder 4, pg. 1.

Derumple, Joseph, Male

DISBROW, Daniel, - Name on a petition, 1754, to the House of Representatives from freeholders of the province opposing the election of Samuel Nevell as a judge of the Supreme Court.- *Manuscript Collection-Legislative Records [New Jersey State Archives],* Box 1-12, Folder 66, pg. 1.

Disbrow, Daniel, Male

DOD, Daniel, Essex County, - Name on petition, 10 Apr 1746, to the General Assembly by freeholders & inhabitants of Essex Co. seeking a repeal of acts for preserving of timber & a duty on imported strong liquors. They cannot build ships because of the present war with France & Spain.- *Manuscript Collection-Legislative Records [New Jersey State Archives],* Box 1-12, Folder 25, pg. 1.

Dod, Daniel, Male

DOD, John, Essex County, - Name on petition, 10 Apr 1746, to the General Assembly by freeholders & inhabitants of Essex Co. seeking a repeal of acts for preserving of timber & a duty on imported strong liquors. They cannot build ships because of the present war with France & Spain.- *Manuscript Collection-Legislative Records [New Jersey State Archives],* Box 1-12, Folder 25, pg. 1.

Dod, John, Male

DOD, John, iuneor, Essex County, - Name on petition, 10 Apr 1746, to the General Assembly by freeholders & inhabitants of Essex Co. seeking a repeal of acts for preserving of timber & a duty on imported strong liquors. They cannot build ships because of the present war with France & Spain.- *Manuscript Collection-Legislative Records [New Jersey State Archives],* Box 1-12, Folder 25, pg. 1.

Dod, John, iuneor, Male

DOD, Joseph, Essex County, - Name on petition, 10 Apr 1746, to the General Assembly by freeholders & inhabitants of Essex Co. seeking a repeal of acts for preserving of timber & a duty on imported strong liquors. They cannot build ships because of the present war with France & Spain.- *Manuscript Collection-Legislative Records [New Jersey State Archives],* Box 1-12, Folder 25, pg. 2.

Dod, Joseph, Male

DOD, Samuell, Essex County, - Name on petition, 10 Apr 1746, to the General Assembly by freeholders & inhabitants of Essex Co. seeking a repeal of acts for preserving of timber & a duty on imported strong liquors. They cannot build ships because of the present war with France & Spain.- *Manuscript Collection-Legislative Records [New Jersey State Archives],* Box 1-12, Folder 25, pg. 1.

Dod, Samuell, Male

DOD, Thomas, Essex County, - Name on petition, 10 Apr 1746, to the General Assembly by freeholders & inhabitants of Essex Co. seeking a repeal of acts for preserving of timber & a duty on imported strong liquors. They cannot build ships because of the present war with France & Spain.- *Manuscript Collection-Legislative Records [New Jersey State Archives],* Box 1-12, Folder 25, pg. 1.

Dod, Thomas, Male

DOND, John, Essex County, - Name on petition, 10 Apr 1746, to the General Assembly by freeholders & inhabitants of Essex Co. seeking a repeal of acts for preserving of timber & a duty on imported strong liquors. They cannot build ships because of the present war with France & Spain.- *Manuscript Collection-Legislative Records [New Jersey State Archives],* Box 1-12, Folder 25, pg. 2.

Dond, John, Male

DOTY, Jonathan, - Name on petition, 1 Mar 1748/9, to the governor, etc., seeking passage of a law forbidding the killing of deer by dogs because the meat and hides are mostly worthless.- *Manuscript Collection-Governors' Papers [New Jersey State Archives]*, Box 1-1, Folder 4, pg. 1.

Doty, Jonathan, Male

DOTY, Moses, - Name on petition, 1 Mar 1748/9, to the governor, etc., seeking passage of a law forbidding the killing of deer by dogs because the meat and hides are mostly worthless.- *Manuscript Collection-Governors' Papers [New Jersey State Archives]*, Box 1-1, Folder 4, pg. 1.

Doty, Moses, Male

DOUGHTY, D . . ., Hunterdon County, Bethlehem - Name on a petition, 12 Jan 1747/8, to Jonathan Belcher, Governor, from inhabitants of Bethlehem in Hunterdon County seeking to have the southerly part of Bethlehem Township made into a new township.- *Legislature-Petitions re: Municipal Boundaries [New Jersey State Archives]*, Box 1, Folder 1, pg. 1.

Doughty, D . . ., Male

DUDLES, Samuel, - Name on petition, 1 Mar 1748/9, to the governor, etc., seeking passage of a law forbidding the killing of deer by dogs because the meat and hides are mostly worthless.- *Manuscript Collection-Governors' Papers [New Jersey State Archives]*, Box 1-1, Folder 4, pg. 1.

Dudles, Samuel, Male

DUNBAR, David, Burlington & Hunterdon Cos., - Name on a petition, 1748/9, to the House of Representatives from inhabitants freeholders of Hunterdon and Burlington Counties seeking for a law requiring every person to record their "Mortgage Deeds" to ensure validity of titles to land.- *Manuscript Collection-Oversized Legislative Papers [New Jersey State Archives]*, Box 1-43, Folder 2, pg. 1.

Dunbar, David, Male

DUNHAM?, Wm, Burlington & Hunterdon Cos., - Name on a petition, 1748/9, to the House of Representatives from inhabitants freeholders of Hunterdon and Burlington Counties seeking for a law requiring every person to record their "Mortgage Deeds" to ensure validity of titles to land.- *Manuscript Collection-Oversized Legislative Papers [New Jersey State Archives]*, Box 1-43, Folder 2, pg. 1.

Dunham?, Wm, Male

DY, John, Middlesex County, Perth Amboy Township - Name on a petition, 1754, to the General Assembly from freeholders/inhabitants of Perth Amboy Township in Middlesex County opposing the election of Samuel Nevill as a judge of the Supreme Court.- *Manuscript Collection-Oversized Legislative Papers [New Jersey State Archives]*, Box 1-43, Folder 2, pg. 1.

Dy, John, Male

DYE, william, Middlesex County, Perth Amboy Township - Name on a petition, 1754, to the General Assembly from freeholders/inhabitants of Perth Amboy Township in Middlesex County opposing the election of Samuel Nevill as a judge of the Supreme Court.- *Manuscript Collection-Oversized Legislative Papers [New Jersey State Archives]*, Box 1-43, Folder 2, pg. 1.

Dye, william, Male -He signed his name with a "w".

EDWARDS, Epharhaser?, Cape May County, - Name on petition, 12 Mar 1745/6, to the House of Representatives from freeholders of Cape May County complaining of the devaluation of their paper money [likely due in part to the present war] and asking for creation of a fund, apparently to stabilize it.- *Manuscript Collection-Legislative Records [New Jersey State Archives]*, Box 1-12, Folder 22, pg. 1.

Edwards, Epharhaser?, Male

EDWARDS, James, Cape May County, - Name on petition, 12 Mar 1745/6, to the House of Representatives from freeholders of Cape May County complaining of the devaluation of their paper money [likely due in part to the present war] and asking for creation of a fund, apparently to stabilize it.- *Manuscript Collection-Legislative Records [New Jersey State Archives]*, Box 1-12, Folder 22, pg. 1.

Edwards, James, Male

ELDIDG?, Obediah, - Name on a petition, 1750/1, the House of Representatives from inhabitants of the province protesting against the great number of taverns in the province.- *Manuscript Collection-Legislative Records [New Jersey State Archives]*, Box 1-12, Folder 59, pg. 1.

Eldidg?, Obediah, Male

ELDREDGE, John, Cape May County, - Name on petition, 12 Mar 1745/6, to the House of Representatives from freeholders of Cape May County complaining of the devaluation of their paper money [likely due in part to the present war] and asking for creation of a fund, apparently to stabilize it.- *Manuscript Collection-Legislative*

Records [New Jersey State Archives], Box 1-12, Folder 22, pg. 1.

Eldredge, John, Male

ELDREDGE, Samuel, Cape May County, - Name on petition, 12 Mar 1745/6, to the House of Representatives from freeholders of Cape May County complaining of the devaluation of their paper money [likely due in part to the present war] and asking for creation of a fund, apparently to stabilize it.- *Manuscript Collection-Legislative Records [New Jersey State Archives],* Box 1-12, Folder 22, pg. 1.

Eldredge, Samuel, Male

ELDREDGE, William, Cape May County, - Name on petition, 12 Mar 1745/6, to the House of Representatives from freeholders of Cape May County complaining of the devaluation of their paper money [likely due in part to the present war] and asking for creation of a fund, apparently to stabilize it.- *Manuscript Collection-Legislative Records [New Jersey State Archives],* Box 1-12, Folder 22, pg. 1.

Eldredge, William, Male

ELDRIDGE, James, - Name on a petition, 24 Sep? 1753, to the House of Representatives from inhabitants of the province expressing distress because of a lack of currency as a medium of trade. They present various arguments for the value of a paper currency.- *Manuscript Collection-Oversized Legislative Papers [New Jersey State Archives],* Box 1-43, Folder 4, pg. 1.

Eldridge, James, Male

ELTON, Revell, Burlington County, Northampton Township - Name on a petition, 30 May 1753, to the House of Representatives from inhabitants in and about Northampton who are requesting an increase in the amount of currency which is scarce. Gold and silver are chiefly transported elsewhere and are scarce also.- *Manuscript Collection-Legislative Records [New Jersey State Archives],* Box 1-12, Folder 65, pg. 1.

Elton, Revell, Male

EMLEY, Elisha, Hunterdon County, Bethlehem - Name on a petition, 12 Jan 1747/8, to Jonathan Belcher, Governor, from inhabitants of Bethlehem in Hunterdon County seeking to have the southerly part of Bethlehem Township made into a new township.- *Legislature-Petitions re: Municipal Boundaries [New Jersey State Archives],* Box 1, Folder 1, pg. 1.

Emley, Elisha, Male

EMLEY, Jno, Jur, Hunterdon County, Bethlehem - Name on a petition, 12 Jan 1747/8, to Jonathan Belcher, Governor, from inhabitants of Bethlehem in Hunterdon County seeking to have the southerly part of Bethlehem Township made into a new township.- *Legislature-Petitions re: Municipal Boundaries [New Jersey State Archives],* Box 1, Folder 1, pg. 1.

Emley, Jno, Jur, Male

EMLEY, Wm, Hunterdon County, Bethlehem - Name on a petition, 12 Jan 1747/8, to Jonathan Belcher, Governor, from inhabitants of Bethlehem in Hunterdon County seeking to have the southerly part of Bethlehem Township made into a new township.- *Legislature-Petitions re: Municipal Boundaries [New Jersey State Archives],* Box 1, Folder 1, pg. 1.

Emley, Wm, Male

EVANS, Tho, Hunterdon County, Bethlehem - Name on a petition, 12 Jan 1747/8, to Jonathan Belcher, Governor, from inhabitants of Bethlehem in Hunterdon County seeking to have the southerly part of Bethlehem Township made into a new township.- *Legislature-Petitions re: Municipal Boundaries [New Jersey State Archives],* Box 1, Folder 1, pg. 1.

Evans, Tho, Male

EVENS, Isaac, - Name on a petition, 24 Sep? 1753, to the House of Representatives from inhabitants of the province expressing distress because of a lack of currency as a medium of trade. They present various arguments for the value of a paper currency.- *Manuscript Collection-Oversized Legislative Papers [New Jersey State Archives],* Box 1-43, Folder 4, pg. 1.

Evens, Isaac, Male

EVENS, William, - Name on a petition, 24 Sep? 1753, to the House of Representatives from inhabitants of the province expressing distress because of a lack of currency as a medium of trade. They present various arguments for the value of a paper currency.- *Manuscript Collection-Oversized Legislative Papers [New Jersey State Archives],* Box 1-43, Folder 4, pg. 1.

Evens, William, Male

EVERITT, John, Hunterdon County, Bethlehem - Name on a petition, 12 Jan 1747/8, to Jonathan Belcher, Governor, from inhabitants of Bethlehem in Hunterdon County seeking to have the southerly part of Bethlehem Township made into a new township.- *Legislature-Petitions re: Municipal*

Boundaries [New Jersey State Archives], Box 1, Folder 1, pg. 1.

Everitt, John, Male

EVINS?, John, Burlington & Hunterdon Cos., - Name on a petition, 1748/9, to the House of Representatives from inhabitants freeholders of Hunterdon and Burlington Counties seeking for a law requiring every person to record their "Mortgage Deeds" to ensure validity of titles to land.- *Manuscript Collection-Oversized Legislative Papers [New Jersey State Archives]*, Box 1-43, Folder 2, pg. 1.

Evins?, John, Male

EWAN, Julius, Burlington County, Northampton Township - Name on a petition, 30 May 1753, to the House of Representatives from inhabitants in and about Northampton who are requesting an increase in the amount of currency which is scarce. Gold and silver are chiefly transported elsewhere and are scarce also.- *Manuscript Collection-Legislative Records [New Jersey State Archives]*, Box 1-12, Folder 65, pg. 1.

Ewan, Julius, Male

FANTUM OR TANTUM, John, Hunterdon County, Bethlehem - On a petition, 12 Jan 1747/8, to Jonathan Belcher, Governor, from inhabitants of Bethlehem in Hunterdon County seeking to have the southerly part of Bethlehem Township made into a new township part of the boundary is an "Island formerly John Fantum's".- *Legislature-Petitions re: Municipal Boundaries [New Jersey State Archives]*, Box 1, Folder 1, pg. 1.

Fantum or Tantum, John, Male

FARNSWORTH, Saml, Burlington & Hunterdon Cos., - Name on a petition, 1748/9, to the House of Representatives from inhabitants freeholders of Hunterdon and Burlington Counties seeking for a law requiring every person to record their "Mortgage Deeds" to ensure validity of titles to land.- *Manuscript Collection-Oversized Legislative Papers [New Jersey State Archives]*, Box 1-43, Folder 2, pg. 1.

Farnsworth, Saml, Male

FARQUHA, Adam, - Name on a petition, 1750/1, the House of Representatives from inhabitants of the province protesting against the great number of taverns in the province.- *Manuscript Collection-Legislative Records [New Jersey State Archives]*, Box 1-12, Folder 59, pg. 1.

farquha, Adam, Male

FERRIS, Robert, Middlesex County, - Name on a petition, 1754, to the House of Representatives from freeholders of the province opposing the election of Samuel Nevell as a judge of the Supreme Court.- *Manuscript Collection-Legislative Records [New Jersey State Archives]*, Box 1-12, Folder 66, pg. 2.

Ferris, Robert, Male

FFARNSWORTH, Henry, Hunterdon County, Bethlehem - Name on a petition, 12 Jan 1747/8, to Jonathan Belcher, Governor, from inhabitants of Bethlehem in Hunterdon County seeking to have the southerly part of Bethlehem Township made into a new township.- *Legislature-Petitions re: Municipal Boundaries [New Jersey State Archives]*, Box 1, Folder 1, pg. 1.

ffarnsworth, Henry, Male

FFARRINGTON, Abrm, - Name on a petition, 1750/1, the House of Representatives from inhabitants of the province protesting against the great number of taverns in the province.- *Manuscript Collection-Legislative Records [New Jersey State Archives]*, Box 1-12, Folder 59, pg. 1.

ffarrington, Abrm, Male

FFORD?, Jacob, Morris County, - Name on a petition, 6 Oct 1751, to Governor Jonathan Belcher from owners of "Bloomaries" in Morris County seeking removal of a tax on their iron works (Bloomeries). Many make 5-6 tons or less a year. They seek instead for a bounty on all they produce.- *Manuscript Collection-MSS Coll., #1-100 [New Jersey State Archives]*, Box 5-1, Folder 28, pg. 2.

Fford?, Jacob, Male

FLOWER, John, Cape May County, - Name on petition, 12 Mar 1745/6, to the House of Representatives from freeholders of Cape May County complaining of the devaluation of their paper money [likely due in part to the present war] and asking for creation of a fund, apparently to stabilize it.- *Manuscript Collection-Legislative Records [New Jersey State Archives]*, Box 1-12, Folder 22, pg. 1.

flower, John, Male

FOLKES, Thos, Burlington & Hunterdon Cos., - Name on a petition, 1748/9, to the House of Representatives from inhabitants freeholders of Hunterdon and Burlington Counties seeking for a law requiring every person to record their "Mortgage Deeds" to ensure validity of titles to land.- *Manuscript Collection-Oversized Legislative*

Papers [New Jersey State Archives], Box 1-43, Folder 2, pg. 1.

Folkes, Thos, Male

FOSTEN? OR FOSTER, Nathall, Cape May County, - Name on petition, 12 Mar 1745/6, to the House of Representatives from freeholders of Cape May County complaining of the devaluation of their paper money [likely due in part to the present war] and asking for creation of a fund, apparently to stabilize it.- *Manuscript Collection-Legislative Records [New Jersey State Archives],* Box 1-12, Folder 22, pg. 1.

Fosten? or Foster, Nathall, Male

FOSTER, Josiah, - Name on a petition, 1750/1, the House of Representatives from inhabitants of the province protesting against the great number of taverns in the province.- *Manuscript Collection-Legislative Records [New Jersey State Archives],* Box 1-12, Folder 59, pg. 1.

Foster, Josiah, Male

FOSTER, Josiah, - Name on a petition, 24 Sep? 1753, to the House of Representatives from inhabitants of the province expressing distress because of a lack of currency as a medium of trade. They present various arguments for the value of a paper currency.- *Manuscript Collection-Oversized Legislative Papers [New Jersey State Archives],* Box 1-43, Folder 4, pg. 1.

Foster, Josiah, Male

FOSTER, William, - Name on a petition, 24 Sep? 1753, to the House of Representatives from inhabitants of the province expressing distress because of a lack of currency as a medium of trade. They present various arguments for the value of a paper currency.- *Manuscript Collection-Oversized Legislative Papers [New Jersey State Archives],* Box 1-43, Folder 4, pg. 1.

Foster, William, Male

FOSTER OR FOSTEN?, Nathall, Cape May County, - Name on petition, 12 Mar 1745/6, to the House of Representatives from freeholders of Cape May County complaining of the devaluation of their paper money [likely due in part to the present war] and asking for creation of a fund, apparently to stabilize it.- *Manuscript Collection-Legislative Records [New Jersey State Archives],* Box 1-12, Folder 22, pg. 1.

Foster or Fosten?, Nathall, Male

FOX, Georg, Hunterdon County, Bethlehem - Name on a petition, 12 Jan 1747/8, to Jonathan Belcher, Governor, from inhabitants of Bethlehem in Hunterdon County seeking to have the southerly part of Bethlehem Township made into a new township.- *Legislature-Petitions re: Municipal Boundaries [New Jersey State Archives],* Box 1, Folder 1, pg. 1.

fox, Georg, Male

FREEMAN, James, - Name on a petition, 1754, to the House of Representatives from freeholders of the province opposing the election of Samuel Nevell as a judge of the Supreme Court.- *Manuscript Collection-Legislative Records [New Jersey State Archives],* Box 1-12, Folder 66, pg. 3.

Freeman, James, Male

FREEMAN, Jedadiah, Essex County, - Name on petition, 10 Apr 1746, to the General Assembly by freeholders & inhabitants of Essex Co. seeking a repeal of acts for preserving of timber & a duty on imported strong liquors. They cannot build ships because of the present war with France & Spain.- *Manuscript Collection-Legislative Records [New Jersey State Archives],* Box 1-12, Folder 25, pg. 1.

Freeman, Jedadiah, Male

FREEMAN, Samll, Essex County, - Name on petition, 10 Apr 1746, to the General Assembly by freeholders & inhabitants of Essex Co. seeking a repeal of acts for preserving of timber & a duty on imported strong liquors. They cannot build ships because of the present war with France & Spain.- *Manuscript Collection-Legislative Records [New Jersey State Archives],* Box 1-12, Folder 25, pg. 1.

Freeman, Samll, Male

FREEMAN, Samuel, Junr, Essex County, - Name on petition, 10 Apr 1746, to the General Assembly by freeholders & inhabitants of Essex Co. seeking a repeal of acts for preserving of timber & a duty on imported strong liquors. They cannot build ships because of the present war with France & Spain.- *Manuscript Collection-Legislative Records [New Jersey State Archives],* Box 1-12, Folder 25, pg. 1.

Freeman, Samuel, Junr, Male

FREEMAN, Timothy, Essex County, - Name on petition, 10 Apr 1746, to the General Assembly by freeholders & inhabitants of Essex Co. seeking a repeal of acts for preserving of timber & a duty on imported strong liquors. They cannot build ships because of the present war with France & Spain.- *Manuscript Collection-Legislative Records [New Jersey State Archives],* Box 1-12, Folder 25, pg. 1.

Freeman, Timothy, Male

FREEMAN?, Beniamin, Essex County, - Name on petition, 10 Apr 1746, to the General Assembly by freeholders & inhabitants of Essex Co. seeking a repeal of acts for preserving of timber & a duty on imported strong liquors. They cannot build ships because of the present war with France & Spain.- *Manuscript Collection-Legislative Records [New Jersey State Archives],* Box 1-12, Folder 25, pg. 1.
Freeman?, Beniamin, Male

FREEMAN?, Richd, Burlington & Hunterdon Cos., - Name on a petition, 1748/9, to the House of Representatives from inhabitants freeholders of Hunterdon and Burlington Counties seeking for a law requiring every person to record their "Mortgage Deeds" to ensure validity of titles to land.- *Manuscript Collection-Oversized Legislative Papers [New Jersey State Archives],* Box 1-43, Folder 2, pg. 1.
freeman?, Richd, Male

FROST, James, Morris County, - Name on a petition, 6 Oct 1751, to Governor Jonathan Belcher from owners of "Bloomaries" in Morris County seeking removal of a tax on their iron works (Bloomeries). Many make 5-6 tons or less a year. They seek instead for a bounty on all they produce.- *Manuscript Collection-MSS Coll., #1-100 [New Jersey State Archives],* Box 5-1, Folder 28, pg. 2.
Frost, James, Male

FURMAN?, Josiah, Burlington & Hunterdon Cos., - Name on a petition, 1748/9, to the House of Representatives from inhabitants freeholders of Hunterdon and Burlington Counties seeking for a law requiring every person to record their "Mortgage Deeds" to ensure validity of titles to land.- *Manuscript Collection-Oversized Legislative Papers [New Jersey State Archives],* Box 1-43, Folder 2, pg. 1.
Furman?, Josiah, Male

GARLICK, Joshua, Cape May County, - Name on petition, 12 Mar 1745/6, to the House of Representatives from freeholders of Cape May County complaining of the devaluation of their paper money [likely due in part to the present war] and asking for creation of a fund, apparently to stabilize it.- *Manuscript Collection-Legislative Records [New Jersey State Archives],* Box 1-12, Folder 22, pg. 1.
Garlick, Joshua, Male

GASKILL, Benieman, - Name on a petition, 1750/1, the House of Representatives from inhabitants of the province protesting against the great number of taverns in the province.- *Manuscript Collection-Legislative Records [New Jersey State Archives],* Box 1-12, Folder 59, pg. 1.
gaskill, Benieman, Male

GASKILL, Ebenezer, - Name on a petition, 1750/1, the House of Representatives from inhabitants of the province protesting against the great number of taverns in the province.- *Manuscript Collection-Legislative Records [New Jersey State Archives],* Box 1-12, Folder 59, pg. 1.
Gaskill, Ebenezer, Male -He signed his name with an "x".

GASKILL, Edward, - Name on a petition, 1750/1, the House of Representatives from inhabitants of the province protesting against the great number of taverns in the province.- *Manuscript Collection-Legislative Records [New Jersey State Archives],* Box 1-12, Folder 59, pg. 1.
gaskill, Edward, Male

GASKILL, Jonathan, - Name on a petition, 1750/1, the House of Representatives from inhabitants of the province protesting against the great number of taverns in the province.- *Manuscript Collection-Legislative Records [New Jersey State Archives],* Box 1-12, Folder 59, pg. 1.
gaskill, Jonathan, Male

GASKILL, Joseph, - Name on a petition, 1750/1, the House of Representatives from inhabitants of the province protesting against the great number of taverns in the province.- *Manuscript Collection-Legislative Records [New Jersey State Archives],* Box 1-12, Folder 59, pg. 1.
Gaskill, Joseph, Male

GASKILL, Solomon, - Name on a petition, 24 Sep? 1753, to the House of Representatives from inhabitants of the province expressing distress because of a lack of currency as a medium of trade. They present various arguments for the value of a paper currency.- *Manuscript Collection-Oversized Legislative Papers [New Jersey State Archives],* Box 1-43, Folder 4, pg. 1.
Gaskill, Solomon, Male

GASKILL, Stephen, - Name on a petition, 1750/1, the House of Representatives from inhabitants of the province protesting against the great number of taverns in the province.- *Manuscript Collection-Legislative Records [New Jersey State Archives],* Box 1-12, Folder 59, pg. 1.

gaskill, Stephen, Male

GASKILL, Zerubbabel, - Name on a petition, 1750/1, the House of Representatives from inhabitants of the province protesting against the great number of taverns in the province.- *Manuscript Collection-Legislative Records [New Jersey State Archives],* Box 1-12, Folder 59, pg. 1.

gaskill, Zerubbabel, Male

GERRETSEN, Gerreth, Essex County, - Name on petition, 10 Apr 1746, to the General Assembly by freeholders & inhabitants of Essex Co. seeking a repeal of acts for preserving of timber & a duty on imported strong liquors. They cannot build ships because of the present war with France & Spain.- *Manuscript Collection-Legislative Records [New Jersey State Archives],* Box 1-12, Folder 25, pg. 2.

Gerretsen, Gerreth, Male

GEY, Jonathan, Burlington & Hunterdon Cos., - Name on a petition, 1748/9, to the House of Representatives from inhabitants freeholders of Hunterdon and Burlington Counties seeking for a law requiring every person to record their "Mortgage Deeds" to ensure validity of titles to land.- *Manuscript Collection-Oversized Legislative Papers [New Jersey State Archives],* Box 1-43, Folder 2, pg. 1.

Gey, Jonathan, Male

GHULECK, Jockem, - Name on a petition, 1754, to the House of Representatives from freeholders of the province opposing the election of Samuel Nevell as a judge of the Supreme Court.- *Manuscript Collection-Legislative Records [New Jersey State Archives],* Box 1-12, Folder 66, pg. 3.

Ghuleck, Jockem, Male

GIFT?, Willm, Morris County, - Name on a petition, 6 Oct 1751, to Governor Jonathan Belcher from owners of "Bloomaries" in Morris County seeking removal of a tax on their iron works (Bloomeries). Many make 5-6 tons or less a year. They seek instead for a bounty on all they produce.- *Manuscript Collection-MSS Coll., #1-100 [New Jersey State Archives],* Box 5-1, Folder 28, pg. 2.

Gift?, Willm, Male

GILDERSLEVE, John, Essex County, - Name on petition, 10 Apr 1746, to the General Assembly by freeholders & inhabitants of Essex Co. seeking a repeal of acts for preserving of timber & a duty on imported strong liquors. They cannot build ships because of the present war with France & Spain.- *Manuscript Collection-Legislative Records [New Jersey State Archives],* Box 1-12, Folder 25, pg. 2.

Gildersleve, John, Male

GILLAM, Charles, Essex County, - Name on petition, 10 Apr 1746, to the General Assembly by freeholders & inhabitants of Essex Co. seeking a repeal of acts for preserving of timber & a duty on imported strong liquors. They cannot build ships because of the present war with France & Spain.- *Manuscript Collection-Legislative Records [New Jersey State Archives],* Box 1-12, Folder 25, pg. 2.

Gillam, Charles, Male

GOLDSWOOD, Jonas?, Essex County, - Name on petition, 10 Apr 1746, to the General Assembly by freeholders & inhabitants of Essex Co. seeking a repeal of acts for preserving of timber & a duty on imported strong liquors. They cannot build ships because of the present war with France & Spain.- *Manuscript Collection-Legislative Records [New Jersey State Archives],* Box 1-12, Folder 25, pg. 2.

Goldswood, Jonas?, Male

GRAY, Abraham, Hunterdon County, Bethlehem - Name on a petition, 12 Jan 1747/8, to Jonathan Belcher, Governor, from inhabitants of Bethlehem in Hunterdon County seeking to have the southerly part of Bethlehem Township made into a new township.- *Legislature-Petitions re: Municipal Boundaries [New Jersey State Archives],* Box 1, Folder 1, pg. 1.

Gray, Abraham, Male

GREEN, ***jamin, Burlington & Hunterdon Cos., - Name on a petition, 1748/9, to the House of Representatives from inhabitants freeholders of Hunterdon and Burlington Counties seeking for a law requiring every person to record their "Mortgage Deeds" to ensure validity of titles to land.- *Manuscript Collection-Oversized Legislative Papers [New Jersey State Archives],* Box 1-43, Folder 2, pg. 1.

green, ***jamin, Male

GREEN, Isaac, Burlington & Hunterdon Cos., - Name on a petition, 1748/9, to the House of Representatives from inhabitants freeholders of Hunterdon and Burlington Counties seeking for a law requiring every person to record their "Mortgage Deeds" to ensure validity of titles to land.- *Manuscript Collection-Oversized Legislative Papers [New Jersey State Archives],* Box 1-43, Folder 2, pg. 1.

Green, Isaac, Male

GREEN, Joseph, Burlington & Hunterdon Cos., - Name on a petition, 1748/9, to the House of Representatives from inhabitants freeholders of Hunterdon and Burlington Counties seeking for a law requiring every person to record their "Mortgage Deeds" to ensure validity of titles to land.- *Manuscript Collection-Oversized Legislative Papers [New Jersey State Archives],* Box 1-43, Folder 2, pg. 1.

Green, Joseph, Male

GREEN, peter, Middlesex County, - Name on a petition, 1754, to the House of Representatives from freeholders of the province opposing the election of Samuel Nevell as a judge of the Supreme Court.- *Manuscript Collection-Legislative Records [New Jersey State Archives],* Box 1-12, Folder 66, pg. 2.

green, peter, Male

GRIGGS, Thomas, Burlington & Hunterdon Cos., - Name on a petition, 1748/9, to the House of Representatives from inhabitants freeholders of Hunterdon and Burlington Counties seeking for a law requiring every person to record their "Mortgage Deeds" to ensure validity of titles to land.- *Manuscript Collection-Oversized Legislative Papers [New Jersey State Archives],* Box 1-43, Folder 2, pg. 1.

griggs, Thomas, Male

GROENENDIJCK, Johannis, - Name on a petition, 1754, to the House of Representatives from freeholders of the province opposing the election of Samuel Nevell as a judge of the Supreme Court.- *Manuscript Collection-Legislative Records [New Jersey State Archives],* Box 1-12, Folder 66, pg. 3.

Groenendijck, Johannis, Male

GUINNELL OR GUINNETT, Thomas, - Name on a petition, 24 Sep? 1753, to the House of Representatives from inhabitants of the province expressing distress because of a lack of currency as a medium of trade. They present various arguments for the value of a paper currency.- *Manuscript Collection-Oversized Legislative Papers [New Jersey State Archives],* Box 1-43, Folder 4, pg. 1.

Guinnell or Guinnett, Thomas, Male

GUINNETT OR GUINNELL, Thomas, - Name on a petition, 24 Sep? 1753, to the House of Representatives from inhabitants of the province expressing distress because of a lack of currency as a medium of trade. They present various arguments for the value of a paper currency.- *Manuscript*

Collection-Oversized Legislative Papers [New Jersey State Archives], Box 1-43, Folder 4, pg. 1.

Guinnett or Guinnell, Thomas, Male

HAINES, Job, - Name on a petition, 1750/1, the House of Representatives from inhabitants of the province protesting against the great number of taverns in the province.- *Manuscript Collection-Legislative Records [New Jersey State Archives],* Box 1-12, Folder 59, pg. 1.

Haines, Job, Male

HAINES, Jonathan, - Name on a petition, 24 Sep? 1753, to the House of Representatives from inhabitants of the province expressing distress because of a lack of currency as a medium of trade. They present various arguments for the value of a paper currency.- *Manuscript Collection-Oversized Legislative Papers [New Jersey State Archives],* Box 1-43, Folder 4, pg. 1.

Haines, Jonathan, Male

HALL, Saml?, - Name on a petition, 1750/1, the House of Representatives from inhabitants of the province protesting against the great number of taverns in the province.- *Manuscript Collection-Legislative Records [New Jersey State Archives],* Box 1-12, Folder 59, pg. 1.

Hall, Saml?, Male

HAMOND, James, - Name on petition, 1 Mar 1748/9, to the governor, etc., seeking passage of a law forbidding the killing of deer by dogs because the meat and hides are mostly worthless.- *Manuscript Collection-Governors' Papers [New Jersey State Archives],* Box 1-1, Folder 4, pg. 1.

Hamond, James, Male

HAND, George, Junr, Cape May County, - Name on petition, 12 Mar 1745/6, to the House of Representatives from freeholders of Cape May County complaining of the devaluation of their paper money [likely due in part to the present war] and asking for creation of a fund, apparently to stabilize it.- *Manuscript Collection-Legislative Records [New Jersey State Archives],* Box 1-12, Folder 22, pg. 1.

Hand, George, Junr, Male

HAND, Isaiah, Cape May County, - Name on petition, 12 Mar 1745/6, to the House of Representatives from freeholders of Cape May County complaining of the devaluation of their paper money [likely due in part to the present war] and asking for creation of a fund, apparently to stabilize it.- *Manuscript Collection-Legislative*

Records [New Jersey State Archives], Box 1-12, Folder 22, pg. 1.

Hand, Isaiah, Male

HAND, Jeremiah, Cape May County, - Name on petition, 12 Mar 1745/6, to the House of Representatives from freeholders of Cape May County complaining of the devaluation of their paper money [likely due in part to the present war] and asking for creation of a fund, apparently to stabilize it.- *Manuscript Collection-Legislative Records [New Jersey State Archives],* Box 1-12, Folder 22, pg. 1.

Hand, Jeremiah, Male

HAND, Nathaniel, Cape May County, - Name on petition, 12 Mar 1745/6, to the House of Representatives from freeholders of Cape May County complaining of the devaluation of their paper money [likely due in part to the present war] and asking for creation of a fund, apparently to stabilize it.- *Manuscript Collection-Legislative Records [New Jersey State Archives],* Box 1-12, Folder 22, pg. 1.

Hand, Nathaniel, Male

HARISON, Adoniiah, Essex County, - Name on petition, 10 Apr 1746, to the General Assembly by freeholders & inhabitants of Essex Co. seeking a repeal of acts for preserving of timber & a duty on imported strong liquors. They cannot build ships because of the present war with France & Spain.- *Manuscript Collection-Legislative Records [New Jersey State Archives],* Box 1-12, Folder 25, pg. 1.

Harison, Adoniiah, Male

HARRISON, Caleb, Essex County, - Name on petition, 10 Apr 1746, to the General Assembly by freeholders & inhabitants of Essex Co. seeking a repeal of acts for preserving of timber & a duty on imported strong liquors. They cannot build ships because of the present war with France & Spain.- *Manuscript Collection-Legislative Records [New Jersey State Archives],* Box 1-12, Folder 25, pg. 1.

Harrison, Caleb, Male

HARRISON, Danl, Essex County, - Name on petition, 10 Apr 1746, to the General Assembly by freeholders & inhabitants of Essex Co. seeking a repeal of acts for preserving of timber & a duty on imported strong liquors. They cannot build ships because of the present war with France & Spain.- *Manuscript Collection-Legislative Records [New Jersey State Archives],* Box 1-12, Folder 25, pg. 1.

Harrison, Danl, Male

HARRISON, Isaac, Essex County, - Name on petition, 10 Apr 1746, to the General Assembly by freeholders & inhabitants of Essex Co. seeking a repeal of acts for preserving of timber & a duty on imported strong liquors. They cannot build ships because of the present war with France & Spain.- *Manuscript Collection-Legislative Records [New Jersey State Archives],* Box 1-12, Folder 25, pg. 1.

Harrison, Isaac, Male

HARRISON, James, Essex County, - Name on petition, 10 Apr 1746, to the General Assembly by freeholders & inhabitants of Essex Co. seeking a repeal of acts for preserving of timber & a duty on imported strong liquors. They cannot build ships because of the present war with France & Spain.- *Manuscript Collection-Legislative Records [New Jersey State Archives],* Box 1-12, Folder 25, pg. 1.

Harrison, James, Male

HARRISON, John, Essex County, - Name on petition, 10 Apr 1746, to the General Assembly by freeholders & inhabitants of Essex Co. seeking a repeal of acts for preserving of timber & a duty on imported strong liquors. They cannot build ships because of the present war with France & Spain.- *Manuscript Collection-Legislative Records [New Jersey State Archives],* Box 1-12, Folder 25, pg. 1.

Harrison, John, Male

HARRISON, Joseph, Essex County, - Name on petition, 10 Apr 1746, to the General Assembly by freeholders & inhabitants of Essex Co. seeking a repeal of acts for preserving of timber & a duty on imported strong liquors. They cannot build ships because of the present war with France & Spain.- *Manuscript Collection-Legislative Records [New Jersey State Archives],* Box 1-12, Folder 25, pg. 1.

Harrison, Joseph, Male

HARRISON, Nathaniel, Essex County, - Name on petition, 10 Apr 1746, to the General Assembly by freeholders & inhabitants of Essex Co. seeking a repeal of acts for preserving of timber & a duty on imported strong liquors. They cannot build ships because of the present war with France & Spain.- *Manuscript Collection-Legislative Records [New Jersey State Archives],* Box 1-12, Folder 25, pg. 1.

Harrison, Nathaniel, Male

HARRISON, Richard, Essex County, - Name on petition, 10 Apr 1746, to the General Assembly by freeholders & inhabitants of Essex Co. seeking a repeal of acts for preserving of timber & a duty on imported strong liquors. They cannot build ships

because of the present war with France & Spain.-
*Manuscript Collection-Legislative Records [New
Jersey State Archives]*, Box 1-12, Folder 25, pg. 1.
Harrison, Richard, Male

HARRISON, Saml, Essex County, - Name on
petition, 10 Apr 1746, to the General Assembly by
freeholders & inhabitants of Essex Co. seeking a
repeal of acts for preserving of timber & a duty on
imported strong liquors. They cannot build ships
because of the present war with France & Spain.-
*Manuscript Collection-Legislative Records [New
Jersey State Archives]*, Box 1-12, Folder 25, pg. 1.
Harrison, Saml, Male

HARRISON, Samuel, Essex County, - Name on
petition, 10 Apr 1746, to the General Assembly by
freeholders & inhabitants of Essex Co. seeking a
repeal of acts for preserving of timber & a duty on
imported strong liquors. They cannot build ships
because of the present war with France & Spain.-
*Manuscript Collection-Legislative Records [New
Jersey State Archives]*, Box 1-12, Folder 25, pg. 1.
Harrison, Samuel, Male

HARRISON, Stephen, Essex County, - Name on
petition, 10 Apr 1746, to the General Assembly by
freeholders & inhabitants of Essex Co. seeking a
repeal of acts for preserving of timber & a duty on
imported strong liquors. They cannot build ships
because of the present war with France & Spain.-
*Manuscript Collection-Legislative Records [New
Jersey State Archives]*, Box 1-12, Folder 25, pg. 1.
Harrison, Stephen, Male

HARRISSON, Geo, Essex County, - Name on
petition, 10 Apr 1746, to the General Assembly by
freeholders & inhabitants of Essex Co. seeking a
repeal of acts for preserving of timber & a duty on
imported strong liquors. They cannot build ships
because of the present war with France & Spain.-
*Manuscript Collection-Legislative Records [New
Jersey State Archives]*, Box 1-12, Folder 25, pg. 1.
Harrisson, Geo, Male

HART, Benjamin, Burlington & Hunterdon Cos.,
- Name on a petition, 1748/9, to the House of
Representatives from inhabitants freeholders of
Hunterdon and Burlington Counties seeking for a
law requiring every person to record their
"Mortgage Deeds" to ensure validity of titles to
land.- *Manuscript Collection-Oversized Legislative
Papers [New Jersey State Archives]*, Box 1-43,
Folder 2, pg. 1.
Hart, Benjamin, Male

HART, Samuel, Burlington & Hunterdon Cos., -
Name on a petition, 1748/9, to the House of
Representatives from inhabitants freeholders of
Hunterdon and Burlington Counties seeking for a
law requiring every person to record their
"Mortgage Deeds" to ensure validity of titles to
land.- *Manuscript Collection-Oversized Legislative
Papers [New Jersey State Archives]*, Box 1-43,
Folder 2, pg. 1.
Hart, Samuel, Male

HATHEWAY, Abraham, Morris County, - Name
on a petition, 6 Oct 1751, to Governor Jonathan
Belcher from owners of "Bloomaries" in Morris
County seeking removal of a tax on their iron
works (Bloomeries). Many make 5-6 tons or less a
year. They seek instead for a bounty on all they
produce.- *Manuscript Collection-MSS Coll., #1-
100 [New Jersey State Archives]*, Box 5-1, Folder
28, pg. 2.
hatheway, Abraham, Male

HATHEWAY, Benjamin, Morris County, - Name
on a petition, 6 Oct 1751, to Governor Jonathan
Belcher from owners of "Bloomaries" in Morris
County seeking removal of a tax on their iron
works (Bloomeries). Many make 5-6 tons or less a
year. They seek instead for a bounty on all they
produce.- *Manuscript Collection-MSS Coll., #1-
100 [New Jersey State Archives]*, Box 5-1, Folder
28, pg. 2.
Hatheway, Benjamin, Male

HATHEWAY, Joseph, Morris County, - Name
on a petition, 6 Oct 1751, to Governor Jonathan
Belcher from owners of "Bloomaries" in Morris
County seeking removal of a tax on their iron
works (Bloomeries). Many make 5-6 tons or less a
year. They seek instead for a bounty on all they
produce.- *Manuscript Collection-MSS Coll., #1-
100 [New Jersey State Archives]*, Box 5-1, Folder
28, pg. 2.
Hatheway, Joseph, Male

HATHEWAY, Shadrack, Morris County, - Name
on a petition, 6 Oct 1751, to Governor Jonathan
Belcher from owners of "Bloomaries" in Morris
County seeking removal of a tax on their iron
works (Bloomeries). Many make 5-6 tons or less a
year. They seek instead for a bounty on all they
produce.- *Manuscript Collection-MSS Coll., #1-
100 [New Jersey State Archives]*, Box 5-1, Folder
28, pg. 2.
Hatheway, Shadrack, Male

HAYES, Robeart, Essex County, - Name on petition, 10 Apr 1746, to the General Assembly by freeholders & inhabitants of Essex Co. seeking a repeal of acts for preserving of timber & a duty on imported strong liquors. They cannot build ships because of the present war with France & Spain.- *Manuscript Collection-Legislative Records [New Jersey State Archives],* Box 1-12, Folder 25, pg. 1.

Hayes, Robeart, Male

HEDDEN, Elmer?, Essex County, - Name on petition, 10 Apr 1746, to the General Assembly by freeholders & inhabitants of Essex Co. seeking a repeal of acts for preserving of timber & a duty on imported strong liquors. They cannot build ships because of the present war with France & Spain.- *Manuscript Collection-Legislative Records [New Jersey State Archives],* Box 1-12, Folder 25, pg. 2.

Hedden, Elmer?, Male

HEDDEN, John, Essex County, - Name on petition, 10 Apr 1746, to the General Assembly by freeholders & inhabitants of Essex Co. seeking a repeal of acts for preserving of timber & a duty on imported strong liquors. They cannot build ships because of the present war with France & Spain.- *Manuscript Collection-Legislative Records [New Jersey State Archives],* Box 1-12, Folder 25, pg. 2.

hedden, John, Male

HEDDEN, Josiah, Essex County, - Name on petition, 10 Apr 1746, to the General Assembly by freeholders & inhabitants of Essex Co. seeking a repeal of acts for preserving of timber & a duty on imported strong liquors. They cannot build ships because of the present war with France & Spain.- *Manuscript Collection-Legislative Records [New Jersey State Archives],* Box 1-12, Folder 25, pg. 2.

Hedden, Josiah, Male

HEDDEN, Nehemiah, Essex County, - Name on petition, 10 Apr 1746, to the General Assembly by freeholders & inhabitants of Essex Co. seeking a repeal of acts for preserving of timber & a duty on imported strong liquors. They cannot build ships because of the present war with France & Spain.- *Manuscript Collection-Legislative Records [New Jersey State Archives],* Box 1-12, Folder 25, pg. 2.

Hedden, Nehemiah, Male

HEDDIN, Elazer, Essex County, - Name on petition, 10 Apr 1746, to the General Assembly by freeholders & inhabitants of Essex Co. seeking a repeal of acts for preserving of timber & a duty on imported strong liquors. They cannot build ships because of the present war with France & Spain.- *Manuscript Collection-Legislative Records [New Jersey State Archives],* Box 1-12, Folder 25, pg. 2.

Heddin, Elazer, Male

HEDGES, James, Cape May County, - Name on petition, 12 Mar 1745/6, to the House of Representatives from freeholders of Cape May County complaining of the devaluation of their paper money [likely due in part to the present war] and asking for creation of a fund, apparently to stabilize it.- *Manuscript Collection-Legislative Records [New Jersey State Archives],* Box 1-12, Folder 22, pg. 1.

Hedges, James, Male

HEGEMAN, Barent, - Name on a petition, 1754, to the House of Representatives from freeholders of the province opposing the election of Samuel Nevell as a judge of the Supreme Court.- *Manuscript Collection-Legislative Records [New Jersey State Archives],* Box 1-12, Folder 66, pg. 1.

Hegeman, Barent, Male

HEGEMAN, denis, Middlesex County, Perth Amboy Township - Name on a petition, 1754, to the General Assembly from freeholders/inhabitants of Perth Amboy Township in Middlesex County opposing the election of Samuel Nevill as a judge of the Supreme Court.- *Manuscript Collection-Oversized Legislative Papers [New Jersey State Archives],* Box 1-43, Folder 2, pg. 1.

Hegeman, denis, Male

HENDRICSON, G, Burlington County, Nottingham - Name on a petition, 18 Nov 1748, to the House of Representatives from inhabitants of Nottingham, Burlington County complaining of those hunting out of season who have killed their hogs and cattle. Sometimes people are in danger of being shot.- *Manuscript Collection-Legislative Records [New Jersey State Archives],* Box 1-12, Folder 46, pg. 1.

Hendricson, G, Male

HEWET, Thmas, Cape May County, - Name on petition, 12 Mar 1745/6, to the House of Representatives from freeholders of Cape May County complaining of the devaluation of their paper money [likely due in part to the present war] and asking for creation of a fund, apparently to stabilize it.- *Manuscript Collection-Legislative Records [New Jersey State Archives],* Box 1-12, Folder 22, pg. 1.

Hewet, Thmas, Male

HIGBEE, Jos, Burlington & Hunterdon Cos., - Name on a petition, 1748/9, to the House of

Representatives from inhabitants freeholders of Hunterdon and Burlington Counties seeking for a law requiring every person to record their "Mortgage Deeds" to ensure validity of titles to land.- *Manuscript Collection-Oversized Legislative Papers [New Jersey State Archives],* Box 1-43, Folder 2, pg. 1.

Higbee, Jos, Male

HILLDRETH, Joshua, Cape May County, - Name on petition, 12 Mar 1745/6, to the House of Representatives from freeholders of Cape May County complaining of the devaluation of their paper money [likely due in part to the present war] and asking for creation of a fund, apparently to stabilize it.- *Manuscript Collection-Legislative Records [New Jersey State Archives],* Box 1-12, Folder 22, pg. 1.

Hilldreth, Joshua, Male

HILLER, Edward, Burlington County, Northampton Township - Name on a petition, 30 May 1753, to the House of Representatives from inhabitants in and about Northampton who are requesting an increase in the amount of currency which is scarce. Gold and silver are chiefly transported elsewhere and are scarce also.- *Manuscript Collection-Legislative Records [New Jersey State Archives],* Box 1-12, Folder 65, pg. 1.

Hiller, Edward, Male

HILLER, John, Burlington County, Northampton Township - Name on a petition, 30 May 1753, to the House of Representatives from inhabitants in and about Northampton who are requesting an increase in the amount of currency which is scarce. Gold and silver are chiefly transported elsewhere and are scarce also.- *Manuscript Collection-Legislative Records [New Jersey State Archives],* Box 1-12, Folder 65, pg. 1.

Hiller, John, Male

HILLS OR WILLS, David, - Name on a petition, 24 Sep? 1753, to the House of Representatives from inhabitants of the province expressing distress because of a lack of currency as a medium of trade. They present various arguments for the value of a paper currency.- *Manuscript Collection-Oversized Legislative Papers [New Jersey State Archives],* Box 1-43, Folder 4, pg. 1.

Hills or Wills, David, Male

HOFF, Charles, Junr, Hunterdon County, Bethlehem - Name on a petition, 12 Jan 1747/8, to Jonathan Belcher, Governor, from inhabitants of Bethlehem in Hunterdon County seeking to have the southerly part of Bethlehem Township made into a new township.- *Legislature-Petitions re: Municipal Boundaries [New Jersey State Archives],* Box 1, Folder 1, pg. 1.

Hoff, Charles, Junr, Male

HOGELOM, John, - Name on a petition, 1754, to the House of Representatives from freeholders of the province opposing the election of Samuel Nevell as a judge of the Supreme Court.- *Manuscript Collection-Legislative Records [New Jersey State Archives],* Box 1-12, Folder 66, pg. 4.

Hogelom, John, Male

HOOPER, Clament, Middlesex County, - Name on a petition, 1754, to the House of Representatives from freeholders of the province opposing the election of Samuel Nevell as a judge of the Supreme Court.- *Manuscript Collection-Legislative Records [New Jersey State Archives],* Box 1-12, Folder 66, pg. 2.

hooper, Clament, Male

HOUGHSWORK?, Leffend, Middlesex County, Perth Amboy Township - Name on a petition, 1754, to the General Assembly from freeholders/inhabitants of Perth Amboy Township in Middlesex County opposing the election of Samuel Nevill as a judge of the Supreme Court.- *Manuscript Collection-Oversized Legislative Papers [New Jersey State Archives],* Box 1-43, Folder 2, pg. 1.

houghswork?, Leffend, Male

HOWELL, Joshua, Burlington & Hunterdon Cos., - Name on a petition, 1748/9, to the House of Representatives from inhabitants freeholders of Hunterdon and Burlington Counties seeking for a law requiring every person to record their "Mortgage Deeds" to ensure validity of titles to land.- *Manuscript Collection-Oversized Legislative Papers [New Jersey State Archives],* Box 1-43, Folder 2, pg. 1.

Howell, Joshua, Male

HUFFE, Lawrance, Snr, Hunterdon County, Bethlehem - Name on a petition, 12 Jan 1747/8, to Jonathan Belcher, Governor, from inhabitants of Bethlehem in Hunterdon County seeking to have the southerly part of Bethlehem Township made into a new township.- *Legislature-Petitions re: Municipal Boundaries [New Jersey State Archives],* Box 1, Folder 1, pg. 1.

Huffe, Lawrance, Snr, Male

HUFFYMEIER, Lawrence, Hunterdon County, Bethlehem - Name on a petition, 12 Jan 1747/8, to

Jonathan Belcher, Governor, from inhabitants of Bethlehem in Hunterdon County seeking to have the southerly part of Bethlehem Township made into a new township.- *Legislature-Petitions re: Municipal Boundaries [New Jersey State Archives],* Box 1, Folder 1, pg. 1.

Huffymeier, Lawrence, Male

HUGHES, Jacob, Cape May County, - Name on petition, 12 Mar 1745/6, to the House of Representatives from freeholders of Cape May County complaining of the devaluation of their paper money [likely due in part to the present war] and asking for creation of a fund, apparently to stabilize it.- *Manuscript Collection-Legislative Records [New Jersey State Archives],* Box 1-12, Folder 22, pg. 1.

Hughes, Jacob, Male

HUIE, Robert, - Name on petition, 1 Mar 1748/9, to the governor, etc., seeking passage of a law forbidding the killing of deer by dogs because the meat and hides are mostly worthless.- *Manuscript Collection-Governors' Papers [New Jersey State Archives],* Box 1-1, Folder 4, pg. 1.

Huie, Robert, Male

HUMPHRIS, Josa, - Name on a petition, 1750/1, the House of Representatives from inhabitants of the province protesting against the great number of taverns in the province.- *Manuscript Collection-Legislative Records [New Jersey State Archives],* Box 1-12, Folder 59, pg. 1.

Humphris, Josa, Male

HUNTINGTON, Simon, Essex County, - Name on petition, 10 Apr 1746, to the General Assembly by freeholders & inhabitants of Essex Co. seeking a repeal of acts for preserving of timber & a duty on imported strong liquors. They cannot build ships because of the present war with France & Spain.- *Manuscript Collection-Legislative Records [New Jersey State Archives],* Box 1-12, Folder 25, pg. 1.

Huntington, Simon, Male

IMLAY, Jno, Burlington & Hunterdon Cos., - Name on a petition, 1748/9, to the House of Representatives from inhabitants freeholders of Hunterdon and Burlington Counties seeking for a law requiring every person to record their "Mortgage Deeds" to ensure validity of titles to land.- *Manuscript Collection-Oversized Legislative Papers [New Jersey State Archives],* Box 1-43, Folder 2, pg. 1.

Imlay, Jno, Male

JACKSON, John, Morris County, - Name on a petition, 6 Oct 1751, to Governor Jonathan Belcher from owners of "Bloomaries" in Morris County seeking removal of a tax on their iron works (Bloomeries). Many make 5-6 tons or less a year. They seek instead for a bounty on all they produce.- *Manuscript Collection-MSS Coll., #1-100 [New Jersey State Archives],* Box 5-1, Folder 28, pg. 2.

Jackson, John, Male

JENKINS, Jno, Burlington & Hunterdon Cos., - Name on a petition, 1748/9, to the House of Representatives from inhabitants freeholders of Hunterdon and Burlington Counties seeking for a law requiring every person to record their "Mortgage Deeds" to ensure validity of titles to land.- *Manuscript Collection-Oversized Legislative Papers [New Jersey State Archives],* Box 1-43, Folder 2, pg. 1.

Jenkins, Jno, Male

JENKINS, Nath:, Junr, Cape May County, - Name on petition, 12 Mar 1745/6, to the House of Representatives from freeholders of Cape May County complaining of the devaluation of their paper money [likely due in part to the present war] and asking for creation of a fund, apparently to stabilize it.- *Manuscript Collection-Legislative Records [New Jersey State Archives],* Box 1-12, Folder 22, pg. 1.

Jenkins, Nath:, Junr, Male

JEWELL, Richard, - Name on a petition, 1754, to the House of Representatives from freeholders of the province opposing the election of Samuel Nevell as a judge of the Supreme Court.- *Manuscript Collection-Legislative Records [New Jersey State Archives],* Box 1-12, Folder 66, pg. 1.

Jewell, Richard, Male

JOB, George, - Name on a petition, 1754, to the House of Representatives from freeholders of the province opposing the election of Samuel Nevell as a judge of the Supreme Court.- *Manuscript Collection-Legislative Records [New Jersey State Archives],* Box 1-12, Folder 66, pg. 4.

Job, George, Male

JOHNSON, Eliphelet, Essex County, - Name on petition, 10 Apr 1746, to the General Assembly by freeholders & inhabitants of Essex Co. seeking a repeal of acts for preserving of timber & a duty on imported strong liquors. They cannot build ships because of the present war with France & Spain.-

Manuscript Collection-Legislative Records [New Jersey State Archives], Box 1-12, Folder 25, pg. 1.

Johnson, Eliphelet, Male

JOHNSON, John, Essex County, - Name on petition, 10 Apr 1746, to the General Assembly by freeholders & inhabitants of Essex Co. seeking a repeal of acts for preserving of timber & a duty on imported strong liquors. They cannot build ships because of the present war with France & Spain.- *Manuscript Collection-Legislative Records [New Jersey State Archives]*, Box 1-12, Folder 25, pg. 1.

Johnson, John, Male

JOHNSON, Josuph, Essex County, - Name on petition, 10 Apr 1746, to the General Assembly by freeholders & inhabitants of Essex Co. seeking a repeal of acts for preserving of timber & a duty on imported strong liquors. They cannot build ships because of the present war with France & Spain.- *Manuscript Collection-Legislative Records [New Jersey State Archives]*, Box 1-12, Folder 25, pg. 1.

Johnson, Josuph, Male

JOHNSON, matthias, - Name on a petition, 1754, to the House of Representatives from freeholders of the province opposing the election of Samuel Nevell as a judge of the Supreme Court.- *Manuscript Collection-Legislative Records [New Jersey State Archives]*, Box 1-12, Folder 66, pg. 1.

Johnson, matthias, Male

JOHNSON, Nathaniel, Essex County, - Name on petition, 10 Apr 1746, to the General Assembly by freeholders & inhabitants of Essex Co. seeking a repeal of acts for preserving of timber & a duty on imported strong liquors. They cannot build ships because of the present war with France & Spain.- *Manuscript Collection-Legislative Records [New Jersey State Archives]*, Box 1-12, Folder 25, pg. 1.

Johnson, Nathaniel, Male

JOHNSON, William, - Name on a petition, 1754, to the House of Representatives from freeholders of the province opposing the election of Samuel Nevell as a judge of the Supreme Court.- *Manuscript Collection-Legislative Records [New Jersey State Archives]*, Box 1-12, Folder 66, pg. 3.

Johnson, William, Male

JONES, Jos, Burlington & Hunterdon Cos., - Name on a petition, 1748/9, to the House of Representatives from inhabitants freeholders of Hunterdon and Burlington Counties seeking for a law requiring every person to record their "Mortgage Deeds" to ensure validity of titles to land.- *Manuscript Collection-Oversized Legislative Papers [New Jersey State Archives]*, Box 1-43, Folder 2, pg. 1.

Jones, Jos, Male

JONES, Joseph, Essex County, - Name on petition, 10 Apr 1746, to the General Assembly by freeholders & inhabitants of Essex Co. seeking a repeal of acts for preserving of timber & a duty on imported strong liquors. They cannot build ships because of the present war with France & Spain.- *Manuscript Collection-Legislative Records [New Jersey State Archives]*, Box 1-12, Folder 25, pg. 1.

Jones, Joseph, Male

JONES, Samll, Essex County, - Name on petition, 10 Apr 1746, to the General Assembly by freeholders & inhabitants of Essex Co. seeking a repeal of acts for preserving of timber & a duty on imported strong liquors. They cannot build ships because of the present war with France & Spain.- *Manuscript Collection-Legislative Records [New Jersey State Archives]*, Box 1-12, Folder 25, pg. 1.

Jones, Samll, Male

JONES? OR JUSTONES?, Jno (if Jones), Burlington & Hunterdon Cos., - Name on a petition, 1748/9, to the House of Representatives from inhabitants freeholders of Hunterdon and Burlington Counties seeking for a law requiring every person to record their "Mortgage Deeds" to ensure validity of titles to land.- *Manuscript Collection-Oversized Legislative Papers [New Jersey State Archives]*, Box 1-43, Folder 2, pg. 1.

Jones? or Justones?, Jno (if Jones), Male

JONS, Daniel, - Name on petition, 1 Mar 1748/9, to the governor, etc., seeking passage of a law forbidding the killing of deer by dogs because the meat and hides are mostly worthless.- *Manuscript Collection-Governors' Papers [New Jersey State Archives]*, Box 1-1, Folder 4, pg. 1.

Jons, Daniel, Male

JONSON, Ezekiel, Essex County, - Name on petition, 10 Apr 1746, to the General Assembly by freeholders & inhabitants of Essex Co. seeking a repeal of acts for preserving of timber & a duty on imported strong liquors. They cannot build ships because of the present war with France & Spain.- *Manuscript Collection-Legislative Records [New Jersey State Archives]*, Box 1-12, Folder 25, pg. 2.

Jonson, Ezekiel, Male

JUSTONES? OR JONES?, Jno (if Jones), Burlington & Hunterdon Cos., - Name on a petition, 1748/9, to the House of Representatives from inhabitants freeholders of Hunterdon and

Burlington Counties seeking for a law requiring every person to record their "Mortgage Deeds" to ensure validity of titles to land.- *Manuscript Collection-Oversized Legislative Papers [New Jersey State Archives], Box 1-43, Folder 2, pg. 1.*

Justones? or Jones?, Jno (if Jones), Male

KARSON, Charles, - Name on a petition, 1754, to the House of Representatives from freeholders of the province opposing the election of Samuel Nevell as a judge of the Supreme Court.- *Manuscript Collection-Legislative Records [New Jersey State Archives], Box 1-12, Folder 66, pg. 4.*

Karson, Charles, Male

KESTOR, Harm?, Hunterdon County, Bethlehem - Name on a petition, 12 Jan 1747/8, to Jonathan Belcher, Governor, from inhabitants of Bethlehem in Hunterdon County seeking to have the southerly part of Bethlehem Township made into a new township.- *Legislature-Petitions re: Municipal Boundaries [New Jersey State Archives], Box 1, Folder 1, pg. 1.*

Kestor, Harm?, Male

KILPATERRICK, alaxalandr, - Name on petition, 1 Mar 1748/9, to the governor, etc., seeking passage of a law forbidding the killing of deer by dogs because the meat and hides are mostly worthless.- *Manuscript Collection-Governors' Papers [New Jersey State Archives], Box 1-1, Folder 4, pg. 1.*

kilpaterrick, alaxalandr, Male

KING, Jos, Senr, Hunterdon County, Bethlehem - Name on a petition, 12 Jan 1747/8, to Jonathan Belcher, Governor, from inhabitants of Bethlehem in Hunterdon County seeking to have the southerly part of Bethlehem Township made into a new township.- *Legislature-Petitions re: Municipal Boundaries [New Jersey State Archives], Box 1, Folder 1, pg. 1.*

King, Jos, Senr, Male

KING, William, Hunterdon County, Bethlehem - Name on a petition, 12 Jan 1747/8, to Jonathan Belcher, Governor, from inhabitants of Bethlehem in Hunterdon County seeking to have the southerly part of Bethlehem Township made into a new township.- *Legislature-Petitions re: Municipal Boundaries [New Jersey State Archives], Box 1, Folder 1, pg. 1.*

King, William, Male

LAKE, Daniel, Hunterdon County, Bethlehem - Name on a petition, 12 Jan 1747/8, to Jonathan Belcher, Governor, from inhabitants of Bethlehem in Hunterdon County seeking to have the southerly part of Bethlehem Township made into a new township.- *Legislature-Petitions re: Municipal Boundaries [New Jersey State Archives], Box 1, Folder 1, pg. 1.*

Lake, Daniel, Male

LANGSTAFF, James, - Name on a petition, 1750/1, the House of Representatives from inhabitants of the province protesting against the great number of taverns in the province.- *Manuscript Collection-Legislative Records [New Jersey State Archives], Box 1-12, Folder 59, pg. 1.*

Langstaff, James, Male

LANING, Danl or Davd, Burlington & Hunterdon Cos., - Name on a petition, 1748/9, to the House of Representatives from inhabitants freeholders of Hunterdon and Burlington Counties seeking for a law requiring every person to record their "Mortgage Deeds" to ensure validity of titles to land.- *Manuscript Collection-Oversized Legislative Papers [New Jersey State Archives], Box 1-43, Folder 2, pg. 1.*

Laning, Danl or Davd, Male

LANING, Stephen, Burlington & Hunterdon Cos., - Name on a petition, 1748/9, to the House of Representatives from inhabitants freeholders of Hunterdon and Burlington Counties seeking for a law requiring every person to record their "Mortgage Deeds" to ensure validity of titles to land.- *Manuscript Collection-Oversized Legislative Papers [New Jersey State Archives], Box 1-43, Folder 2, pg. 1.*

Laning, Stephen, Male

LARGE, Jacob, Hunterdon County, Bethlehem - Name on a petition, 12 Jan 1747/8, to Jonathan Belcher, Governor, from inhabitants of Bethlehem in Hunterdon County seeking to have the southerly part of Bethlehem Township made into a new township.- *Legislature-Petitions re: Municipal Boundaries [New Jersey State Archives], Box 1, Folder 1, pg. 1.*

Large, Jacob, Male

LARGE, Robert, Hunterdon County, Bethlehem - Name on a petition, 12 Jan 1747/8, to Jonathan Belcher, Governor, from inhabitants of Bethlehem in Hunterdon County seeking to have the southerly part of Bethlehem Township made into a new township.- *Legislature-Petitions re: Municipal Boundaries [New Jersey State Archives], Box 1, Folder 1, pg. 1.*

Large, Robert, Male

LARGE, Saml, Jur, Hunterdon County, Bethlehem - Name on a petition, 12 Jan 1747/8, to Jonathan Belcher, Governor, from inhabitants of Bethlehem in Hunterdon County seeking to have the southerly part of Bethlehem Township made into a new township.- *Legislature-Petitions re: Municipal Boundaries [New Jersey State Archives],* Box 1, Folder 1, pg. 1.
Large, Saml, Jur, Male

LARGE, Samll, Senr, Hunterdon County, Bethlehem - Name on a petition, 12 Jan 1747/8, to Jonathan Belcher, Governor, from inhabitants of Bethlehem in Hunterdon County seeking to have the southerly part of Bethlehem Township made into a new township.- *Legislature-Petitions re: Municipal Boundaries [New Jersey State Archives],* Box 1, Folder 1, pg. 1.
Large, Samll, Senr, Male

LARRENCE, John, Burlington & Hunterdon Cos., - Name on a petition, 1748/9, to the House of Representatives from inhabitants freeholders of Hunterdon and Burlington Counties seeking for a law requiring every person to record their "Mortgage Deeds" to ensure validity of titles to land.- *Manuscript Collection-Oversized Legislative Papers [New Jersey State Archives],* Box 1-43, Folder 2, pg. 1.
Larrence, John, Male

LAYTEN, Danel, - Name on petition, 1 Mar 1748/9, to the governor, etc., seeking passage of a law forbidding the killing of deer by dogs because the meat and hides are mostly worthless.- *Manuscript Collection-Governors' Papers [New Jersey State Archives],* Box 1-1, Folder 4, pg. 1.
Layten, Danel, Male

LEEDS?, Vincent, Burlington County, Northampton Township - Name on a petition, 30 May 1753, to the House of Representatives from inhabitants in and about Northampton who are requesting an increase in the amount of currency which is scarce. Gold and silver are chiefly transported elsewhere and are scarce also.- *Manuscript Collection-Legislative Records [New Jersey State Archives],* Box 1-12, Folder 65, pg. 1.
Leeds?, Vincent, Male

LENSLI, Elehu, Essex County, - Name on petition, 10 Apr 1746, to the General Assembly by freeholders & inhabitants of Essex Co. seeking a repeal of acts for preserving of timber & a duty on imported strong liquors. They cannot build ships because of the present war with France & Spain.- *Manuscript Collection-Legislative Records [New Jersey State Archives],* Box 1-12, Folder 25, pg. 2.
Lensli, Elehu, Male

LEONARD, Henry, Cape May County, - Name on petition, 12 Mar 1745/6, to the House of Representatives from freeholders of Cape May County complaining of the devaluation of their paper money [likely due in part to the present war] and asking for creation of a fund, apparently to stabilize it.- *Manuscript Collection-Legislative Records [New Jersey State Archives],* Box 1-12, Folder 22, pg. 1.
Leonard, Henry, Male

LEONARD, John, Cape May County, - Name on petition, 12 Mar 1745/6, to the House of Representatives from freeholders of Cape May County complaining of the devaluation of their paper money [likely due in part to the present war] and asking for creation of a fund, apparently to stabilize it.- *Manuscript Collection-Legislative Records [New Jersey State Archives],* Box 1-12, Folder 22, pg. 1.
Leonard, John, Male

LEONARD, Samuel, Cape May County, - Name on petition, 12 Mar 1745/6, to the House of Representatives from freeholders of Cape May County complaining of the devaluation of their paper money [likely due in part to the present war] and asking for creation of a fund, apparently to stabilize it.- *Manuscript Collection-Legislative Records [New Jersey State Archives],* Box 1-12, Folder 22, pg. 1.
Leonard, Samuel, Male

LEUGHTON, Benjamin, Cape May County, - Name on petition, 12 Mar 1745/6, to the House of Representatives from freeholders of Cape May County complaining of the devaluation of their paper money [likely due in part to the present war] and asking for creation of a fund, apparently to stabilize it.- *Manuscript Collection-Legislative Records [New Jersey State Archives],* Box 1-12, Folder 22, pg. 1.
Leughton, Benjamin, Male

LEVINGSTON, Neil, Burlington & Hunterdon Cos., - Name on a petition, 1748/9, to the House of Representatives from inhabitants freeholders of Hunterdon and Burlington Counties seeking for a law requiring every person to record their "Mortgage Deeds" to ensure validity of titles to land.- *Manuscript Collection-Oversized Legislative*

Papers [New Jersey State Archives], Box 1-43, Folder 2, pg. 1.

Levingston, Neil, Male

LINDALL, John, Middlesex County, - Name on a petition, 1754, to the House of Representatives from freeholders of the province opposing the election of Samuel Nevell as a judge of the Supreme Court.- *Manuscript Collection-Legislative Records [New Jersey State Archives],* Box 1-12, Folder 66, pg. 2.

Lindall, John, Male

LINSLE, Beniman, Essex County, - Name on petition, 10 Apr 1746, to the General Assembly by freeholders & inhabitants of Essex Co. seeking a repeal of acts for preserving of timber & a duty on imported strong liquors. They cannot build ships because of the present war with France & Spain.- *Manuscript Collection-Legislative Records [New Jersey State Archives],* Box 1-12, Folder 25, pg. 2.

Linsle, Beniman, Male

LINSLE, Josiah, Essex County, - Name on petition, 10 Apr 1746, to the General Assembly by freeholders & inhabitants of Essex Co. seeking a repeal of acts for preserving of timber & a duty on imported strong liquors. They cannot build ships because of the present war with France & Spain.- *Manuscript Collection-Legislative Records [New Jersey State Archives],* Box 1-12, Folder 25, pg. 2.

Linsle, Josiah, Male

LION, David, Essex County, - Name on petition, 10 Apr 1746, to the General Assembly by freeholders & inhabitants of Essex Co. seeking a repeal of acts for preserving of timber & a duty on imported strong liquors. They cannot build ships because of the present war with France & Spain.- *Manuscript Collection-Legislative Records [New Jersey State Archives],* Box 1-12, Folder 25, pg. 2.

lion, David, Male

LIPPINCOTT, James, - Name on a petition, 1750/1, the House of Representatives from inhabitants of the province protesting against the great number of taverns in the province.- *Manuscript Collection-Legislative Records [New Jersey State Archives],* Box 1-12, Folder 59, pg. 1.

Lippincott, James, Male

LIPPINCOTT, James, Burlington County, Northampton Township - Name on a petition, 30 May 1753, to the House of Representatives from inhabitants in and about Northampton who are requesting an increase in the amount of currency which is scarce. Gold and silver are chiefly transported elsewhere and are scarce also.- *Manuscript Collection-Legislative Records [New Jersey State Archives],* Box 1-12, Folder 65, pg. 1.

Lippincott, James, Male

LIPPINCOTT, Joseph, - Name on a petition, 1750/1, the House of Representatives from inhabitants of the province protesting against the great number of taverns in the province.- *Manuscript Collection-Legislative Records [New Jersey State Archives],* Box 1-12, Folder 59, pg. 1.

Lippincott, Joseph, Male

LIPPINCOTT, Samuel, - Name on a petition, 1750/1, the House of Representatives from inhabitants of the province protesting against the great number of taverns in the province.- *Manuscript Collection-Legislative Records [New Jersey State Archives],* Box 1-12, Folder 59, pg. 1.

Lippincott, Samuel, Male

LONGSTREET, Awrey?, - Name on a petition, 1754, to the House of Representatives from freeholders of the province opposing the election of Samuel Nevell as a judge of the Supreme Court.- *Manuscript Collection-Legislative Records [New Jersey State Archives],* Box 1-12, Folder 66, pg. 3.

Longstreet, Awrey?, Male

LONGWORTH, Thos, Essex County, - Name on petition, 10 Apr 1746, to the General Assembly by freeholders & inhabitants of Essex Co. seeking a repeal of acts for preserving of timber & a duty on imported strong liquors. They cannot build ships because of the present war with France & Spain.- *Manuscript Collection-Legislative Records [New Jersey State Archives],* Box 1-12, Folder 25, pg. 1.

Longworth, Thos, Male

LOUDRICH?, Abraham, Essex County, - Name on petition, 10 Apr 1746, to the General Assembly by freeholders & inhabitants of Essex Co. seeking a repeal of acts for preserving of timber & a duty on imported strong liquors. They cannot build ships because of the present war with France & Spain.- *Manuscript Collection-Legislative Records [New Jersey State Archives],* Box 1-12, Folder 25, pg. 1.

Loudrich?, Abraham, Male

LOW, John, Essex County, - Name on petition, 10 Apr 1746, to the General Assembly by freeholders & inhabitants of Essex Co. seeking a repeal of acts for preserving of timber & a duty on imported strong liquors. They cannot build ships because of the present war with France & Spain.- *Manuscript*

Collection-Legislative Records [New Jersey State Archives], Box 1-12, Folder 25, pg. 1.

Low, John, Male

LUPTON, Christopher, Cape May County, - Name on petition, 12 Mar 1745/6, to the House of Representatives from freeholders of Cape May County complaining of the devaluation of their paper money [likely due in part to the present war] and asking for creation of a fund, apparently to stabilize it.- *Manuscript Collection-Legislative Records [New Jersey State Archives]*, Box 1-12, Folder 22, pg. 1.

Lupton, Christopher, Male

LYON, John, Essex County, - Name on petition, 10 Apr 1746, to the General Assembly by freeholders & inhabitants of Essex Co. seeking a repeal of acts for preserving of timber & a duty on imported strong liquors. They cannot build ships because of the present war with France & Spain.- *Manuscript Collection-Legislative Records [New Jersey State Archives]*, Box 1-12, Folder 25, pg. 1.

Lyon, John, Male

LYORN?, Thomas, Essex County, - Name on petition, 10 Apr 1746, to the General Assembly by freeholders & inhabitants of Essex Co. seeking a repeal of acts for preserving of timber & a duty on imported strong liquors. They cannot build ships because of the present war with France & Spain.- *Manuscript Collection-Legislative Records [New Jersey State Archives]*, Box 1-12, Folder 25, pg. 2.

Lyorn?, Thomas, Male

MACK OR ST MARK?, *eykee?, Middlesex County, Perth Amboy Township - Name on a petition, 1754, to the General Assembly from freeholders/inhabitants of Perth Amboy Township in Middlesex County opposing the election of Samuel Nevill as a judge of the Supreme Court.- *Manuscript Collection-Oversized Legislative Papers [New Jersey State Archives]*, Box 1-43, Folder 2, pg. 1.

mack or St mark?, *eykee?, Male

MAOS?, Denes, - Name on petition, 1 Mar 1748/9, to the governor, etc., seeking passage of a law forbidding the killing of deer by dogs because the meat and hides are mostly worthless.- *Manuscript Collection-Governors' Papers [New Jersey State Archives]*, Box 1-1, Folder 4, pg. 1.

maos?, Denes, Male

MAPET, Bengman, - Name on a petition, 1754, to the House of Representatives from freeholders of the province opposing the election of Samuel Nevell as a judge of the Supreme Court.- *Manuscript Collection-Legislative Records [New Jersey State Archives]*, Box 1-12, Folder 66, pg. 3.

mapet, Bengman, Male -He signed his name with an "x".

MAROT OR MASCOT, Philip, Burlington & Hunterdon Cos., - Name on a petition, 1748/9, to the House of Representatives from inhabitants freeholders of Hunterdon and Burlington Counties seeking for a law requiring every person to record their "Mortgage Deeds" to ensure validity of titles to land.- *Manuscript Collection-Oversized Legislative Papers [New Jersey State Archives]*, Box 1-43, Folder 2, pg. 1.

Marot or Mascot, Philip, Male

MARSELIS, jo*n?, Burlington & Hunterdon Cos., - Name on a petition, 1748/9, to the House of Representatives from inhabitants freeholders of Hunterdon and Burlington Counties seeking for a law requiring every person to record their "Mortgage Deeds" to ensure validity of titles to land.- *Manuscript Collection-Oversized Legislative Papers [New Jersey State Archives]*, Box 1-43, Folder 2, pg. 1.

marselis, jo*n?, Male

MARTIN, C D?, Burlington & Hunterdon Cos., - Name on a petition, 1748/9, to the House of Representatives from inhabitants freeholders of Hunterdon and Burlington Counties seeking for a law requiring every person to record their "Mortgage Deeds" to ensure validity of titles to land.- *Manuscript Collection-Oversized Legislative Papers [New Jersey State Archives]*, Box 1-43, Folder 2, pg. 1.

Martin, C D?, Male

MASCOT OR MAROT, Philip, Burlington & Hunterdon Cos., - Name on a petition, 1748/9, to the House of Representatives from inhabitants freeholders of Hunterdon and Burlington Counties seeking for a law requiring every person to record their "Mortgage Deeds" to ensure validity of titles to land.- *Manuscript Collection-Oversized Legislative Papers [New Jersey State Archives]*, Box 1-43, Folder 2, pg. 1.

Mascot or Marot, Philip, Male

MATTHEWS, Samuel, Cape May County, - Name on petition, 12 Mar 1745/6, to the House of Representatives from freeholders of Cape May County complaining of the devaluation of their paper money [likely due in part to the present war] and asking for creation of a fund, apparently to stabilize it.- *Manuscript Collection-Legislative Records [New Jersey State Archives],* Box 1-12, Folder 22, pg. 1.

Matthews, Samuel, Male

MEEDON OR MEEDOR, Isaac, Burlington & Hunterdon Cos., - Name on a petition, 1748/9, to the House of Representatives from inhabitants freeholders of Hunterdon and Burlington Counties seeking for a law requiring every person to record their "Mortgage Deeds" to ensure validity of titles to land.- *Manuscript Collection-Oversized Legislative Papers [New Jersey State Archives],* Box 1-43, Folder 2, pg. 1.

Meedon or Meedor, Isaac, Male

MEEDOR OR MEEDON, Isaac, Burlington & Hunterdon Cos., - Name on a petition, 1748/9, to the House of Representatives from inhabitants freeholders of Hunterdon and Burlington Counties seeking for a law requiring every person to record their "Mortgage Deeds" to ensure validity of titles to land.- *Manuscript Collection-Oversized Legislative Papers [New Jersey State Archives],* Box 1-43, Folder 2, pg. 1.

Meedor or Meedon, Isaac, Male

MERRET, Abraham, Burlington County, Northampton Township - Name on a petition, 30 May 1753, to the House of Representatives from inhabitants in and about Northampton who are requesting an increase in the amount of currency which is scarce. Gold and silver are chiefly transported elsewhere and are scarce also.- *Manuscript Collection-Legislative Records [New Jersey State Archives],* Box 1-12, Folder 65, pg. 1.

Merret, Abraham, Male

MERRIT, Abraham, - Name on a petition, 1750/1, the House of Representatives from inhabitants of the province protesting against the great number of taverns in the province.- *Manuscript Collection-Legislative Records [New Jersey State Archives],* Box 1-12, Folder 59, pg. 1.

Merrit, Abraham, Male

MERSHON, Houghton, Burlington & Hunterdon Cos., - Name on a petition, 1748/9, to the House of Representatives from inhabitants freeholders of Hunterdon and Burlington Counties seeking for a law requiring every person to record their "Mortgage Deeds" to ensure validity of titles to land.- *Manuscript Collection-Oversized Legislative Papers [New Jersey State Archives],* Box 1-43, Folder 2, pg. 1.

mershon, Houghton, Male

MIDDLETON, Thomas, - Name on a petition, 24 Sep? 1753, to the House of Representatives from inhabitants of the province expressing distress because of a lack of currency as a medium of trade. They present various arguments for the value of a paper currency.- *Manuscript Collection-Oversized Legislative Papers [New Jersey State Archives],* Box 1-43, Folder 4, pg. 1.

Middleton, Thomas, Male

MILES, John, Essex County, - Name on petition, 10 Apr 1746, to the General Assembly by freeholders & inhabitants of Essex Co. seeking a repeal of acts for preserving of timber & a duty on imported strong liquors. They cannot build ships because of the present war with France & Spain.- *Manuscript Collection-Legislative Records [New Jersey State Archives],* Box 1-12, Folder 25, pg. 2.

miles, John, Male

MILLER, Nitham?, - Name on petition, 1 Mar 1748/9, to the governor, etc., seeking passage of a law forbidding the killing of deer by dogs because the meat and hides are mostly worthless.- *Manuscript Collection-Governors' Papers [New Jersey State Archives],* Box 1-1, Folder 4, pg. 1.

miller, Nitham?, Male

MIONDS?, Geo., - Name on a petition, 24 Sep? 1753, to the House of Representatives from inhabitants of the province expressing distress because of a lack of currency as a medium of trade. They present various arguments for the value of a paper currency.- *Manuscript Collection-Oversized Legislative Papers [New Jersey State Archives],* Box 1-43, Folder 4, pg. 1.

Mionds?, Geo., Male

MONROW?, John, Burlington County, Northampton Township - Name on a petition, 30 May 1753, to the House of Representatives from inhabitants in and about Northampton who are requesting an increase in the amount of currency which is scarce. Gold and silver are chiefly transported elsewhere and are scarce also.- *Manuscript Collection-Legislative Records [New Jersey State Archives],* Box 1-12, Folder 65, pg. 1.

Monrow?, John, Male

MONY, Danel, - Name on petition, 1 Mar 1748/9, to the governor, etc., seeking passage of a law forbidding the killing of deer by dogs because the meat and hides are mostly worthless.- *Manuscript Collection-Governors' Papers [New Jersey State Archives],* Box 1-1, Folder 4, pg. 1.

mony, Danel, Male

MOOR, Benjamin, Burlington & Hunterdon Cos., - Name on a petition, 1748/9, to the House of Representatives from inhabitants freeholders of Hunterdon and Burlington Counties seeking for a law requiring every person to record their "Mortgage Deeds" to ensure validity of titles to land.- *Manuscript Collection-Oversized Legislative Papers [New Jersey State Archives],* Box 1-43, Folder 2, pg. 1.
moor, Benjamin, Male

MOOR, James, - Name on petition, 1 Mar 1748/9, to the governor, etc., seeking passage of a law forbidding the killing of deer by dogs because the meat and hides are mostly worthless.- *Manuscript Collection-Governors' Papers [New Jersey State Archives],* Box 1-1, Folder 4, pg. 1.
Moor, James, Male

MOORE, Robarte, - Name on petition, 1 Mar 1748/9, to the governor, etc., seeking passage of a law forbidding the killing of deer by dogs because the meat and hides are mostly worthless.- *Manuscript Collection-Governors' Papers [New Jersey State Archives],* Box 1-1, Folder 4, pg. 1.
Moore, Robarte, Male

MOORE, William, Essex County, - Name on petition, 10 Apr 1746, to the General Assembly by freeholders & inhabitants of Essex Co. seeking a repeal of acts for preserving of timber & a duty on imported strong liquors. They cannot build ships because of the present war with France & Spain.- *Manuscript Collection-Legislative Records [New Jersey State Archives],* Box 1-12, Folder 25, pg. 1.
Moore, William, Male

MOORE, Zebediah, Essex County, - Name on petition, 10 Apr 1746, to the General Assembly by freeholders & inhabitants of Essex Co. seeking a repeal of acts for preserving of timber & a duty on imported strong liquors. They cannot build ships because of the present war with France & Spain.- *Manuscript Collection-Legislative Records [New Jersey State Archives],* Box 1-12, Folder 25, pg. 1.
Moore, Zebediah, Male

MORGAN?, [Missing], Junir?, Essex County, - Name on petition, 10 Apr 1746, to the General Assembly by freeholders & inhabitants of Essex Co. seeking a repeal of acts for preserving of timber & a duty on imported strong liquors. They cannot build ships because of the present war with France & Spain.- *Manuscript Collection-Legislative Records [New Jersey State Archives],* Box 1-12, Folder 25, pg. 1.
Morgan?, [Missing], Junir?, Male

MORISON?, Tho, Middlesex County, Perth Amboy Township - Name on a petition, 1754, to the General Assembly from freeholders/inhabitants of Perth Amboy Township in Middlesex County opposing the election of Samuel Nevill as a judge of the Supreme Court.- *Manuscript Collection-Oversized Legislative Papers [New Jersey State Archives],* Box 1-43, Folder 2, pg. 1.
morison?, Tho, Male

MORRESSON, John, - Name on petition, 1 Mar 1748/9, to the governor, etc., seeking passage of a law forbidding the killing of deer by dogs because the meat and hides are mostly worthless.- *Manuscript Collection-Governors' Papers [New Jersey State Archives],* Box 1-1, Folder 4, pg. 1.
morresson, John, Male

MORRIS, w, Burlington & Hunterdon Cos., - Name on a petition, 1748/9, to the House of Representatives from inhabitants freeholders of Hunterdon and Burlington Counties seeking for a law requiring every person to record their "Mortgage Deeds" to ensure validity of titles to land.- *Manuscript Collection-Oversized Legislative Papers [New Jersey State Archives],* Box 1-43, Folder 2, pg. 1.
morris, w, Male

MORRISLY, Willm, Burlington & Hunterdon Cos., - Name on a petition, 1748/9, to the House of Representatives from inhabitants freeholders of Hunterdon and Burlington Counties seeking for a law requiring every person to record their "Mortgage Deeds" to ensure validity of titles to land.- *Manuscript Collection-Oversized Legislative Papers [New Jersey State Archives],* Box 1-43, Folder 2, pg. 1.
Morrisly, Willm, Male

MORRISON, Andrew, Morris County, - Name on a petition, 6 Oct 1751, to Governor Jonathan Belcher from owners of "Bloomaries" in Morris County seeking removal of a tax on their iron works (Bloomeries). Many make 5-6 tons or less a year. They seek instead for a bounty on all they produce.- *Manuscript Collection-MSS Coll., #1-100 [New Jersey State Archives],* Box 5-1, Folder 28, pg. 2.
Morrison, Andrew, Male

MORTON?, David?, - Name on a petition, 24 Sep? 1753, to the House of Representatives from inhabitants of the province expressing distress because of a lack of currency as a medium of trade.

They present various arguments for the value of a paper currency.- *Manuscript Collection-Oversized Legislative Papers [New Jersey State Archives],* Box 1-43, Folder 4, pg. 1.

morton?, David?, Male

MOUNT?, Humphry, - Name on a petition, 1754, to the House of Representatives from freeholders of the province opposing the election of Samuel Nevell as a judge of the Supreme Court.- *Manuscript Collection-Legislative Records [New Jersey State Archives],* Box 1-12, Folder 66, pg. 1.

mount?, Humphry, Male

MOUNT?, Matthias, Middlesex County, - Name on a petition, 1754, to the House of Representatives from freeholders of the province opposing the election of Samuel Nevell as a judge of the Supreme Court.- *Manuscript Collection-Legislative Records [New Jersey State Archives],* Box 1-12, Folder 66, pg. 2.

mount?, Matthias, Male

MULFORD, Wiliam, Cape May County, - Name on petition, 12 Mar 1745/6, to the House of Representatives from freeholders of Cape May County complaining of the devaluation of their paper money [likely due in part to the present war] and asking for creation of a fund, apparently to stabilize it.- *Manuscript Collection-Legislative Records [New Jersey State Archives],* Box 1-12, Folder 22, pg. 1.

Mulford, Wiliam, Male

MULLEN, Joseph, Burlington County, Northampton Township - Name on a petition, 30 May 1753, to the House of Representatives from inhabitants in and about Northampton who are requesting an increase in the amount of currency which is scarce. Gold and silver are chiefly transported elsewhere and are scarce also.- *Manuscript Collection-Legislative Records [New Jersey State Archives],* Box 1-12, Folder 65, pg. 1.

Mullen, Joseph, Male

MURPIN?, William, Burlington County, Nottingham - Name on a petition, 18 Nov 1748, to the House of Representatives from inhabitants of Nottingham, Burlington County complaining of those hunting out of season who have killed their hogs and cattle. Sometimes people are in danger of being shot.- *Manuscript Collection-Legislative Records [New Jersey State Archives],* Box 1-12, Folder 46, pg. 1.

Murpin?, William, Male

MYERS, John, Hunterdon County, Bethlehem - Name on a petition, 12 Jan 1747/8, to Jonathan Belcher, Governor, from inhabitants of Bethlehem in Hunterdon County seeking to have the southerly part of Bethlehem Township made into a new township.- *Legislature-Petitions re: Municipal Boundaries [New Jersey State Archives],* Box 1, Folder 1, pg. 1.

Myers, John, Male

MYERS, Joseph, Hunterdon County, Bethlehem - Name on a petition, 12 Jan 1747/8, to Jonathan Belcher, Governor, from inhabitants of Bethlehem in Hunterdon County seeking to have the southerly part of Bethlehem Township made into a new township.- *Legislature-Petitions re: Municipal Boundaries [New Jersey State Archives],* Box 1, Folder 1, pg. 1.

Myers, Joseph, Male

NEVILE?, Tobeyas, - Name on a petition, 1754, to the House of Representatives from freeholders of the province opposing the election of Samuel Nevell as a judge of the Supreme Court.- *Manuscript Collection-Legislative Records [New Jersey State Archives],* Box 1-12, Folder 66, pg. 4.

Nevile?, Tobeyas, Male

NITZENGER?, joseph, - Name on petition, 1 Mar 1748/9, to the governor, etc., seeking passage of a law forbidding the killing of deer by dogs because the meat and hides are mostly worthless.- *Manuscript Collection-Governors' Papers [New Jersey State Archives],* Box 1-1, Folder 4, pg. 1.

nitzenger?, joseph, Male

NORTON, Nathanel, Cape May County, - Name on petition, 12 Mar 1745/6, to the House of Representatives from freeholders of Cape May County complaining of the devaluation of their paper money [likely due in part to the present war] and asking for creation of a fund, apparently to stabilize it.- *Manuscript Collection-Legislative Records [New Jersey State Archives],* Box 1-12, Folder 22, pg. 1.

norton, Nathanel, Male

OATS?, Jno, Hunterdon County, Bethlehem - Name on a petition, 12 Jan 1747/8, to Jonathan Belcher, Governor, from inhabitants of Bethlehem in Hunterdon County seeking to have the southerly part of Bethlehem Township made into a new township.- *Legislature-Petitions re: Municipal Boundaries [New Jersey State Archives],* Box 1, Folder 1, pg. 1.

Oats?, Jno, Male

OGDEN, David, Jun, Essex County, - Name on petition, 10 Apr 1746, to the General Assembly by freeholders & inhabitants of Essex Co. seeking a repeal of acts for preserving of timber & a duty on imported strong liquors. They cannot build ships because of the present war with France & Spain.- *Manuscript Collection-Legislative Records [New Jersey State Archives],* Box 1-12, Folder 25, pg. 1.

Ogden, David, Jun, Male

OGDEN, John, Jun, Essex County, - Name on petition, 10 Apr 1746, to the General Assembly by freeholders & inhabitants of Essex Co. seeking a repeal of acts for preserving of timber & a duty on imported strong liquors. They cannot build ships because of the present war with France & Spain.- *Manuscript Collection-Legislative Records [New Jersey State Archives],* Box 1-12, Folder 25, pg. 1.

Ogden, John, Jun, Male

OGDEN, Nathanel, Essex County, - Name on petition, 10 Apr 1746, to the General Assembly by freeholders & inhabitants of Essex Co. seeking a repeal of acts for preserving of timber & a duty on imported strong liquors. They cannot build ships because of the present war with France & Spain.- *Manuscript Collection-Legislative Records [New Jersey State Archives],* Box 1-12, Folder 25, pg. 1.

Ogden, Nathanel, Male

OGDEN, Samuel, Essex County, - Name on petition, 10 Apr 1746, to the General Assembly by freeholders & inhabitants of Essex Co. seeking a repeal of acts for preserving of timber & a duty on imported strong liquors. They cannot build ships because of the present war with France & Spain.- *Manuscript Collection-Legislative Records [New Jersey State Archives],* Box 1-12, Folder 25, pg. 1.

ogden, Samuel, Male

OGDEN, Sussion?, Essex County, - Name on petition, 10 Apr 1746, to the General Assembly by freeholders & inhabitants of Essex Co. seeking a repeal of acts for preserving of timber & a duty on imported strong liquors. They cannot build ships because of the present war with France & Spain.- *Manuscript Collection-Legislative Records [New Jersey State Archives],* Box 1-12, Folder 25, pg. 1.

ogden, Sussion?, Male

OGDEN, Uzal?, Sr?, Essex County, - Name on petition, 10 Apr 1746, to the General Assembly by freeholders & inhabitants of Essex Co. seeking a repeal of acts for preserving of timber & a duty on imported strong liquors. They cannot build ships because of the present war with France & Spain.- *Manuscript Collection-Legislative Records [New Jersey State Archives],* Box 1-12, Folder 25, pg. 1.

Ogden, Uzal?, Sr?, Male

OSBORN, Arenias?, Cape May County, - Name on petition, 12 Mar 1745/6, to the House of Representatives from freeholders of Cape May County complaining of the devaluation of their paper money [likely due in part to the present war] and asking for creation of a fund, apparently to stabilize it.- *Manuscript Collection-Legislative Records [New Jersey State Archives],* Box 1-12, Folder 22, pg. 1.

Osborn, Arenias?, Male

OSBORNE, Nathan, Cape May County, - Name on petition, 12 Mar 1745/6, to the House of Representatives from freeholders of Cape May County complaining of the devaluation of their paper money [likely due in part to the present war] and asking for creation of a fund, apparently to stabilize it.- *Manuscript Collection-Legislative Records [New Jersey State Archives],* Box 1-12, Folder 22, pg. 1.

Osborne, Nathan, Male

OSEAMEL?, John, - Name on a petition, 1754, to the House of Representatives from freeholders of the province opposing the election of Samuel Nevell as a judge of the Supreme Court.- *Manuscript Collection-Legislative Records [New Jersey State Archives],* Box 1-12, Folder 66, pg. 4.

OSeamel?, John, Male

PAGE, Joseph, Cape May County, - Name on petition, 12 Mar 1745/6, to the House of Representatives from freeholders of Cape May County complaining of the devaluation of their paper money [likely due in part to the present war] and asking for creation of a fund, apparently to stabilize it.- *Manuscript Collection-Legislative Records [New Jersey State Archives],* Box 1-12, Folder 22, pg. 1.

Page, Joseph, Male

PALMERE, Samll, Morris County, - Name on a petition, 6 Oct 1751, to Governor Jonathan Belcher from owners of "Bloomaries" in Morris County seeking removal of a tax on their iron works (Bloomeries). Many make 5-6 tons or less a year. They seek instead for a bounty on all they produce.- *Manuscript Collection-MSS Coll., #1-100 [New Jersey State Archives],* Box 5-1, Folder 28, pg. 2.

Palmere, Samll, Male

PAN, John, Juner, - Name on a petition, 1754, to the House of Representatives from freeholders of the province opposing the election of Samuel Nevell as a judge of the Supreme Court.- *Manuscript Collection-Legislative Records [New Jersey State Archives],* Box 1-12, Folder 66, pg. 4.

pan, John, Juner, Male

PANCOOST? OR BANCROFT, Thos, Burlington & Hunterdon Cos., - Name on a petition, 1748/9, to the House of Representatives from inhabitants freeholders of Hunterdon and Burlington Counties seeking for a law requiring every person to record their "Mortgage Deeds" to ensure validity of titles to land.- *Manuscript Collection-Oversized Legislative Papers [New Jersey State Archives],* Box 1-43, Folder 2, pg. 1.

Pancoost? or Bancroft, Thos, Male

PARKHURST, Samuel, Essex County, - Name on petition, 10 Apr 1746, to the General Assembly by freeholders & inhabitants of Essex Co. seeking a repeal of acts for preserving of timber & a duty on imported strong liquors. They cannot build ships because of the present war with France & Spain.- *Manuscript Collection-Legislative Records [New Jersey State Archives],* Box 1-12, Folder 25, pg. 1.

parkhurst, Samuel, Male

PARSON, Thomas, Essex County, - Name on petition, 10 Apr 1746, to the General Assembly by freeholders & inhabitants of Essex Co. seeking a repeal of acts for preserving of timber & a duty on imported strong liquors. They cannot build ships because of the present war with France & Spain.- *Manuscript Collection-Legislative Records [New Jersey State Archives],* Box 1-12, Folder 25, pg. 2.

parson, Thomas, Male

PAXSON, Henry, Burlington County, Northampton Township - Name on a petition, 30 May 1753, to the House of Representatives from inhabitants in and about Northampton who are requesting an increase in the amount of currency which is scarce. Gold and silver are chiefly transported elsewhere and are scarce also.- *Manuscript Collection-Legislative Records [New Jersey State Archives],* Box 1-12, Folder 65, pg. 1.

Paxson, Henry, Male

PAXTON, Jos, Burlington & Hunterdon Cos., - Name on a petition, 1748/9, to the House of Representatives from inhabitants freeholders of Hunterdon and Burlington Counties seeking for a law requiring every person to record their

"Mortgage Deeds" to ensure validity of titles to land.- *Manuscript Collection-Oversized Legislative Papers [New Jersey State Archives],* Box 1-43, Folder 2, pg. 1.

Paxton, Jos, Male

PEAIRS, James, - Name on a petition, 1754, to the House of Representatives from freeholders of the province opposing the election of Samuel Nevell as a judge of the Supreme Court.- *Manuscript Collection-Legislative Records [New Jersey State Archives],* Box 1-12, Folder 66, pg. 1.

Peairs, James, Male

PEARSON, Robart, Burlington County, Nottingham - Name on a petition, 18 Nov 1748, to the House of Representatives from inhabitants of Nottingham, Burlington County complaining of those hunting out of season who have killed their hogs and cattle. Sometimes people are in danger of being shot.- *Manuscript Collection-Legislative Records [New Jersey State Archives],* Box 1-12, Folder 46, pg. 1.

Pearson, Robart, Male

PECK?, Joseph, Essex County, - Name on petition, 10 Apr 1746, to the General Assembly by freeholders & inhabitants of Essex Co. seeking a repeal of acts for preserving of timber & a duty on imported strong liquors. They cannot build ships because of the present war with France & Spain.- *Manuscript Collection-Legislative Records [New Jersey State Archives],* Box 1-12, Folder 25, pg. 1.

Peck?, Joseph, Male

PECK?, Joseph, iunior, Essex County, - Name on petition, 10 Apr 1746, to the General Assembly by freeholders & inhabitants of Essex Co. seeking a repeal of acts for preserving of timber & a duty on imported strong liquors. They cannot build ships because of the present war with France & Spain.- *Manuscript Collection-Legislative Records [New Jersey State Archives],* Box 1-12, Folder 25, pg. 1.

Peck?, Joseph, iunior, Male

PEIRSON, Bethuel?, Essex County, - Name on petition, 10 Apr 1746, to the General Assembly by freeholders & inhabitants of Essex Co. seeking a repeal of acts for preserving of timber & a duty on imported strong liquors. They cannot build ships because of the present war with France & Spain.- *Manuscript Collection-Legislative Records [New Jersey State Archives],* Box 1-12, Folder 25, pg. 2.

Peirson, Bethuel?, Male

PEIRSON, Samuel, Essex County, - Name on petition, 10 Apr 1746, to the General Assembly by freeholders & inhabitants of Essex Co. seeking a repeal of acts for preserving of timber & a duty on imported strong liquors. They cannot build ships because of the present war with France & Spain.- *Manuscript Collection-Legislative Records [New Jersey State Archives]*, Box 1-12, Folder 25, pg. 1.

peirson, Samuel, Male

PERINE, Henry, - Name on a petition, 1754, to the House of Representatives from freeholders of the province opposing the election of Samuel Nevell as a judge of the Supreme Court.- *Manuscript Collection-Legislative Records [New Jersey State Archives]*, Box 1-12, Folder 66, pg. 1.

Perine, Henry, Male

PHILLIPS, John, Essex County, - Name on petition, 10 Apr 1746, to the General Assembly by freeholders & inhabitants of Essex Co. seeking a repeal of acts for preserving of timber & a duty on imported strong liquors. They cannot build ships because of the present war with France & Spain.- *Manuscript Collection-Legislative Records [New Jersey State Archives]*, Box 1-12, Folder 25, pg. 2.

Phillips, John, Male

PHILLIPS, John, Burlington & Hunterdon Cos., - Name on a petition, 1748/9, to the House of Representatives from inhabitants freeholders of Hunterdon and Burlington Counties seeking for a law requiring every person to record their "Mortgage Deeds" to ensure validity of titles to land.- *Manuscript Collection-Oversized Legislative Papers [New Jersey State Archives]*, Box 1-43, Folder 2, pg. 1.

Phillips, John, Male

PICKITT OR RICKITT, Jacob, - Name on a petition, 24 Sep? 1753, to the House of Representatives from inhabitants of the province expressing distress because of a lack of currency as a medium of trade. They present various arguments for the value of a paper currency.- *Manuscript Collection-Oversized Legislative Papers [New Jersey State Archives]*, Box 1-43, Folder 4, pg. 1.

Pickitt or Rickitt, Jacob, Male

PIERSONE?, Joseph?, Essex County, - Name on petition, 10 Apr 1746, to the General Assembly by freeholders & inhabitants of Essex Co. seeking a repeal of acts for preserving of timber & a duty on imported strong liquors. They cannot build ships because of the present war with France & Spain.- *Manuscript Collection-Legislative Records [New Jersey State Archives]*, Box 1-12, Folder 25, pg. 2.

Piersone?, Joseph?, Male

PIRTTY, John, Hunterdon County, Bethlehem - Name on a petition, 12 Jan 1747/8, to Jonathan Belcher, Governor, from inhabitants of Bethlehem in Hunterdon County seeking to have the southerly part of Bethlehem Township made into a new township.- *Legislature-Petitions re: Municipal Boundaries [New Jersey State Archives]*, Box 1, Folder 1, pg. 1.

pirtty, John, Male

POBAG?, Bengaman, Burlington County, Nottingham - Name on a petition, 18 Nov 1748, to the House of Representatives from inhabitants of Nottingham, Burlington County complaining of those hunting out of season who have killed their hogs and cattle. Sometimes people are in danger of being shot.- *Manuscript Collection-Legislative Records [New Jersey State Archives]*, Box 1-12, Folder 46, pg. 1.

Pobag?, Bengaman, Male

POOG, John, - Name on petition, 1 Mar 1748/9, to the governor, etc., seeking passage of a law forbidding the killing of deer by dogs because the meat and hides are mostly worthless.- *Manuscript Collection-Governors' Papers [New Jersey State Archives]*, Box 1-1, Folder 4, pg. 1.

Poog, John, Male

POULSEN, John, Essex County, - Name on petition, 10 Apr 1746, to the General Assembly by freeholders & inhabitants of Essex Co. seeking a repeal of acts for preserving of timber & a duty on imported strong liquors. They cannot build ships because of the present war with France & Spain.- *Manuscript Collection-Legislative Records [New Jersey State Archives]*, Box 1-12, Folder 25, pg. 2.

Poulsen, John, Male

POWELL, Isaac, - Name on a petition, 24 Sep? 1753, to the House of Representatives from inhabitants of the province expressing distress because of a lack of currency as a medium of trade. They present various arguments for the value of a paper currency.- *Manuscript Collection-Oversized Legislative Papers [New Jersey State Archives]*, Box 1-43, Folder 4, pg. 1.

Powell, Isaac, Male

POWELL, John, - Name on a petition, 1750/1, the House of Representatives from inhabitants of the province protesting against the great number of taverns in the province.- *Manuscript Collection-Legislative Records [New Jersey State Archives]*, Box 1-12, Folder 59, pg. 1.

Powell, John, Male

POWELL, Robert, - Name on a petition, 24 Sep? 1753, to the House of Representatives from inhabitants of the province expressing distress because of a lack of currency as a medium of trade. They present various arguments for the value of a paper currency.- *Manuscript Collection-Oversized Legislative Papers [New Jersey State Archives],* Box 1-43, Folder 4, pg. 1.

Powell, Robert, Male

PRICE, Thos, Burlington & Hunterdon Cos., - Name on a petition, 1748/9, to the House of Representatives from inhabitants freeholders of Hunterdon and Burlington Counties seeking for a law requiring every person to record their "Mortgage Deeds" to ensure validity of titles to land.- *Manuscript Collection-Oversized Legislative Papers [New Jersey State Archives],* Box 1-43, Folder 2, pg. 1.

Price, Thos, Male

PRICE, Tomson, Hunterdon County, Bethlehem - Name on a petition, 12 Jan 1747/8, to Jonathan Belcher, Governor, from inhabitants of Bethlehem in Hunterdon County seeking to have the southerly part of Bethlehem Township made into a new township.- *Legislature-Petitions re: Municipal Boundaries [New Jersey State Archives],* Box 1, Folder 1, pg. 1.

price, Tomson, Male

PRINC?, peter, Middlesex County, Perth Amboy Township - Name on a petition, 1754, to the General Assembly from freeholders/inhabitants of Perth Amboy Township in Middlesex County opposing the election of Samuel Nevill as a judge of the Supreme Court.- *Manuscript Collection-Oversized Legislative Papers [New Jersey State Archives],* Box 1-43, Folder 2, pg. 1.

princ?, peter, Male

RECKLESS, Jos, Junr, Burlington & Hunterdon Cos., - Name on a petition, 1748/9, to the House of Representatives from inhabitants freeholders of Hunterdon and Burlington Counties seeking for a law requiring every person to record their "Mortgage Deeds" to ensure validity of titles to land.- *Manuscript Collection-Oversized Legislative Papers [New Jersey State Archives],* Box 1-43, Folder 2, pg. 1.

Reckless, Jos, Junr, Male

REED, Andrew, Burlington & Hunterdon Cos., - Name on a petition, 1748/9, to the House of Representatives from inhabitants freeholders of Hunterdon and Burlington Counties seeking for a law requiring every person to record their "Mortgage Deeds" to ensure validity of titles to land.- *Manuscript Collection-Oversized Legislative Papers [New Jersey State Archives],* Box 1-43, Folder 2, pg. 1.

Reed, Andrew, Male

REED, John, - Name on a petition, 1754, to the House of Representatives from freeholders of the province opposing the election of Samuel Nevell as a judge of the Supreme Court.- *Manuscript Collection-Legislative Records [New Jersey State Archives],* Box 1-12, Folder 66, pg. 4.

Reed, John, Male

REESEN?, William, Burlington & Hunterdon Cos., - Name on a petition, 1748/9, to the House of Representatives from inhabitants freeholders of Hunterdon and Burlington Counties seeking for a law requiring every person to record their "Mortgage Deeds" to ensure validity of titles to land.- *Manuscript Collection-Oversized Legislative Papers [New Jersey State Archives],* Box 1-43, Folder 2, pg. 1.

Reesen?, William, Male

REYNOLDS, John, - Name on a petition, 1754, to the House of Representatives from freeholders of the province opposing the election of Samuel Nevell as a judge of the Supreme Court.- *Manuscript Collection-Legislative Records [New Jersey State Archives],* Box 1-12, Folder 66, pg. 3.

Reynolds, John, Male

RICHARD, Thoms, Essex County, - Name on petition, 10 Apr 1746, to the General Assembly by freeholders & inhabitants of Essex Co. seeking a repeal of acts for preserving of timber & a duty on imported strong liquors. They cannot build ships because of the present war with France & Spain.- *Manuscript Collection-Legislative Records [New Jersey State Archives],* Box 1-12, Folder 25, pg. 1.

Richard, Thoms, Male

RICHARDSON, Jacob, Cape May County, - Name on petition, 12 Mar 1745/6, to the House of Representatives from freeholders of Cape May County complaining of the devaluation of their paper money [likely due in part to the present war] and asking for creation of a fund, apparently to stabilize it.- *Manuscript Collection-Legislative Records [New Jersey State Archives],* Box 1-12, Folder 22, pg. 1.

Richardson, Jacob, Male

RICKERDIKE OR BICKERDIKE, Gideon, Burlington & Hunterdon Cos., - Name on a petition, 1748/9, to the House of Representatives from inhabitants freeholders of Hunterdon and Burlington Counties seeking for a law requiring every person to record their "Mortgage Deeds" to ensure validity of titles to land.- *Manuscript Collection-Oversized Legislative Papers [New Jersey State Archives]*, Box 1-43, Folder 2, pg. 1.

Rickerdike or Bickerdike, Gideon, Male

RICKITT OR PICKITT, Jacob, - Name on a petition, 24 Sep? 1753, to the House of Representatives from inhabitants of the province expressing distress because of a lack of currency as a medium of trade. They present various arguments for the value of a paper currency.- *Manuscript Collection-Oversized Legislative Papers [New Jersey State Archives]*, Box 1-43, Folder 4, pg. 1.

Rickitt or Pickitt, Jacob, Male

RIDGWAY, Joseph, Burlington County, Northampton Township - Name on a petition, 30 May 1753, to the House of Representatives from inhabitants in and about Northampton who are requesting an increase in the amount of currency which is scarce. Gold and silver are chiefly transported elsewhere and are scarce also.- *Manuscript Collection-Legislative Records [New Jersey State Archives]*, Box 1-12, Folder 65, pg. 1.

Ridgway, Joseph, Male

RIDGWAY, Solomon, - Name on a petition, 24 Sep? 1753, to the House of Representatives from inhabitants of the province expressing distress because of a lack of currency as a medium of trade. They present various arguments for the value of a paper currency.- *Manuscript Collection-Oversized Legislative Papers [New Jersey State Archives]*, Box 1-43, Folder 4, pg. 1.

Ridgway, Solomon, Male

RIGGS, Daniel, Essex County, - Name on petition, 10 Apr 1746, to the General Assembly by freeholders & inhabitants of Essex Co. seeking a repeal of acts for preserving of timber & a duty on imported strong liquors. They cannot build ships because of the present war with France & Spain.- *Manuscript Collection-Legislative Records [New Jersey State Archives]*, Box 1-12, Folder 25, pg. 2.

Riggs, Daniel, Male

RIGGS, Gideon, Essex County, - Name on petition, 10 Apr 1746, to the General Assembly by freeholders & inhabitants of Essex Co. seeking a repeal of acts for preserving of timber & a duty on imported strong liquors. They cannot build ships because of the present war with France & Spain.- *Manuscript Collection-Legislative Records [New Jersey State Archives]*, Box 1-12, Folder 25, pg. 2.

Riggs, Gideon, Male

RIGGS, Samuel, Morris County, - Name on a petition, 6 Oct 1751, to Governor Jonathan Belcher from owners of "Bloomaries" in Morris County seeking removal of a tax on their iron works (Bloomeries). Many make 5-6 tons or less a year. They seek instead for a bounty on all they produce.- *Manuscript Collection-MSS Coll., #1-100 [New Jersey State Archives]*, Box 5-1, Folder 28, pg. 2.

Riggs, Samuel, Male

RIGGS, Simeon, Essex County, - Name on petition, 10 Apr 1746, to the General Assembly by freeholders & inhabitants of Essex Co. seeking a repeal of acts for preserving of timber & a duty on imported strong liquors. They cannot build ships because of the present war with France & Spain.- *Manuscript Collection-Legislative Records [New Jersey State Archives]*, Box 1-12, Folder 25, pg. 1.

Riggs, Simeon, Male

RIKY, Brice, - Name on petition, 1 Mar 1748/9, to the governor, etc., seeking passage of a law forbidding the killing of deer by dogs because the meat and hides are mostly worthless.- *Manuscript Collection-Governors' Papers [New Jersey State Archives]*, Box 1-1, Folder 4, pg. 1.

Riky, Brice, Male

ROBERSON?, John, Cape May County, - Name on petition, 12 Mar 1745/6, to the House of Representatives from freeholders of Cape May County complaining of the devaluation of their paper money [likely due in part to the present war] and asking for creation of a fund, apparently to stabilize it.- *Manuscript Collection-Legislative Records [New Jersey State Archives]*, Box 1-12, Folder 22, pg. 1.

Roberson?, John, Male

ROGERS, Robert, Middlesex County, - Name on a petition, 1754, to the House of Representatives from freeholders of the province opposing the election of Samuel Nevell as a judge of the Supreme Court.- *Manuscript Collection-Legislative Records [New Jersey State Archives]*, Box 1-12, Folder 66, pg. 2.

Rogers, Robert, Male

ROGERS, Samll, Burlington & Hunterdon Cos., - Name on a petition, 1748/9, to the House of Representatives from inhabitants freeholders of Hunterdon and Burlington Counties seeking for a law requiring every person to record their "Mortgage Deeds" to ensure validity of titles to land.- *Manuscript Collection-Oversized Legislative Papers [New Jersey State Archives]*, Box 1-43, Folder 2, pg. 1.

Rogers, Samll, Male

ROGERS, Wm, Burlington County, Northampton Township - Name on a petition, 30 May 1753, to the House of Representatives from inhabitants in and about Northampton who are requesting an increase in the amount of currency which is scarce. Gold and silver are chiefly transported elsewhere and are scarce also.- *Manuscript Collection-Legislative Records [New Jersey State Archives]*, Box 1-12, Folder 65, pg. 1.

Rogers, Wm, Male

ROMINE?, Peter, Hunterdon County, Bethlehem - Name on a petition, 12 Jan 1747/8, to Jonathan Belcher, Governor, from inhabitants of Bethlehem in Hunterdon County seeking to have the southerly part of Bethlehem Township made into a new township.- *Legislature-Petitions re: Municipal Boundaries [New Jersey State Archives]*, Box 1, Folder 1, pg. 1.

Romine?, Peter, Male

ROSS, Alexd, Burlington County, Northampton Township - Name on a petition, 30 May 1753, to the House of Representatives from inhabitants in and about Northampton who are requesting an increase in the amount of currency which is scarce. Gold and silver are chiefly transported elsewhere and are scarce also.- *Manuscript Collection-Legislative Records [New Jersey State Archives]*, Box 1-12, Folder 65, pg. 1.

Ross, Alexd, Male

ROSS, Thomas, Cape May County, - Name on petition, 12 Mar 1745/6, to the House of Representatives from freeholders of Cape May County complaining of the devaluation of their paper money [likely due in part to the present war] and asking for creation of a fund, apparently to stabilize it.- *Manuscript Collection-Legislative Records [New Jersey State Archives]*, Box 1-12, Folder 22, pg. 1.

Ross, Thomas, Male

ROSTEDO?, peter, Essex County, - Name on petition, 10 Apr 1746, to the General Assembly by freeholders & inhabitants of Essex Co. seeking a repeal of acts for preserving of timber & a duty on imported strong liquors. They cannot build ships because of the present war with France & Spain.- *Manuscript Collection-Legislative Records [New Jersey State Archives]*, Box 1-12, Folder 25, pg. 1.

Rostedo?, peter, Male

ROWS OR BOWS, Thos, Essex County, - Name on petition, 10 Apr 1746, to the General Assembly by freeholders & inhabitants of Essex Co. seeking a repeal of acts for preserving of timber & a duty on imported strong liquors. They cannot build ships because of the present war with France & Spain.- *Manuscript Collection-Legislative Records [New Jersey State Archives]*, Box 1-12, Folder 25, pg. 1.

Rows or Bows, Thos, Male

ROYSE?, John, Morris County, - Name on a petition, 6 Oct 1751, to Governor Jonathan Belcher from owners of "Bloomaries" in Morris County seeking removal of a tax on their iron works (Bloomeries). Many make 5-6 tons or less a year. They seek instead for a bounty on all they produce.- *Manuscript Collection-MSS Coll., #1-100 [New Jersey State Archives]*, Box 5-1, Folder 28, pg. 2.

Royse?, John, Male

RUCKMAN, John, Hunterdon County, Bethlehem - Name on a petition, 12 Jan 1747/8, to Jonathan Belcher, Governor, from inhabitants of Bethlehem in Hunterdon County seeking to have the southerly part of Bethlehem Township made into a new township.- *Legislature-Petitions re: Municipal Boundaries [New Jersey State Archives]*, Box 1, Folder 1, pg. 1.

Ruckman, John, Male

RUCKMAN, Thomas, Hunterdon County, Bethlehem - Name on a petition, 12 Jan 1747/8, to Jonathan Belcher, Governor, from inhabitants of Bethlehem in Hunterdon County seeking to have the southerly part of Bethlehem Township made into a new township.- *Legislature-Petitions re: Municipal Boundaries [New Jersey State Archives]*, Box 1, Folder 1, pg. 1.

Ruckman, Thomas, Male

RUE, Joseph, - Name on a petition, 1754, to the House of Representatives from freeholders of the province opposing the election of Samuel Nevell as a judge of the Supreme Court.- *Manuscript Collection-Legislative Records [New Jersey State Archives]*, Box 1-12, Folder 66, pg. 1.

Rue, Joseph, Male

RUE, matthew, Middlesex County, Perth Amboy Township - Name on a petition, 1754, to the General Assembly from freeholders/inhabitants of

Perth Amboy Township in Middlesex County opposing the election of Samuel Nevill as a judge of the Supreme Court.- *Manuscript Collection-Oversized Legislative Papers [New Jersey State Archives]*, Box 1-43, Folder 2, pg. 1.

Rue, matthew, Male

RULON?, David, Burlington County, Nottingham - Name on a petition, 18 Nov 1748, to the House of Representatives from inhabitants of Nottingham, Burlington County complaining of those hunting out of season who have killed their hogs and cattle. Sometimes people are in danger of being shot.- *Manuscript Collection-Legislative Records [New Jersey State Archives]*, Box 1-12, Folder 46, pg. 1.

rulon?, David, Male

RUNYON, Reuben, - Name on a petition, 1754, to the House of Representatives from freeholders of the province opposing the election of Samuel Nevell as a judge of the Supreme Court.- *Manuscript Collection-Legislative Records [New Jersey State Archives]*, Box 1-12, Folder 66, pg. 3.

Runyon, Reuben, Male

SCHANCK, Luycas, - Name on a petition, 1754, to the House of Representatives from freeholders of the province opposing the election of Samuel Nevell as a judge of the Supreme Court.- *Manuscript Collection-Legislative Records [New Jersey State Archives]*, Box 1-12, Folder 66, pg. 1.

Schanck, Luycas, Male

SCHENCK, Albert, Middlesex County, - Name on a petition, 1754, to the House of Representatives from freeholders of the province opposing the election of Samuel Nevell as a judge of the Supreme Court.- *Manuscript Collection-Legislative Records [New Jersey State Archives]*, Box 1-12, Folder 66, pg. 2.

Schenck, Albert, Male

SCHENCK, John, Middlesex County, - Name on a petition, 1754, to the House of Representatives from freeholders of the province opposing the election of Samuel Nevell as a judge of the Supreme Court.- *Manuscript Collection-Legislative Records [New Jersey State Archives]*, Box 1-12, Folder 66, pg. 2.

Schenck, John, Male

SCHILLINGER?, Cornelius, Cape May County, - Name on petition, 12 Mar 1745/6, to the House of Representatives from freeholders of Cape May County complaining of the devaluation of their paper money [likely due in part to the present war] and asking for creation of a fund, apparently to stabilize it.- *Manuscript Collection-Legislative Records [New Jersey State Archives]*, Box 1-12, Folder 22, pg. 1.

Schillinger?, Cornelius, Male

SCHMUCK, Peter, Hunterdon County, Bethlehem - Name on a petition, 12 Jan 1747/8, to Jonathan Belcher, Governor, from inhabitants of Bethlehem in Hunterdon County seeking to have the southerly part of Bethlehem Township made into a new township.- *Legislature-Petitions re: Municipal Boundaries [New Jersey State Archives]*, Box 1, Folder 1, pg. 1.

Schmuck, Peter, Male

SERGEANT, Jann, Essex County, - Name on petition, 10 Apr 1746, to the General Assembly by freeholders & inhabitants of Essex Co. seeking a repeal of acts for preserving of timber & a duty on imported strong liquors. They cannot build ships because of the present war with France & Spain.- *Manuscript Collection-Legislative Records [New Jersey State Archives]*, Box 1-12, Folder 25, pg. 1.

Sergeant, Jann, Male

SEVERNS, Theo., Burlington & Hunterdon Cos., - Name on a petition, 1748/9, to the House of Representatives from inhabitants freeholders of Hunterdon and Burlington Counties seeking for a law requiring every person to record their "Mortgage Deeds" to ensure validity of titles to land.- *Manuscript Collection-Oversized Legislative Papers [New Jersey State Archives]*, Box 1-43, Folder 2, pg. 1.

Severns, Theo., Male

SEWARD, Eliakim, Essex County, - Name on petition, 10 Apr 1746, to the General Assembly by freeholders & inhabitants of Essex Co. seeking a repeal of acts for preserving of timber & a duty on imported strong liquors. They cannot build ships because of the present war with France & Spain.- *Manuscript Collection-Legislative Records [New Jersey State Archives]*, Box 1-12, Folder 25, pg. 1.

Seward, Eliakim, Male

SHARP, John, - Name on a petition, 24 Sep? 1753, to the House of Representatives from inhabitants of the province expressing distress because of a lack of currency as a medium of trade. They present various arguments for the value of a paper currency.- *Manuscript Collection-Oversized Legislative Papers [New Jersey State Archives]*, Box 1-43, Folder 4, pg. 1.

Sharp, John, Male

SHARP, Saml, - Name on a petition, 24 Sep? 1753, to the House of Representatives from inhabitants of the province expressing distress because of a lack of currency as a medium of trade. They present various arguments for the value of a paper currency.- *Manuscript Collection-Oversized Legislative Papers [New Jersey State Archives],* Box 1-43, Folder 4, pg. 1.

Sharp, Saml, Male

SHARP, William, - Name on a petition, 24 Sep? 1753, to the House of Representatives from inhabitants of the province expressing distress because of a lack of currency as a medium of trade. They present various arguments for the value of a paper currency.- *Manuscript Collection-Oversized Legislative Papers [New Jersey State Archives],* Box 1-43, Folder 4, pg. 1.

Sharp, William, Male

SHINN, Jacob, - Name on a petition, 1750/1, the House of Representatives from inhabitants of the province protesting against the great number of taverns in the province.- *Manuscript Collection-Legislative Records [New Jersey State Archives],* Box 1-12, Folder 59, pg. 1.

Shinn, Jacob, Male

SHINN, Tho, - Name on a petition, 1750/1, the House of Representatives from inhabitants of the province protesting against the great number of taverns in the province.- *Manuscript Collection-Legislative Records [New Jersey State Archives],* Box 1-12, Folder 59, pg. 1.

Shinn, Tho, Male

SHINN, Thos, Burlington County, Northampton Township - Name on a petition, 30 May 1753, to the House of Representatives from inhabitants in and about Northampton who are requesting an increase in the amount of currency which is scarce. Gold and silver are chiefly transported elsewhere and are scarce also.- *Manuscript Collection-Legislative Records [New Jersey State Archives],* Box 1-12, Folder 65, pg. 1.

Shinn, Thos, Male

SHIPMAN, David, Essex County, - Name on petition, 10 Apr 1746, to the General Assembly by freeholders & inhabitants of Essex Co. seeking a repeal of acts for preserving of timber & a duty on imported strong liquors. They cannot build ships because of the present war with France & Spain.- *Manuscript Collection-Legislative Records [New Jersey State Archives],* Box 1-12, Folder 25, pg. 1.

Shipman, David, Male

SHIPMAN, Jonathan, Essex County, - Name on petition, 10 Apr 1746, to the General Assembly by freeholders & inhabitants of Essex Co. seeking a repeal of acts for preserving of timber & a duty on imported strong liquors. They cannot build ships because of the present war with France & Spain.- *Manuscript Collection-Legislative Records [New Jersey State Archives],* Box 1-12, Folder 25, pg. 2.

Shipman, Jonathan, Male

SHORDT?, Jonthon, Essex County, - Name on petition, 10 Apr 1746, to the General Assembly by freeholders & inhabitants of Essex Co. seeking a repeal of acts for preserving of timber & a duty on imported strong liquors. They cannot build ships because of the present war with France & Spain.- *Manuscript Collection-Legislative Records [New Jersey State Archives],* Box 1-12, Folder 25, pg. 1.

Shordt?, Jonthon, Male

SHOURDE, Samll, junr, Burlington & Hunterdon Cos., - Name on a petition, 1748/9, to the House of Representatives from inhabitants freeholders of Hunterdon and Burlington Counties seeking for a law requiring every person to record their "Mortgage Deeds" to ensure validity of titles to land.- *Manuscript Collection-Oversized Legislative Papers [New Jersey State Archives],* Box 1-43, Folder 2, pg. 1.

Shourde, Samll, junr, Male

SIRATEN?, John, Essex County, - Name on petition, 10 Apr 1746, to the General Assembly by freeholders & inhabitants of Essex Co. seeking a repeal of acts for preserving of timber & a duty on imported strong liquors. They cannot build ships because of the present war with France & Spain.- *Manuscript Collection-Legislative Records [New Jersey State Archives],* Box 1-12, Folder 25, pg. 1.

Siraten?, John, Male

SMITH, Andrew?, Essex County, - Name on petition, 10 Apr 1746, to the General Assembly by freeholders & inhabitants of Essex Co. seeking a repeal of acts for preserving of timber & a duty on imported strong liquors. They cannot build ships because of the present war with France & Spain.- *Manuscript Collection-Legislative Records [New Jersey State Archives],* Box 1-12, Folder 25, pg. 1.

Smith, Andrew?, Male

SMITH, Charles, Hunterdon County, Bethlehem - Name on a petition, 12 Jan 1747/8, to Jonathan Belcher, Governor, from inhabitants of Bethlehem in Hunterdon County seeking to have the southerly part of Bethlehem Township made into a new township.- *Legislature-Petitions re: Municipal Boundaries [New Jersey State Archives]*, Box 1, Folder 1, pg. 1.

Smith, Charles, Male

SMITH, isaac, Essex County, - Name on petition, 10 Apr 1746, to the General Assembly by freeholders & inhabitants of Essex Co. seeking a repeal of acts for preserving of timber & a duty on imported strong liquors. They cannot build ships because of the present war with France & Spain.- *Manuscript Collection-Legislative Records [New Jersey State Archives]*, Box 1-12, Folder 25, pg. 2.

Smith, isaac, Male

SMITH, Isreall, Essex County, - Name on petition, 10 Apr 1746, to the General Assembly by freeholders & inhabitants of Essex Co. seeking a repeal of acts for preserving of timber & a duty on imported strong liquors. They cannot build ships because of the present war with France & Spain.- *Manuscript Collection-Legislative Records [New Jersey State Archives]*, Box 1-12, Folder 25, pg. 1.

Smith, Isreall, Male

SMITH, James, Essex County, - Name on petition, 10 Apr 1746, to the General Assembly by freeholders & inhabitants of Essex Co. seeking a repeal of acts for preserving of timber & a duty on imported strong liquors. They cannot build ships because of the present war with France & Spain.- *Manuscript Collection-Legislative Records [New Jersey State Archives]*, Box 1-12, Folder 25, pg. 1.

Smith, James, Male

SMITH, John, Essex County, - Name on petition, 10 Apr 1746, to the General Assembly by freeholders & inhabitants of Essex Co. seeking a repeal of acts for preserving of timber & a duty on imported strong liquors. They cannot build ships because of the present war with France & Spain.- *Manuscript Collection-Legislative Records [New Jersey State Archives]*, Box 1-12, Folder 25, pg. 1.

Smith, John, Male

SMITH, John, Cape May County, - Name on petition, 12 Mar 1745/6, to the House of Representatives from freeholders of Cape May County complaining of the devaluation of their paper money [likely due in part to the present war] and asking for creation of a fund, apparently to stabilize it.- *Manuscript Collection-Legislative Records [New Jersey State Archives]*, Box 1-12, Folder 22, pg. 1.

Smith, John, Male

SMITH, Jonathan, Cape May County, - Name on petition, 12 Mar 1745/6, to the House of Representatives from freeholders of Cape May County complaining of the devaluation of their paper money [likely due in part to the present war] and asking for creation of a fund, apparently to stabilize it.- *Manuscript Collection-Legislative Records [New Jersey State Archives]*, Box 1-12, Folder 22, pg. 1.

Smith, Jonathan, Male

SMITH, Joseph, Essex County, - Name on petition, 10 Apr 1746, to the General Assembly by freeholders & inhabitants of Essex Co. seeking a repeal of acts for preserving of timber & a duty on imported strong liquors. They cannot build ships because of the present war with France & Spain.- *Manuscript Collection-Legislative Records [New Jersey State Archives]*, Box 1-12, Folder 25, pg. 1.

Smith, Joseph, Male

SMITH, Richard, Cape May County, - Name on petition, 12 Mar 1745/6, to the House of Representatives from freeholders of Cape May County complaining of the devaluation of their paper money [likely due in part to the present war] and asking for creation of a fund, apparently to stabilize it.- *Manuscript Collection-Legislative Records [New Jersey State Archives]*, Box 1-12, Folder 22, pg. 1.

Smith, Richard, Male

SMITH, Samel, Morris County, - Name on a petition, 6 Oct 1751, to Governor Jonathan Belcher from owners of "Bloomaries" in Morris County seeking removal of a tax on their iron works (Bloomeries). Many make 5-6 tons or less a year. They seek instead for a bounty on all they produce.- *Manuscript Collection-MSS Coll., #1-100 [New Jersey State Archives]*, Box 5-1, Folder 28, pg. 2.

Smith, Samel, Male

SMITH, Thomas, - Name on a petition, 24 Sep? 1753, to the House of Representatives from inhabitants of the province expressing distress because of a lack of currency as a medium of trade. They present various arguments for the value of a paper currency.- *Manuscript Collection-Oversized Legislative Papers [New Jersey State Archives]*, Box 1-43, Folder 4, pg. 1.

Smith, Thomas, Male

SMITH, William, Cape May County, - Name on petition, 12 Mar 1745/6, to the House of Representatives from freeholders of Cape May

County complaining of the devaluation of their paper money [likely due in part to the present war] and asking for creation of a fund, apparently to stabilize it.- *Manuscript Collection-Legislative Records [New Jersey State Archives],* Box 1-12, Folder 22, pg. 1.

Smith, William, Male

SMITH, William, Essex County, - Name on petition, 10 Apr 1746, to the General Assembly by freeholders & inhabitants of Essex Co. seeking a repeal of acts for preserving of timber & a duty on imported strong liquors. They cannot build ships because of the present war with France & Spain.- *Manuscript Collection-Legislative Records [New Jersey State Archives],* Box 1-12, Folder 25, pg. 2.

Smith, William, Male

SMITH, william, Essex County, - Name on petition, 10 Apr 1746, to the General Assembly by freeholders & inhabitants of Essex Co. seeking a repeal of acts for preserving of timber & a duty on imported strong liquors. They cannot build ships because of the present war with France & Spain.- *Manuscript Collection-Legislative Records [New Jersey State Archives],* Box 1-12, Folder 25, pg. 2.

Smith, william, Male

SMITH, [Illegible], Essex County, - Name on petition, 10 Apr 1746, to the General Assembly by freeholders & inhabitants of Essex Co. seeking a repeal of acts for preserving of timber & a duty on imported strong liquors. They cannot build ships because of the present war with France & Spain.- *Manuscript Collection-Legislative Records [New Jersey State Archives],* Box 1-12, Folder 25, pg. 1.

Smith, Thos?, Male

SNEDEKER, Isaac, Middlesex County, Perth Amboy Township - Name on a petition, 1754, to the General Assembly from freeholders/inhabitants of Perth Amboy Township in Middlesex County opposing the election of Samuel Nevill as a judge of the Supreme Court.- *Manuscript Collection-Oversized Legislative Papers [New Jersey State Archives],* Box 1-43, Folder 2, pg. 1.

Snedeker, Isaac, Male

SNOWDEN, Wm, Burlington & Hunterdon Cos., - Name on a petition, 1748/9, to the House of Representatives from inhabitants freeholders of Hunterdon and Burlington Counties seeking for a law requiring every person to record their "Mortgage Deeds" to ensure validity of titles to land.- *Manuscript Collection-Oversized Legislative Papers [New Jersey State Archives],* Box 1-43, Folder 2, pg. 1.

Snowden, Wm, Male

SOUTHWICK, Jams, - Name on a petition, 1750/1, the House of Representatives from inhabitants of the province protesting against the great number of taverns in the province.- *Manuscript Collection-Legislative Records [New Jersey State Archives],* Box 1-12, Folder 59, pg. 1.

Southwick, Jams, Male

ST MARK? OR MACK, *eykee?, Middlesex County, Perth Amboy Township - Name on a petition, 1754, to the General Assembly from freeholders/inhabitants of Perth Amboy Township in Middlesex County opposing the election of Samuel Nevill as a judge of the Supreme Court.- *Manuscript Collection-Oversized Legislative Papers [New Jersey State Archives],* Box 1-43, Folder 2, pg. 1.

St mark? or mack, *eykee?, Male

STABACK?, David?, Middlesex County, - Name on a petition, 1754, to the House of Representatives from freeholders of the province opposing the election of Samuel Nevell as a judge of the Supreme Court.- *Manuscript Collection-Legislative Records [New Jersey State Archives],* Box 1-12, Folder 66, pg. 2.

Staback?, David?, Male

STAMBARY?, Elisha, Essex County, - Name on petition, 10 Apr 1746, to the General Assembly by freeholders & inhabitants of Essex Co. seeking a repeal of acts for preserving of timber & a duty on imported strong liquors. They cannot build ships because of the present war with France & Spain.- *Manuscript Collection-Legislative Records [New Jersey State Archives],* Box 1-12, Folder 25, pg. 2.

Stambary?, Elisha, Male

STEVENSON, Samll?, Hunterdon County, Bethlehem - Name on a petition, 12 Jan 1747/8, to Jonathan Belcher, Governor, from inhabitants of Bethlehem in Hunterdon County seeking to have the southerly part of Bethlehem Township made into a new township.- *Legislature-Petitions re: Municipal Boundaries [New Jersey State Archives],* Box 1, Folder 1, pg. 1.

Stevenson, Samll?, Male

STILLERALL?, Richard, Cape May County, - Name on petition, 12 Mar 1745/6, to the House of Representatives from freeholders of Cape May County complaining of the devaluation of their paper money [likely due in part to the present war] and asking for creation of a fund, apparently to stabilize it.- *Manuscript Collection-Legislative Records [New Jersey State Archives]*, Box 1-12, Folder 22, pg. 1.

Stillerall?, Richard, Male

STITCH, Nicholas, - Name on a petition, 24 Sep? 1753, to the House of Representatives from inhabitants of the province expressing distress because of a lack of currency as a medium of trade. They present various arguments for the value of a paper currency.- *Manuscript Collection-Oversized Legislative Papers [New Jersey State Archives]*, Box 1-43, Folder 4, pg. 1.

Stitch, Nicholas, Male

STITES, George, Cape May County, - Name on petition, 12 Mar 1745/6, to the House of Representatives from freeholders of Cape May County complaining of the devaluation of their paper money [likely due in part to the present war] and asking for creation of a fund, apparently to stabilize it.- *Manuscript Collection-Legislative Records [New Jersey State Archives]*, Box 1-12, Folder 22, pg. 1.

Stites, George, Male

STITS, Richard, Cape May County, - Name on petition, 12 Mar 1745/6, to the House of Representatives from freeholders of Cape May County complaining of the devaluation of their paper money [likely due in part to the present war] and asking for creation of a fund, apparently to stabilize it.- *Manuscript Collection-Legislative Records [New Jersey State Archives]*, Box 1-12, Folder 22, pg. 1.

Stits, Richard, Male

STOKES, Joseph, jur, - Name on a petition, 24 Sep? 1753, to the House of Representatives from inhabitants of the province expressing distress because of a lack of currency as a medium of trade. They present various arguments for the value of a paper currency.- *Manuscript Collection-Oversized Legislative Papers [New Jersey State Archives]*, Box 1-43, Folder 4, pg. 1.

Stokes, Joseph, jur, Male

STORY, John, - Name on a petition, 1754, to the House of Representatives from freeholders of the province opposing the election of Samuel Nevell as a judge of the Supreme Court.- *Manuscript Collection-Legislative Records [New Jersey State Archives]*, Box 1-12, Folder 66, pg. 4.

Story, John, Male

STORY, Joseph, - Name on a petition, 1754, to the House of Representatives from freeholders of the province opposing the election of Samuel Nevell as a judge of the Supreme Court.- *Manuscript Collection-Legislative Records [New Jersey State Archives]*, Box 1-12, Folder 66, pg. 4.

Story, Joseph, Male

STORY, Thomas, - Name on a petition, 1754, to the House of Representatives from freeholders of the province opposing the election of Samuel Nevell as a judge of the Supreme Court.- *Manuscript Collection-Legislative Records [New Jersey State Archives]*, Box 1-12, Folder 66, pg. 4.

Story, Thomas, Male

STRATTON, Dan:, - Name on a petition, 24 Sep? 1753, to the House of Representatives from inhabitants of the province expressing distress because of a lack of currency as a medium of trade. They present various arguments for the value of a paper currency.- *Manuscript Collection-Oversized Legislative Papers [New Jersey State Archives]*, Box 1-43, Folder 4, pg. 1.

Stratton, Dan:, Male

SUTTEN, Beniamien, Middlesex County, - Name on a petition, 1754, to the House of Representatives from freeholders of the province opposing the election of Samuel Nevell as a judge of the Supreme Court.- *Manuscript Collection-Legislative Records [New Jersey State Archives]*, Box 1-12, Folder 66, pg. 2.

sutten, Beniamien, Male

SUTTON, Thos, Burlington & Hunterdon Cos., - Name on a petition, 1748/9, to the House of Representatives from inhabitants freeholders of Hunterdon and Burlington Counties seeking for a law requiring every person to record their "Mortgage Deeds" to ensure validity of titles to land.- *Manuscript Collection-Oversized Legislative Papers [New Jersey State Archives]*, Box 1-43, Folder 2, pg. 1.

Sutton, Thos, Male

SWAINE, Daniel, Cape May County, - Name on petition, 12 Mar 1745/6, to the House of Representatives from freeholders of Cape May County complaining of the devaluation of their paper money [likely due in part to the present war] and asking for creation of a fund, apparently to stabilize it.- *Manuscript Collection-Legislative Records [New Jersey State Archives]*, Box 1-12, Folder 22, pg. 1.

Swaine, Daniel, Male

SWAINE, Ebenezer, Cape May County, - Name on petition, 12 Mar 1745/6, to the House of Representatives from freeholders of Cape May County complaining of the devaluation of their paper money [likely due in part to the present war] and asking for creation of a fund, apparently to stabilize it.- *Manuscript Collection-Legislative Records [New Jersey State Archives],* Box 1-12, Folder 22, pg. 1.
Swaine, Ebenezer, Male

TALMAN, Jos, Burlington & Hunterdon Cos., - Name on a petition, 1748/9, to the House of Representatives from inhabitants freeholders of Hunterdon and Burlington Counties seeking for a law requiring every person to record their "Mortgage Deeds" to ensure validity of titles to land.- *Manuscript Collection-Oversized Legislative Papers [New Jersey State Archives],* Box 1-43, Folder 2, pg. 1.
Talman, Jos, Male

TANTUM OR FANTUM, John, Hunterdon County, Bethlehem - On a petition, 12 Jan 1747/8, to Jonathan Belcher, Governor, from inhabitants of Bethlehem in Hunterdon County seeking to have the southerly part of Bethlehem Township made into a new township part of the boundary is an "Island formerly John Fantum's".- *Legislature-Petitions re: Municipal Boundaries [New Jersey State Archives],* Box 1, Folder 1, pg. 1.
Tantum or Fantum, John, Male

TATCHER, Jaremijah, Hunterdon County, Bethlehem - Name on a petition, 12 Jan 1747/8, to Jonathan Belcher, Governor, from inhabitants of Bethlehem in Hunterdon County seeking to have the southerly part of Bethlehem Township made into a new township.- *Legislature-Petitions re: Municipal Boundaries [New Jersey State Archives],* Box 1, Folder 1, pg. 1.
Tatcher, Jaremijah, Male

TAYLER, Ephraim, Essex County, - Name on petition, 10 Apr 1746, to the General Assembly by freeholders & inhabitants of Essex Co. seeking a repeal of acts for preserving of timber & a duty on imported strong liquors. They cannot build ships because of the present war with France & Spain.- *Manuscript Collection-Legislative Records [New Jersey State Archives],* Box 1-12, Folder 25, pg. 2.
Tayler, Ephraim, Male

TAYLOR, Elis, Cape May County, - Name on petition, 12 Mar 1745/6, to the House of Representatives from freeholders of Cape May County complaining of the devaluation of their paper money [likely due in part to the present war] and asking for creation of a fund, apparently to stabilize it.- *Manuscript Collection-Legislative Records [New Jersey State Archives],* Box 1-12, Folder 22, pg. 1.
Taylor, Elis, Male

TAYLOR, John, Hunterdon County, Bethlehem - Name on a petition, 12 Jan 1747/8, to Jonathan Belcher, Governor, from inhabitants of Bethlehem in Hunterdon County seeking to have the southerly part of Bethlehem Township made into a new township.- *Legislature-Petitions re: Municipal Boundaries [New Jersey State Archives],* Box 1, Folder 1, pg. 1.
Taylor, John, Male

TAYLOR, John, - Name on a petition, 1754, to the House of Representatives from freeholders of the province opposing the election of Samuel Nevell as a judge of the Supreme Court.- *Manuscript Collection-Legislative Records [New Jersey State Archives],* Box 1-12, Folder 66, pg. 4.
Taylor, John, Male

TAYLOR, Rob, Burlington & Hunterdon Cos., - Name on a petition, 1748/9, to the House of Representatives from inhabitants freeholders of Hunterdon and Burlington Counties seeking for a law requiring every person to record their "Mortgage Deeds" to ensure validity of titles to land.- *Manuscript Collection-Oversized Legislative Papers [New Jersey State Archives],* Box 1-43, Folder 2, pg. 1.
Taylor, Rob, Male

TERHUNE, John, - Name on a petition, 1754, to the House of Representatives from freeholders of the province opposing the election of Samuel Nevell as a judge of the Supreme Court.- *Manuscript Collection-Legislative Records [New Jersey State Archives],* Box 1-12, Folder 66, pg. 3.
Terhune, John, Male

THATCHER, James, Hunterdon County, Bethlehem - Name on a petition, 12 Jan 1747/8, to Jonathan Belcher, Governor, from inhabitants of Bethlehem in Hunterdon County seeking to have the southerly part of Bethlehem Township made into a new township.- *Legislature-Petitions re: Municipal Boundaries [New Jersey State Archives],* Box 1, Folder 1, pg. 1.
Thatcher, James, Male

THICHENOR, Jonathan, Senr, Essex County, - Name on petition, 10 Apr 1746, to the General

Assembly by freeholders & inhabitants of Essex Co. seeking a repeal of acts for preserving of timber & a duty on imported strong liquors. They cannot build ships because of the present war with France & Spain.- *Manuscript Collection-Legislative Records [New Jersey State Archives],* Box 1-12, Folder 25, pg. 2.

Thichenor, Jonathan, Senr, Male

THICHNOR, Jonathan, Essex County, - Name on petition, 10 Apr 1746, to the General Assembly by freeholders & inhabitants of Essex Co. seeking a repeal of acts for preserving of timber & a duty on imported strong liquors. They cannot build ships because of the present war with France & Spain.- *Manuscript Collection-Legislative Records [New Jersey State Archives],* Box 1-12, Folder 25, pg. 2.

Thichnor, Jonathan, Male

THORN, John, Burlington & Hunterdon Cos., - Name on a petition, 1748/9, to the House of Representatives from inhabitants freeholders of Hunterdon and Burlington Counties seeking for a law requiring every person to record their "Mortgage Deeds" to ensure validity of titles to land.- *Manuscript Collection-Oversized Legislative Papers [New Jersey State Archives],* Box 1-43, Folder 2, pg. 1.

Thorn, John, Male

TICHENOR, John, Essex County, - Name on petition, 10 Apr 1746, to the General Assembly by freeholders & inhabitants of Essex Co. seeking a repeal of acts for preserving of timber & a duty on imported strong liquors. They cannot build ships because of the present war with France & Spain.- *Manuscript Collection-Legislative Records [New Jersey State Archives],* Box 1-12, Folder 25, pg. 2.

Tichenor, John, Male

TINDALL, Thomas, Middlesex County, - Name on a petition, 1754, to the House of Representatives from freeholders of the province opposing the election of Samuel Nevell as a judge of the Supreme Court.- *Manuscript Collection-Legislative Records [New Jersey State Archives],* Box 1-12, Folder 66, pg. 2.

Tindall, Thomas, Male

TOMSON, John, - Name on a petition, 1754, to the House of Representatives from freeholders of the province opposing the election of Samuel Nevell as a judge of the Supreme Court.- *Manuscript Collection-Legislative Records [New Jersey State Archives],* Box 1-12, Folder 66, pg. 3.

Tomson, John, Male

TOY?, Nicholas, Burlington County, Northampton Township - Name on a petition, 30 May 1753, to the House of Representatives from inhabitants in and about Northampton who are requesting an increase in the amount of currency which is scarce. Gold and silver are chiefly transported elsewhere and are scarce also.- *Manuscript Collection-Legislative Records [New Jersey State Archives],* Box 1-12, Folder 65, pg. 1.

Toy?, Nicholas, Male

TROST, Ezekiel, Morris County, - Name on a petition, 6 Oct 1751, to Governor Jonathan Belcher from owners of "Bloomaries" in Morris County seeking removal of a tax on their iron works (Bloomeries). Many make 5-6 tons or less a year. They seek instead for a bounty on all they produce.- *Manuscript Collection-MSS Coll., #1-100 [New Jersey State Archives],* Box 5-1, Folder 28, pg. 2.

Trost, Ezekiel, Male

UPDIKE, William, Middlesex County, - Name on a petition, 1754, to the House of Representatives from freeholders of the province opposing the election of Samuel Nevell as a judge of the Supreme Court.- *Manuscript Collection-Legislative Records [New Jersey State Archives],* Box 1-12, Folder 66, pg. 2.

Updike, William, Male

VAN DIJCK, Thomas, - Name on a petition, 1754, to the House of Representatives from freeholders of the province opposing the election of Samuel Nevell as a judge of the Supreme Court.- *Manuscript Collection-Legislative Records [New Jersey State Archives],* Box 1-12, Folder 66, pg. 3.

Van Dijck, Thomas, Male

VAN DIKE, Mathias, - Name on a petition, 1754, to the House of Representatives from freeholders of the province opposing the election of Samuel Nevell as a judge of the Supreme Court.- *Manuscript Collection-Legislative Records [New Jersey State Archives],* Box 1-12, Folder 66, pg. 3.

Van Dike, Mathias, Male

VAN HORNE, Mathias, Hunterdon County, Bethlehem - Name on a petition, 12 Jan 1747/8, to Jonathan Belcher, Governor, from inhabitants of Bethlehem in Hunterdon County seeking to have the southerly part of Bethlehem Township made into a new township.- *Legislature-Petitions re:*

Municipal Boundaries [New Jersey State Archives], Box 1, Folder 1, pg. 1.

Van horne, Mathias, Male

VAN PELT, John, - Name on a petition, 1754, to the House of Representatives from freeholders of the province opposing the election of Samuel Nevell as a judge of the Supreme Court.- *Manuscript Collection-Legislative Records [New Jersey State Archives],* Box 1-12, Folder 66, pg. 3.

Van Pelt, John, Male

VANCE, John, Essex County, - Name on petition, 10 Apr 1746, to the General Assembly by freeholders & inhabitants of Essex Co. seeking a repeal of acts for preserving of timber & a duty on imported strong liquors. They cannot build ships because of the present war with France & Spain.- *Manuscript Collection-Legislative Records [New Jersey State Archives],* Box 1-12, Folder 25, pg. 1.

Vance, John, Male

VANCE, Patrick, Middlesex County, Perth Amboy Township - Name on a petition, 1754, to the General Assembly from freeholders/inhabitants of Perth Amboy Township in Middlesex County opposing the election of Samuel Nevill as a judge of the Supreme Court.- *Manuscript Collection-Oversized Legislative Papers [New Jersey State Archives],* Box 1-43, Folder 2, pg. 1.

Vance, Patrick, Male

VANCE, Patrick, - Name on petition, 1 Mar 1748/9, to the governor, etc., seeking passage of a law forbidding the killing of deer by dogs because the meat and hides are mostly worthless.- *Manuscript Collection-Governors' Papers [New Jersey State Archives],* Box 1-1, Folder 4, pg. 1.

Vance, Patrick, Male

VANGILDER, Isaac, - Name on a petition, 1754, to the House of Representatives from freeholders of the province opposing the election of Samuel Nevell as a judge of the Supreme Court.- *Manuscript Collection-Legislative Records [New Jersey State Archives],* Box 1-12, Folder 66, pg. 4.

Vangilder, Isaac, Male

VANHIGE?, John, - Name on a petition, 1754, to the House of Representatives from freeholders of the province opposing the election of Samuel Nevell as a judge of the Supreme Court.- *Manuscript Collection-Legislative Records [New Jersey State Archives],* Box 1-12, Folder 66, pg. 4.

vanhige?, John, Male

VANKIRK, Arthur, Middlesex County, - Name on a petition, 1754, to the House of Representatives from freeholders of the province opposing the election of Samuel Nevell as a judge of the Supreme Court.- *Manuscript Collection-Legislative Records [New Jersey State Archives],* Box 1-12, Folder 66, pg. 2.

Vankirk, Arthur, Male

VINCENT, John, Essex County, - Name on petition, 10 Apr 1746, to the General Assembly by freeholders & inhabitants of Essex Co. seeking a repeal of acts for preserving of timber & a duty on imported strong liquors. They cannot build ships because of the present war with France & Spain.- *Manuscript Collection-Legislative Records [New Jersey State Archives],* Box 1-12, Folder 25, pg. 1.

Vincent, John, Male

VINCENT, Levi, Essex County, - Name on petition, 10 Apr 1746, to the General Assembly by freeholders & inhabitants of Essex Co. seeking a repeal of acts for preserving of timber & a duty on imported strong liquors. They cannot build ships because of the present war with France & Spain.- *Manuscript Collection-Legislative Records [New Jersey State Archives],* Box 1-12, Folder 25, pg. 1.

vincent, Levi, Male

VOORHIES, Cornelis, Middlesex County, - Name on a petition, 1754, to the House of Representatives from freeholders of the province opposing the election of Samuel Nevell as a judge of the Supreme Court.- *Manuscript Collection-Legislative Records [New Jersey State Archives],* Box 1-12, Folder 66, pg. 2.

Voorhies, Cornelis, Male

VOORHIES, Koert, Middlesex County, - Name on a petition, 1754, to the House of Representatives from freeholders of the province opposing the election of Samuel Nevell as a judge of the Supreme Court.- *Manuscript Collection-Legislative Records [New Jersey State Archives],* Box 1-12, Folder 66, pg. 2.

Voorhies, Koert, Male

VOREHEES, William, Hunterdon County, Bethlehem - Name on a petition, 12 Jan 1747/8, to Jonathan Belcher, Governor, from inhabitants of Bethlehem in Hunterdon County seeking to have the southerly part of Bethlehem Township made into a new township.- *Legislature-Petitions re: Municipal Boundaries [New Jersey State Archives],* Box 1, Folder 1, pg. 1.

Vorehees, William, Male

VREELAND, micheal, Essex County, - Name on petition, 10 Apr 1746, to the General Assembly by

freeholders & inhabitants of Essex Co. seeking a repeal of acts for preserving of timber & a duty on imported strong liquors. They cannot build ships because of the present war with France & Spain.- *Manuscript Collection-Legislative Records [New Jersey State Archives],* Box 1-12, Folder 25, pg. 1.
    Vreeland, micheal, Male

VREELANDT, micheal, Essex County, - Name on petition, 10 Apr 1746, to the General Assembly by freeholders & inhabitants of Essex Co. seeking a repeal of acts for preserving of timber & a duty on imported strong liquors. They cannot build ships because of the present war with France & Spain.- *Manuscript Collection-Legislative Records [New Jersey State Archives],* Box 1-12, Folder 25, pg. 2.
    Vreelandt, micheal, Male

WARD, Able, Essex County, - Name on petition, 10 Apr 1746, to the General Assembly by freeholders & inhabitants of Essex Co. seeking a repeal of acts for preserving of timber & a duty on imported strong liquors. They cannot build ships because of the present war with France & Spain.- *Manuscript Collection-Legislative Records [New Jersey State Archives],* Box 1-12, Folder 25, pg. 2.
    Ward, Able, Male

WARD, abner, Essex County, - Name on petition, 10 Apr 1746, to the General Assembly by freeholders & inhabitants of Essex Co. seeking a repeal of acts for preserving of timber & a duty on imported strong liquors. They cannot build ships because of the present war with France & Spain.- *Manuscript Collection-Legislative Records [New Jersey State Archives],* Box 1-12, Folder 25, pg. 1.
    ward, abner, Male

WARD, Bethel, Essex County, - Name on petition, 10 Apr 1746, to the General Assembly by freeholders & inhabitants of Essex Co. seeking a repeal of acts for preserving of timber & a duty on imported strong liquors. They cannot build ships because of the present war with France & Spain.- *Manuscript Collection-Legislative Records [New Jersey State Archives],* Box 1-12, Folder 25, pg. 1.
    ward, Bethel, Male

WARD, Caleb, Essex County, - Name on petition, 10 Apr 1746, to the General Assembly by freeholders & inhabitants of Essex Co. seeking a repeal of acts for preserving of timber & a duty on imported strong liquors. They cannot build ships because of the present war with France & Spain.- *Manuscript Collection-Legislative Records [New Jersey State Archives],* Box 1-12, Folder 25, pg. 1.
    Ward, Caleb, Male

WARD, Daniel, Essex County, - Name on petition, 10 Apr 1746, to the General Assembly by freeholders & inhabitants of Essex Co. seeking a repeal of acts for preserving of timber & a duty on imported strong liquors. They cannot build ships because of the present war with France & Spain.- *Manuscript Collection-Legislative Records [New Jersey State Archives],* Box 1-12, Folder 25, pg. 1.
    Ward, Daniel, Male

WARD, Elihu, Essex County, - Name on petition, 10 Apr 1746, to the General Assembly by freeholders & inhabitants of Essex Co. seeking a repeal of acts for preserving of timber & a duty on imported strong liquors. They cannot build ships because of the present war with France & Spain.- *Manuscript Collection-Legislative Records [New Jersey State Archives],* Box 1-12, Folder 25, pg. 2.
    ward, Elihu, Male

WARD, Isaac, Essex County, - Name on petition, 10 Apr 1746, to the General Assembly by freeholders & inhabitants of Essex Co. seeking a repeal of acts for preserving of timber & a duty on imported strong liquors. They cannot build ships because of the present war with France & Spain.- *Manuscript Collection-Legislative Records [New Jersey State Archives],* Box 1-12, Folder 25, pg. 1.
    Ward, Isaac, Male

WARD, James, Essex County, - Name on petition, 10 Apr 1746, to the General Assembly by freeholders & inhabitants of Essex Co. seeking a repeal of acts for preserving of timber & a duty on imported strong liquors. They cannot build ships because of the present war with France & Spain.- *Manuscript Collection-Legislative Records [New Jersey State Archives],* Box 1-12, Folder 25, pg. 1.
    ward, James, Male

WARD, John, Essex County, - Name on petition, 10 Apr 1746, to the General Assembly by freeholders & inhabitants of Essex Co. seeking a repeal of acts for preserving of timber & a duty on imported strong liquors. They cannot build ships because of the present war with France & Spain.- *Manuscript Collection-Legislative Records [New Jersey State Archives],* Box 1-12, Folder 25, pg. 1.
    Ward, John, Male

WARD, Jonathan, Essex County, - Name on petition, 10 Apr 1746, to the General Assembly by freeholders & inhabitants of Essex Co. seeking a repeal of acts for preserving of timber & a duty on imported strong liquors. They cannot build ships because of the present war with France & Spain.- *Manuscript Collection-Legislative Records [New Jersey State Archives]*, Box 1-12, Folder 25, pg. 2.

Ward, Jonathan, Male

WARD, Josiah, Essex County, - Name on petition, 10 Apr 1746, to the General Assembly by freeholders & inhabitants of Essex Co. seeking a repeal of acts for preserving of timber & a duty on imported strong liquors. They cannot build ships because of the present war with France & Spain.- *Manuscript Collection-Legislative Records [New Jersey State Archives]*, Box 1-12, Folder 25, pg. 1.

ward, Josiah, Male

WARD, Josiah, Jun, Essex County, - Name on petition, 10 Apr 1746, to the General Assembly by freeholders & inhabitants of Essex Co. seeking a repeal of acts for preserving of timber & a duty on imported strong liquors. They cannot build ships because of the present war with France & Spain.- *Manuscript Collection-Legislative Records [New Jersey State Archives]*, Box 1-12, Folder 25, pg. 1.

Ward, Josiah, Jun, Male

WARD, Lemuel, Essex County, - Name on petition, 10 Apr 1746, to the General Assembly by freeholders & inhabitants of Essex Co. seeking a repeal of acts for preserving of timber & a duty on imported strong liquors. They cannot build ships because of the present war with France & Spain.- *Manuscript Collection-Legislative Records [New Jersey State Archives]*, Box 1-12, Folder 25, pg. 1.

Ward, Lemuel, Male

WARD, Nathan, Essex County, - Name on petition, 10 Apr 1746, to the General Assembly by freeholders & inhabitants of Essex Co. seeking a repeal of acts for preserving of timber & a duty on imported strong liquors. They cannot build ships because of the present war with France & Spain.- *Manuscript Collection-Legislative Records [New Jersey State Archives]*, Box 1-12, Folder 25, pg. 2.

ward, Nathan, Male

WARFORD, Janios or James, Hunterdon County, Bethlehem - Name on a petition, 12 Jan 1747/8, to Jonathan Belcher, Governor, from inhabitants of Bethlehem in Hunterdon County seeking to have the southerly part of Bethlehem Township made into a new township.- *Legislature-Petitions re: Municipal Boundaries [New Jersey State Archives]*, Box 1, Folder 1, pg. 1.

warford, Janios or James, Male

WARFORD, John, Hunterdon County, Bethlehem - Name on a petition, 12 Jan 1747/8, to Jonathan Belcher, Governor, from inhabitants of Bethlehem in Hunterdon County seeking to have the southerly part of Bethlehem Township made into a new township.- *Legislature-Petitions re: Municipal Boundaries [New Jersey State Archives]*, Box 1, Folder 1, pg. 1.

Warford, John, Male

WARRAN?, Samll, Essex County, - Name on petition, 10 Apr 1746, to the General Assembly by freeholders & inhabitants of Essex Co. seeking a repeal of acts for preserving of timber & a duty on imported strong liquors. They cannot build ships because of the present war with France & Spain.- *Manuscript Collection-Legislative Records [New Jersey State Archives]*, Box 1-12, Folder 25, pg. 1.

Warran?, Samll, Male

WARREN, John, Burlington & Hunterdon Cos., - Name on a petition, 1748/9, to the House of Representatives from inhabitants freeholders of Hunterdon and Burlington Counties seeking for a law requiring every person to record their "Mortgage Deeds" to ensure validity of titles to land.- *Manuscript Collection-Oversized Legislative Papers [New Jersey State Archives]*, Box 1-43, Folder 2, pg. 1.

Warren, John, Male

WATERHOUS, Joshua, Hunterdon County, Bethlehem - Name on a petition, 12 Jan 1747/8, to Jonathan Belcher, Governor, from inhabitants of Bethlehem in Hunterdon County seeking to have the southerly part of Bethlehem Township made into a new township.- *Legislature-Petitions re: Municipal Boundaries [New Jersey State Archives]*, Box 1, Folder 1, pg. 1.

Waterhous, Joshua, Male

WATSON, Isaac, Burlington County, Nottingham - Name on a petition, 18 Nov 1748, to the House of Representatives from inhabitants of Nottingham, Burlington County complaining of those hunting out of season who have killed their hogs and cattle. Sometimes people are in danger of being shot.- *Manuscript Collection-Legislative Records [New Jersey State Archives]*, Box 1-12, Folder 46, pg. 1.

Watson, Isaac, Male

WA[R?]D, Nathaniel, Essex County, - Name on petition, 10 Apr 1746, to the General Assembly by freeholders & inhabitants of Essex Co. seeking a repeal of acts for preserving of timber & a duty on imported strong liquors. They cannot build ships because of the present war with France & Spain.- *Manuscript Collection-Legislative Records [New Jersey State Archives]*, Box 1-12, Folder 25, pg. 1.

wa[r?]d, Nathaniel, Male

WEBB OR WILLS?, Daniel, - Name on a petition, 24 Sep? 1753, to the House of Representatives from inhabitants of the province expressing distress because of a lack of currency as a medium of trade. They present various arguments for the value of a paper currency.- *Manuscript Collection-Oversized Legislative Papers [New Jersey State Archives]*, Box 1-43, Folder 4, pg. 1.

Webb or Wills?, Daniel, Male

WETHERILL, Georg, - Name on a petition, 1754, to the House of Representatives from freeholders of the province opposing the election of Samuel Nevell as a judge of the Supreme Court.- *Manuscript Collection-Legislative Records [New Jersey State Archives]*, Box 1-12, Folder 66, pg. 3.

Wetherill, Georg, Male

WHEATCRAFT, Edward, Burlington & Hunterdon Cos., - Name on a petition, 1748/9, to the House of Representatives from inhabitants freeholders of Hunterdon and Burlington Counties seeking for a law requiring every person to record their "Mortgage Deeds" to ensure validity of titles to land.- *Manuscript Collection-Oversized Legislative Papers [New Jersey State Archives]*, Box 1-43, Folder 2, pg. 1.

Wheatcraft, Edward, Male

WHELER, Samuell, Essex County, - Name on petition, 10 Apr 1746, to the General Assembly by freeholders & inhabitants of Essex Co. seeking a repeal of acts for preserving of timber & a duty on imported strong liquors. They cannot build ships because of the present war with France & Spain.- *Manuscript Collection-Legislative Records [New Jersey State Archives]*, Box 1-12, Folder 25, pg. 1.

Wheler, Samuell, Male

WHITE, Edward, - Name on petition, 1 Mar 1748/9, to the governor, etc., seeking passage of a law forbidding the killing of deer by dogs because the meat and hides are mostly worthless.- *Manuscript Collection-Governors' Papers [New Jersey State Archives]*, Box 1-1, Folder 4, pg. 1.

White, Edward, Male

WHITE, Josiah, Burlington County, Northampton Township - Name on a petition, 30 May 1753, to the House of Representatives from inhabitants in and about Northampton who are requesting an increase in the amount of currency which is scarce. Gold and silver are chiefly transported elsewhere and are scarce also.- *Manuscript Collection-Legislative Records [New Jersey State Archives]*, Box 1-12, Folder 65, pg. 1.

White, Josiah, Male

WHITE, Josiah, - Name on a petition, 1750/1, the House of Representatives from inhabitants of the province protesting against the great number of taverns in the province.- *Manuscript Collection-Legislative Records [New Jersey State Archives]*, Box 1-12, Folder 59, pg. 1.

White, Josiah, Male

WICOFE?, Art, - Name on a petition, 1754, to the House of Representatives from freeholders of the province opposing the election of Samuel Nevell as a judge of the Supreme Court.- *Manuscript Collection-Legislative Records [New Jersey State Archives]*, Box 1-12, Folder 66, pg. 4.

Wicofe?, Art, Male

WIJCKOFF, Cornelis, - Name on a petition, 1754, to the House of Representatives from freeholders of the province opposing the election of Samuel Nevell as a judge of the Supreme Court.- *Manuscript Collection-Legislative Records [New Jersey State Archives]*, Box 1-12, Folder 66, pg. 4.

Wijckoff, Cornelis, Male

WILKINS, **red, - Name on a petition, 24 Sep? 1753, to the House of Representatives from inhabitants of the province expressing distress because of a lack of currency as a medium of trade. They present various arguments for the value of a paper currency.- *Manuscript Collection-Oversized Legislative Papers [New Jersey State Archives]*, Box 1-43, Folder 4, pg. 1.

Wilkins, **red, Male

WILKINS, Isaac, - Name on a petition, 24 Sep? 1753, to the House of Representatives from inhabitants of the province expressing distress because of a lack of currency as a medium of trade. They present various arguments for the value of a paper currency.- *Manuscript Collection-Oversized Legislative Papers [New Jersey State Archives]*, Box 1-43, Folder 4, pg. 1.

Wilkins, Isaac, Male

WILKINS, Thomas, - Name on a petition, 24 Sep? 1753, to the House of Representatives from inhabitants of the province expressing distress because of a lack of currency as a medium of trade. They present various arguments for the value of a paper currency.- *Manuscript Collection-Oversized Legislative Papers [New Jersey State Archives],* Box 1-43, Folder 4, pg. 1.

Wilkins, Thomas, Male

WILLIAMES, Josiah, Essex County, - Name on petition, 10 Apr 1746, to the General Assembly by freeholders & inhabitants of Essex Co. seeking a repeal of acts for preserving of timber & a duty on imported strong liquors. They cannot build ships because of the present war with France & Spain.- *Manuscript Collection-Legislative Records [New Jersey State Archives],* Box 1-12, Folder 25, pg. 1.

williames, Josiah, Male

WILLIAMS, Amos, Essex County, - Name on petition, 10 Apr 1746, to the General Assembly by freeholders & inhabitants of Essex Co. seeking a repeal of acts for preserving of timber & a duty on imported strong liquors. They cannot build ships because of the present war with France & Spain.- *Manuscript Collection-Legislative Records [New Jersey State Archives],* Box 1-12, Folder 25, pg. 1.

Williams, Amos, Male

WILLIAMS, David, Essex County, - Name on petition, 10 Apr 1746, to the General Assembly by freeholders & inhabitants of Essex Co. seeking a repeal of acts for preserving of timber & a duty on imported strong liquors. They cannot build ships because of the present war with France & Spain.- *Manuscript Collection-Legislative Records [New Jersey State Archives],* Box 1-12, Folder 25, pg. 1.

Williams, David, Male

WILLIAMS, Jeremiah, Hunterdon County, Bethlehem - Name on a petition, 12 Jan 1747/8, to Jonathan Belcher, Governor, from inhabitants of Bethlehem in Hunterdon County seeking to have the southerly part of Bethlehem Township made into a new township.- *Legislature-Petitions re: Municipal Boundaries [New Jersey State Archives],* Box 1, Folder 1, pg. 1.

Williams, Jeremiah, Male

WILLIAMS, Matthew, Essex County, - Name on petition, 10 Apr 1746, to the General Assembly by freeholders & inhabitants of Essex Co. seeking a repeal of acts for preserving of timber & a duty on imported strong liquors. They cannot build ships because of the present war with France & Spain.- *Manuscript Collection-Legislative Records [New Jersey State Archives],* Box 1-12, Folder 25, pg. 1.

Williams, Matthew, Male

WILLIAMS, Samll, Essex County, - Name on petition, 10 Apr 1746, to the General Assembly by freeholders & inhabitants of Essex Co. seeking a repeal of acts for preserving of timber & a duty on imported strong liquors. They cannot build ships because of the present war with France & Spain.- *Manuscript Collection-Legislative Records [New Jersey State Archives],* Box 1-12, Folder 25, pg. 1.

Williams, Samll, Male

WILLIAMS, Thomas, Essex County, - Name on petition, 10 Apr 1746, to the General Assembly by freeholders & inhabitants of Essex Co. seeking a repeal of acts for preserving of timber & a duty on imported strong liquors. They cannot build ships because of the present war with France & Spain.- *Manuscript Collection-Legislative Records [New Jersey State Archives],* Box 1-12, Folder 25, pg. 1.

williams, Thomas, Male

WILLIAS, Geershom, Essex County, - Name on petition, 10 Apr 1746, to the General Assembly by freeholders & inhabitants of Essex Co. seeking a repeal of acts for preserving of timber & a duty on imported strong liquors. They cannot build ships because of the present war with France & Spain.- *Manuscript Collection-Legislative Records [New Jersey State Archives],* Box 1-12, Folder 25, pg. 1.

willias, Geershom, Male

WILLS OR HILLS, David, - Name on a petition, 24 Sep? 1753, to the House of Representatives from inhabitants of the province expressing distress because of a lack of currency as a medium of trade. They present various arguments for the value of a paper currency.- *Manuscript Collection-Oversized Legislative Papers [New Jersey State Archives],* Box 1-43, Folder 4, pg. 1.

Wills or Hills, David, Male

WILLS? OR WEBB, Daniel, jnr, - Name on a petition, 24 Sep? 1753, to the House of Representatives from inhabitants of the province expressing distress because of a lack of currency as a medium of trade. They present various arguments for the value of a paper currency.- *Manuscript Collection-Oversized Legislative Papers [New Jersey State Archives],* Box 1-43, Folder 4, pg. 1.

Wills? or Webb, Daniel, jnr, Male

WILSON?, James, Hunterdon County, Bethlehem - Name on a petition, 12 Jan 1747/8, to Jonathan Belcher, Governor, from inhabitants of Bethlehem in Hunterdon County seeking to have the southerly part of Bethlehem Township made into a new township.- *Legislature-Petitions re: Municipal Boundaries [New Jersey State Archives],* Box 1, Folder 1, pg. 1.

Wilson?, James, Male

WOOD, Joseph, Morris County, - Name on a petition, 6 Oct 1751, to Governor Jonathan Belcher from owners of "Bloomaries" in Morris County seeking removal of a tax on their iron works (Bloomeries). Many make 5-6 tons or less a year. They seek instead for a bounty on all they produce.- *Manuscript Collection-MSS Coll., #1-100 [New Jersey State Archives],* Box 5-1, Folder 28, pg. 2.

Wood, Joseph, Male

WOODRUFF?, Charls, Essex County, - Name on petition, 10 Apr 1746, to the General Assembly by freeholders & inhabitants of Essex Co. seeking a repeal of acts for preserving of timber & a duty on imported strong liquors. They cannot build ships because of the present war with France & Spain.- *Manuscript Collection-Legislative Records [New Jersey State Archives],* Box 1-12, Folder 25, pg. 1.

woodruff?, Charls, Male

WOOLMAN, John, - Name on a petition, 1750/1, the House of Representatives from inhabitants of the province protesting against the great number of taverns in the province.- *Manuscript Collection-Legislative Records [New Jersey State Archives],* Box 1-12, Folder 59, pg. 1.

Woolman, John, Male

WORTH, James, Middlesex County, - Name on a petition, 1754, to the House of Representatives from freeholders of the province opposing the election of Samuel Nevell as a judge of the Supreme Court.- *Manuscript Collection-Legislative Records [New Jersey State Archives],* Box 1-12, Folder 66, pg. 2.

Worth, James, Male

WORTH, Samll, Middlesex County, - Name on a petition, 1754, to the House of Representatives from freeholders of the province opposing the election of Samuel Nevell as a judge of the Supreme Court.- *Manuscript Collection-Legislative Records [New Jersey State Archives],* Box 1-12, Folder 66, pg. 2.

Worth, Samll, Male

WORTH, Wm, Middlesex County, - Name on a petition, 1754, to the House of Representatives from freeholders of the province opposing the election of Samuel Nevell as a judge of the Supreme Court.- *Manuscript Collection-Legislative Records [New Jersey State Archives],* Box 1-12, Folder 66, pg. 2.

Worth, Wm, Male

WOST?, John, Burlington County, Northampton Township - Name on a petition, 30 May 1753, to the House of Representatives from inhabitants in and about Northampton who are requesting an increase in the amount of currency which is scarce. Gold and silver are chiefly transported elsewhere and are scarce also.- *Manuscript Collection-Legislative Records [New Jersey State Archives],* Box 1-12, Folder 65, pg. 1.

Wost?, John, Male

WRIGHT, William, Hunterdon County, Bethlehem - Name on a petition, 12 Jan 1747/8, to Jonathan Belcher, Governor, from inhabitants of Bethlehem in Hunterdon County seeking to have the southerly part of Bethlehem Township made into a new township.- *Legislature-Petitions re: Municipal Boundaries [New Jersey State Archives],* Box 1, Folder 1, pg. 1.

Wright, William, Male

WRIGHT?, John?, - Name on a petition, 1754, to the House of Representatives from freeholders of the province opposing the election of Samuel Nevell as a judge of the Supreme Court.- *Manuscript Collection-Legislative Records [New Jersey State Archives],* Box 1-12, Folder 66, pg. 1.

Wright?, John?, Male

YARD, Benja, Burlington & Hunterdon Cos., - Name on a petition, 1748/9, to the House of Representatives from inhabitants freeholders of Hunterdon and Burlington Counties seeking for a law requiring every person to record their "Mortgage Deeds" to ensure validity of titles to land.- *Manuscript Collection-Oversized Legislative Papers [New Jersey State Archives],* Box 1-43, Folder 2, pg. 1.

yard, Benja, Male

YOUNG, John, Essex County, - Name on petition, 10 Apr 1746, to the General Assembly by freeholders & inhabitants of Essex Co. seeking a repeal of acts for preserving of timber & a duty on imported strong liquors. They cannot build ships because of the present war with France & Spain.- *Manuscript Collection-Legislative Records [New Jersey State Archives],* Box 1-12, Folder 25, pg. 1.

Young, John, Male

ZNICK, John, Hunterdon County, Bethlehem - Name on a petition, 12 Jan 1747/8, to Jonathan Belcher, Governor, from inhabitants of Bethlehem in Hunterdon County seeking to have the southerly part of Bethlehem Township made into a new township.- *Legislature-Petitions re: Municipal*

Boundaries [New Jersey State Archives], Box 1, Folder 1, pg. 1.

Znick, John, Male

ZUTPHEN, Jacob, - Name on a petition, 1754, to the House of Representatives from freeholders of the province opposing the election of Samuel Nevell as a judge of the Supreme Court.- *Manuscript Collection-Legislative Records [New Jersey State Archives]*, Box 1-12, Folder 66, pg. 3.

Zutphen, Jacob, Male

[CAN'T READ], [Can't read], Burlington County, Nottingham - Name on a petition, 18 Nov 1748, to the House of Representatives from inhabitants of Nottingham, Burlington County complaining of those hunting out of season who have killed their hogs and cattle. Sometimes people are in danger of being shot.- *Manuscript Collection-Legislative Records [New Jersey State Archives]*, Box 1-12, Folder 46, pg. 1.

[Can't read], [Can't read], Male

[MISSING], Samuel, Essex County, - Name on petition, 10 Apr 1746, to the General Assembly by freeholders & inhabitants of Essex Co. seeking a repeal of acts for preserving of timber & a duty on imported strong liquors. They cannot build ships because of the present war with France & Spain.- *Manuscript Collection-Legislative Records [New Jersey State Archives]*, Box 1-12, Folder 25, pg. 1.

[missing], Samuel, Male

[MISSING], [Illegible], Essex County, - Name on petition, 10 Apr 1746, to the General Assembly by freeholders & inhabitants of Essex Co. seeking a repeal of acts for preserving of timber & a duty on imported strong liquors. They cannot build ships because of the present war with France & Spain.- *Manuscript Collection-Legislative Records [New Jersey State Archives]*, Box 1-12, Folder 25, pg. 1.

[missing], [Illegible], Male

[UNREADABLE], [Missing], Essex County, - Name on petition, 10 Apr 1746, to the General Assembly by freeholders & inhabitants of Essex Co. seeking a repeal of acts for preserving of timber & a duty on imported strong liquors. They cannot build ships because of the present war with France & Spain.- *Manuscript Collection-Legislative Records [New Jersey State Archives]*, Box 1-12, Folder 25, pg. 1.

[Unreadable], [Missing], Male

[UNREADABLE], [Unreadable], Middlesex County, Perth Amboy Township - Name on a petition, 1754, to the General Assembly from freeholders/inhabitants of Perth Amboy Township in Middlesex County opposing the election of Samuel Nevill as a judge of the Supreme Court.- *Manuscript Collection-Oversized Legislative Papers [New Jersey State Archives]*, Box 1-43, Folder 2, pg. 1.

[Unreadable], [Unreadable], Male

[UNREADABLE], [Unreadable], Essex County, - Name on petition, 10 Apr 1746, to the General Assembly by freeholders & inhabitants of Essex Co. seeking a repeal of acts for preserving of timber & a duty on imported strong liquors. They cannot build ships because of the present war with France & Spain.- *Manuscript Collection-Legislative Records [New Jersey State Archives]*, Box 1-12, Folder 25, pg. 1.

[Unreadable], [Unreadable], Male

STEMMONS PUBLISHING, 1078 Shields Lane, South Jordan, Utah 84095, 801-254-2152 (Call between 9:00 a.m. and 5:00 p.m. Monday through Friday. If no one answers, please leave a message.), stemmonspublishing@gmail.com

The importance of census records and other population lists cannot be overstated in terms of the help they are in locating people in a specific area. This allows one to examine other records in that area. This is one of our main goals and why we do business. What we are trying to accomplish is a work in progress. We hope to improve as we go along. Thank you for your patience.

Petitions are an important example of these population lists.

Thank you for the opportunity to serve you.

Sincerely,
John Stemmons

A LIST OF OUR GENEALOGY BOOKS

AL-01 ALABAMA 1800 PETITIONERS [-1804]© Compiled by John D Stemmons, 2021. This book compiled from *Territorial Papers of the United States* contains 253 entries for a very early period in Alabama's history. It may contain some biographical details and clues to prior residence. It can help substitute for the missing federal census. For information on how to obtain this book search by the title or "Books by John Stemmons" at Amazon.com. This comes automatically with a paperback binding. It includes but is not limited to petitions regarding:

- Seeking new territory due to the rapid migration from Georgia, etc.
- Petition seeking confirmation of land grants obtained from other governments.

36 Pages $7.20

AL-02 ALABAMA 1810 PETITIONERS, ETC., [1805-1814]© Compiled by John D Stemmons, 2021. This book compiled from *Territorial Papers of the United States* contains 1687 entries for a very early period in Alabama's history. It includes a census of Madison County, taken Jan 1809. It may contain some biographical details and clues to prior residence. It can help substitute for the missing federal census. For information on how to obtain this book search by the title or "Books by John Stemmons" at Amazon.com. This comes automatically with a paperback binding. It includes but is not limited to petitions regarding:

- Issues relating to land.
- Petition of inhabitants east of Pearl River seeking to form a new territory.
- 1809 census of Madison County.
- Inhabitants of Tombigbee seeking for their purchases from the Spanish to be duty free at "Fort Stoddart".

176 Pages $35.20

AL-03 ALABAMA 1820 PETITIONERS, ETC., [1815-1824]© Compiled by John D Stemmons, 2021. This book compiled from *Territorial Papers of the United States* contains 3913 entries for a fast-growing period in Alabama's history. It may contain some biographical details and clues to prior residence. It can help substitute for the missing federal census. For information on how to obtain this book search by the title or "Books by John Stemmons" at Amazon.com. This comes automatically with a paperback binding. It includes but is not limited to petitions regarding:

- Merchants and traders of St. Stephens seeking to establish that town as a port of delivery.
- Inhabitants of eastern part of MS territory, who lost much income/property in the wars with England & Indians.
- Inhabitants of Alabama Territory opposing the "settlements on the western side of the Mobile & Tombigby rivers" being made part of Mississippi.
- List of Letters, 9 Jan 1819, remaining in Huntsville Post Office.
- Issues about military and local officers.
- Memorial, ref. 20 Jan 1817, to Congress from inhabitants of Mobile complaining that Ft Charlotte is indefensible.

407 Pages $81.40

AR-01 ARKANSAS PETITIONERS, ETC. 1800, 1810 [1795-1814]© Compiled by John D Stemmons, 2021. This book compiled from *Territorial Papers of the United States* contains 261 entries and is a partial replacement for the missing federal censuses of 1800 and 1810. As a result, it is a very helpful resource in establishing residence of people in Arkansas during that early formative period in the state's history. These people include some of earliest you will find that established the foundation of what was to become the great state that

Arkansas now is. This also makes it possible to determine what other records might be available for further research. Some additional biographical details may be included, and possible relationships with others may be revealed. For information on how to obtain this book search by the title or "Books by John Stemmons" at Amazon.com. This comes automatically with a paperback binding. It includes but is not limited to petitions regarding:

- Issues relating to land.
- Inhabitants of Arkansas District expressing concern about the hostile attitude of the Cherokees nearby.
- Issues about military and local officers.

43 Pages $8.60

AR-02 ARKANSAS PETITIONERS, ETC. 1820 [1815-1824]© Compiled by John D Stemmons, 2021. This book compiled from *Territorial Papers of the United States* contains 1936 entries and is a partial replacement for the missing federal census of 1820. As a result, it is a very helpful resource in establishing residence of people in Arkansas during that fast-growing territorial period prior to becoming a state. Unfortunately, the 1820 census is not available to help track these people. That is why this new book can help. It is even better in some respects than the census because it helps us understand some of the challenges they faced. It also makes possible the determination of other records that might be available for further research. Some additional biographical details may be included, and possible relationships with others may be revealed. Even the names of some Native Americans are included as well as a few potential residents of Oklahoma. For information on how to obtain this book search by the title or "Books by John Stemmons" at Amazon.com. This comes automatically with a paperback binding. It includes but is not limited to petitions regarding:

- Issues relating to land.
- Issues relating to Native Americans.
- Citizens of Arkansas County describing the good location of the Town of Arkansas.
- Appointments about military and local officers, etc.
- Inhabitants of Arkansas and Phillips Counties seeking a mail route from the Town of Arkansas to the "Post of Ouachita in Louisianna."
- Abstract of Grand and Petit Jurors, Oct term, 1824 listing compensation for their attendance at a Superior Court held at Little Rock.

216 Pages $43.20

1001-GEORGIA PETITIONS 1778-1784© Compiled by John D Stemmons, 2004. This book contains 256 entries for a very early period in Georgia's history. For information on how to obtain this book search by the title or "Books by John Stemmons" at Amazon.com. This comes automatically with a paperback binding. It includes but is not limited to petitions regarding:

- A desire for a new district.
- A request for local courts.
- Issues about military and local officers.
- Request for protection against enemies.
- A request for pardon, amnesty, etc.
- Description of hardship.

44 pages $8.80

1002-GEORGIA PETITIONS 1785-1794© Compiled by John D Stemmons, 2004. Contains 3720 entries which includes about 25% of the heads of household in Georgia at that time. As such this publication is an excellent substitute for the missing Georgia 1790 federal census. It even includes many names for Burke and Washington Counties which suffered severe record loss in the early years. For information on how to obtain this book search by the title or "Books by John Stemmons" at Amazon.com. This comes automatically with a paperback binding. It includes but is not limited to petitions regarding:

- Issues regarding local agencies, boundary changes, etc.
- Issues regarding religion and churches.
- Issues about military and local officers.
- Asking for measures to control slaves.
- Recommendation for a business opportunity.
- Seeking resolution of land problems, land fraud, etc.
- Asking for increased tobacco inspection fees.
- Request for protection against Indians.
- Issues about crimes, pardon, amnesty, etc.
- Description of hardship.

367 pages $73.40

IL-01 ILLINOIS PETITIONS, ETC., 1760-1810 [1755-1814]© Compiled by John D Stemmons, 2021, this book contains 3680 names from *The Territorial Papers of the U.S.* This covers a period of time even before the federal census of 1790. And while no federal censuses exists for Illinois from 1790-1810, these records nicely substitute for those missing documents. It should be noted that 1004-**A PARTIAL CENSUS FOR INDIANA TERRITORY 1810** includes most if not all the names for 1810. A study to determine that they were the same was inconclusive and so, just in the outside chance there might be some that were not the same, it was felt that they should be included. The convenience of having them together outweighs their exclusion. These records include an incredible amount of information about these early people. One can see the change from a mostly French culture to that of English. The transition was not always peaceful. Included are census records, lists of inhabitants, and much more. While the federal censuses are missing that would help track these people, these records are even better in some respects than the census because it helps us understand some of the challenges they faced. That is why this new book can help. Some additional biographical details may be included, plus possible relationships with other family members. For information on how to obtain this book search by the title or "Books by John Stemmons" at Amazon.com. This comes automatically with a paperback binding. It includes but is not limited to petitions regarding:

- Issues relating to land.
- Issues relating to Native Americans.
- List of inhabitants at Kaskaskias before 1783.
- Appointments about military and local officers, etc.
- Lands claimed and possessed by inhabitants of the District of Cahokia on or before 1783 that still existed after 29 May 1790.
- Applications for lands in the District of Cahokia by persons claiming as settlers under the state of Virginia, if the settlements were made on or before 1783 that still existed after 29 May 1790.
- List of families at the Prairie du Pont, undated, but enclosed in St. Clair's report 10 Feb 1791.

349 Pages $69.80

IN-01 THE TERRITORY NORTHWEST OF THE RIVER OHIO, PETITIONERS, ETC., 1790-1800 [1785-1804] (Present day Indiana)© Compiled by John D Stemmons, 2021. This book was compiled from *Territorial Papers of the United States*. 1790 contains 242 names found on petitions, etc., including a census of heads of household for Vincennes. 1800 only includes 76 names and so is not as valuable as 1790. The population of Indiana would have increased significantly between 1790 and 1800. This is still a very early time prior to Indiana becoming a state. Unfortunately, there is no 1790 or 1800 census existing to help track these people. Therefore, we must do what we can with what is available. That is why this new book is so helpful. It is even better in some respects than the census because it helps us understand some of the challenges they faced. It also makes possible the determination of other records that might be available for further research such as land grants. Even the names of some Native

Americans are listed. Some additional biographical details may be included, plus possible relationships with other family members. For information on how to obtain this book search by the title or "Books by John Stemmons" at Amazon.com. This comes automatically with a paperback binding. It includes but is not limited to petitions regarding:

- Issues relating to land.
- Heads of families settled at Post Vincennes on or before 1783 and residents at this time [13 Jul 1790] who are entitled to donation lands.
- Issues relating to Native Americans.
- Inhabitants of Vincennes who migrated to Vincennes around 1786 and received land, but never obtained a deed.
- Appointments about military and local officers, etc.

38 Pages $7.60

1003-INDIANA ELECTION RETURNS 1809, 1812© Compiled by John D and E. Diane Stemmons, 2004. This compilation of 3576 entries includes the names found in the territorial election returns which documents are in the Indiana Historical Society. Also included is a poll book of an election for Dearborn County in 1809 as found in *Territorial Papers of the United States*. All entries in this book are also found in *A Partial Census for Indiana Territory 1810*. The book *Indiana Election Returns, 1809, 1812* was compiled for just the election returns simply because they are one entire record source and may have some value in that. For information on how to obtain this book search by the title or "Books by John Stemmons" at Amazon.com. This comes automatically with a paperback binding.

285 pages $57.00

1004-A PARTIAL CENSUS FOR INDIANA TERRITORY 1810© Compiled by John D and E. Diane Stemmons, 2021. With 8602 entries this book includes name lists found in *Territorial Papers of the United States* for Indiana Territory during the period 1805 through 1814. It also provides the names in *Indiana Election Returns 1809, 1812* listed above. Since there were approximately 4300 heads of households in the territory in 1810, *A Partial Census for Indiana Territory 1810* probably lists virtually every head of household in Indiana Territory for the time period. It makes an excellent substitute for the missing federal census for 1810. In addition, it includes names of people living in what is now Illinois, but which was part of Indiana Territory before 1809. Therefore, *A Partial Census for Indiana Territory 1810* is also a partial census of Illinois in the years between 1805 to 1809. For information on how to obtain this book search by the title or "Books by John Stemmons" at Amazon.com. This comes automatically with a paperback binding. It includes but is not limited to petitions regarding:

- Issues relating to land.
- Heads of families settled at Post Vincennes on or before 1783 and residents at this time [13 Jul 1790] who are entitled to donation lands.
- Issues relating to Native Americans.
- Inhabitants of Vincennes who migrated to Vincennes around 1786 and received land, but never obtained a deed.
- Appointments about military and local officers, etc.

574 pages $114.80

KY-01 KENTUCKY 1800, BARREN COUNTY TAX BOOK© Compiled by John D Stemmons, 2021. It contains 494 names from the Barren County tax list and 1 from *The Territorial Papers of the U.S.* Even though the 1800 census is missing this list it provides an amazing amount of information that substitutes nicely for that missing census, including white and black males aged 16-21 and those 21 and over. This is the kind of information one would expect to find on the census for that period. This list includes all taxable heads of household. Some additional biographical details may be included, plus possible relationships with other family members. The names of the blacks may be found in court, land, and probate records. For information on how to obtain this book search by the title or "Books

by John Stemmons" at Amazon.com. This comes automatically with a paperback binding.
65 Pages $13.00

LA-01 ARKANSAS PETITIONS 1800 [1795-1804] and ORLEANS TERRITORY (NOW LOUISIANA) PETITIONS, ETC., 1800 [1795-1804]© Compiled by John D Stemmons, 2021. This book was compiled from *Territorial Papers of the United States* and contains 495 names for Louisiana and 3 from Arkansas. Since no federal census exists for Arkansas and Louisiana for 1800, these records nicely substitute for those missing documents. These records include an incredible amount of information about these early people. While the federal censuses are missing that would help track these people, these records are even better in some respects than the census because it helps us understand some of the challenges they faced. That is why this new book can help. Some additional biographical details may be included, plus possible relationships with other family members. For information on how to obtain this book search by the title or "Books by John Stemmons" at Amazon.com. This comes automatically with a paperback binding. It includes but is not limited to petitions regarding:

- Inhabitants of Pointe Coupee to Gov. Claiborne, requesting military aid because of fears of a slave revolt.
- Characterization of New Orleans residents, 1 July 1804.
- Address from the free people of color Jan. 1804, volunteering for military service.
- Memorial to Congress from merchants of New Orleans, 9 Jan 1804, offering allegiance to the US.
- Appointments about military and local officers, etc.

47 Pages $9.40

MO-01 MISSOURI PETITIONERS, ETC., 1780-1820 [1775-1824]© Compiled by John D Stemmons, 2021. This book was compiled from *Territorial Papers of the United States* and contains 1 name for 1780, 12 names for 1790, 19 names for 1800, 5057 names for 1810, and 1509 names for 1820. The later lists begin to approach the number needed to include most heads of household, and nicely substitute for missing or no censuses. These records include an incredible amount of information about these early people. While censuses help track people, the records this book includes are even better in some respects than the census because it helps us understand some of their personal feelings and challenges, they faced. Some additional biographical details may be included, plus possible relationships with other family members. For information on how to obtain this book search by the title or "Books by John Stemmons" at Amazon.com. This comes automatically with a paperback binding. It includes but is not limited to petitions, etc., regarding:

- Resolution recommending distinction between Americans and Frenchmen should be done away.
- Letter from U.S. President to Chief White Hairs and the warriors of the Osages, informing them of the Lewis and Clark expedition, and promising them a resident agent.
- Many petitions, etc., expressing their support and confidence in Governor Wilkinson. He was involved in scandals and controversies.
- Memorial recommending replacements for Governor Wilkinson.
- Petition expressing concern about changing the form of territorial government before they are adequately prepared.
- Memorial concerning the large number of their Spanish land claims that are being rejected.
- Lists of civil and military officers.
- Petition seeking a grant of a township of land for the support of the school as had been done in other areas.
- Petition seeking pre-emption rights for the services given in defending the frontier in Boon's Lick Settlement around 1815.
- Petitions relating to the New Madrid & Little Prairie earthquake.

- Petitions asking for new post offices and routes, etc.

552 pages $110.40

MI-01 MICHIGAN PETITIONS, ETC. 1790-1810 [1785-1814]© Compiled by John D Stemmons, 2021. This book was compiled from *Territorial Papers of the United States*. It contains 1 name for 1790, 794 names for 1800, and 1335 names for 1810. Clearly, that is not enough for 1790, but the others begin to approach the number needed. Especially is this so for 1810 because we are fortunate enough to have much of what appears to be the federal 1810 census. Since no federal census exists for 1800, these records nicely substitute for those missing documents. These records include an incredible amount of information about these early people. While censuses help track people, the records this book includes are even better in some respects than the census because it helps us understand some of their personal feelings and challenges, they faced. Some additional biographical details may be included, plus possible relationships with other family members. For information on how to obtain this book search by the title or "Books by John Stemmons" at Amazon.com. This comes automatically with a paperback binding. It includes but is not limited to petitions regarding:

- Inhabitants of Detroit seeking new territory because of distance to travel to the headquarters of Indiana Territory.
- Appointments about military and local officers, etc.
- Inhabitants of Wayne County seeking clarification of the status of their land.
- 1810 Census of the District of Detroit.
- Inhabitants of Michigan Ter. seeking time to file claims to their land.
- List, 23 Jul 1812, of patents received from the General Land Office for private claims in the District of Detroit.
- Petition from inhabitants of Michigan Territory asking that the new territorial code be printed also in French.
- Petition to Thomas Jefferson, from inhabitants of Michigan Territory complaining of Governor William Hull and Supreme Court Chief Justice Augustus B. Woodward.

222 Pages $44.40

MS-01 MISSISSIPPI TERRITORIAL PETITIONERS, ETC. 1800 [1795-1804]© Compiled by John D Stemmons, 2021. This book was compiled from *Territorial Papers of the United States and* contains 2566 names found on petitions, etc., from Mississippi Territory for this time period. This was during a fast-growing era prior to Mississippi becoming a state. Unfortunately, there is no 1800 census existing to help track these people. That is why this new book can help. It is even better in some respects than the census because it helps us understand some of the challenges they faced. It also makes possible the determination of other records that might be available for further research such as Spanish land grants. Some additional biographical details may be included, plus possible relationships with other family members. For information on how to obtain this book search by the title or "Books by John Stemmons" at Amazon.com. This comes automatically with a paperback binding. It includes but is not limited to petitions regarding:

- Citizens of territory asking land office to be in the area, settlers have pre-emption right, & suffrage be for males of age and US citizens & residents of territory for 6 months.
- Memorial by citizens of the territory, who obtained land before the area became part of the US.
- Testimonials, ca 1802, by individuals regarding the service of John Steele, secretary of the territory.
- Memorial by citizens of the territory seeking that "moderate grants [be] made to actual settlers on unappropriated lands,"
- Merchants of Natchez, complaining of the extra duties they must pay for merchandise shipped from the US.

209 Pages $41.80

MS-02 **MISSISSIPPI TERRITORIAL PETITIONS, ETC. 1810 [1805-1814] and WEST FLORIDA 1820 PETITIONERS [1815-1824]**© Compiled by John D Stemmons, 2021. This book was compiled from *Territorial Papers of the United States* and contains 1061 names found on petitions, etc., from Mississippi Territory for the period 1810 [1805-1814]. It also includes a list of 76 names on a petition to Congress, 11 Dec 1816, by inhabitants of Jackson County, Mississippi Territory, many of whom settled on land in West Florida while under Spanish control and now seek for their grant to be confirmed by the US. It is being included with Mississippi Territory because it is basically the same time period and place of residence. This was during a fast-growing time prior to Mississippi and Florida becoming states. Unfortunately, there is no 1810 or 1820 census existing to help track these people. That is why this new book can help. It is even better in some respects than the census because it helps us understand some of the challenges they faced. It also makes possible the determination of other records that might be available for further research. Some additional biographical details may be included, and possible relationships with others may be revealed. For information on how to obtain this book search by the title or "Books by John Stemmons" at Amazon.com. This comes automatically with a paperback binding. It includes but is not limited to petitions regarding:

- Inhabitants of the territory seeking adjustment of land claims obtained from the British Government.
- Inhabitants of the territory seek for a road to be built that follows the Pearl River which would shorten the route from Nashville to New Orleans.
- Inhabitants of Amite and Wilkinson Counties seek establishment of a post office.
- Memorial by citizens of the territory (Americans by birth?) seeking a postponement of statehood for the territory.
- Inhabitants of Jackson Co., Mississippi Territory, many of whom settled on land in West Florida while under Spanish control seek for their grant to be confirmed by the US.

108 Pages $21.60

NJ-01-**NEW JERSEY PETITIONS 1740, 1745 THROUGH 1754**© Compiled by John D Stemmons, 2021. It contains 740 entries for a period of time in New Jersey when records are sparse. While that may not seem like very many names, it was during the time when the population was small, and the residence of people was sometimes hard to track. In looking through these petitions, it appears that the people of this era had basically the same concerns we have. One can see the forces of democracy beginning to stir that were to result in independence from Great Britain just a short three decades away. We can obtain a hint of the personal concerns of these people and what was important to them in this exciting historical time. Even at this time of great distress and hardship life had to go on. These petitions are almost like an open window into the lives of these people. For information on how to obtain this book search by the title or "Books by John Stemmons" at Amazon.com. This comes automatically with a paperback binding. It includes but is not limited to petitions regarding:

- Issues regarding exports and imports.
- Issues regarding devaluation of currency, money supply, etc.
- Issues regarding local agencies, boundary changes, etc.
- Seeking new legislation.
- Issues about military and government officers.
- Seeking resolution of land problems, etc.
- Protesting against the great number of taverns.
- Resolution of tax issues.
- Issues about crimes, pardon, amnesty, etc.

84 pages $16.80

NJ-02-**NEW JERSEY PETITIONS 1755-1764**© Compiled by John D Stemmons, 2004. Contains 2389 entries from many petitions submitted because of concerns about the French and Indian War. This book is an excellent census substitute. For information on how to obtain this book search by the title or "Books by John Stemmons" at Amazon.com. This comes automatically with a paperback binding. It includes petitions regarding:

- Issues regarding local agencies, boundary changes, etc.
- Issues about roads, bridges, etc.
- Opposition to importing slaves.
- Seeking naturalization.
- Seeking new legislation.
- Issues about military and government affairs.
- Request for reimbursement from the government.
- Request for protection against enemies.
- Seeking resolution of land problems, etc.
- Protesting against dispensing of "spirituous liquors"
- Issues about crimes, pardon, amnesty, etc.
- Description of hardship.

246 pages $49.20

NJ-03-**NEW JERSEY PETITIONS 1765-1774**© Compiled by John D Stemmons, 2004. This book contains 806 entries. While a small percent of the population, it represents the time leading up to the Revolution. For information on how to obtain this book search by the title or "Books by John Stemmons" at Amazon.com. This comes automatically with a paperback binding. It includes but is not limited to petitions regarding:

- Issues regarding agriculture, exports and imports.
- Request for permission to beg, financial support, etc.
- Issues about religion and churches.
- Request for medical standards.
- Issues regarding devaluation of currency, money supply, etc.
- Issues regarding local agencies, boundary changes, etc.
- Issues on hunting, fishing, etc.
- Issues about roads, bridges, etc.
- Issues relating to slavery.
- Issues about military and government affairs.
- Seeking resolution of land problems, etc.
- Issues about crimes, pardon, amnesty, etc.

99 pages $19.80

NJ-04-**NEW JERSEY PETITIONS 1775-1784**© Compiled by John D Stemmons, 2005. This book contains 6201 entries which is about 29% of the heads of household living in New Jersey at that time (not counting duplicate names.) It represents the historic period during the Revolution. For information on how to obtain this book search by the title or "Books by John Stemmons" at Amazon.com. This comes automatically with a paperback binding. It includes but is not limited to petitions regarding:

- Issues regarding trade, exports, and imports.
- Issues regarding devaluation of currency, money supply, price controls, etc.
- Issues on religion and churches.
- Issues regarding local agencies, boundary changes or disputes, etc.
- Issues on court cases.
- Request for guardianship of children.
- Issues about roads, bridges, canals, etc.
- Issues on slavery.
- Seeking new legislation or repealing old laws.
- Issues about military and government affairs and officers.
- Issues about payment from the government.
- Issues on independence and the Revolutionary War.
- Request for protection against enemies.
- Seeking resolution of property and land problems, etc.
- Issues about crimes, pardon, amnesty, etc.
- Resolution of tax issues.

559 pages $111.80

NJ-05-**NEW JERSEY PETITIONS 1785-1794 Volumes 1-2**©
Compiled by John D Stemmons, 2005. This book contains 10,353
entries which covers about 35% of the heads of household for that
time, not counting duplicate names. For information on how to obtain
this book search by the title or "Books by John Stemmons" at
Amazon.com. This comes automatically with a paperback binding. It
includes but is not limited to petitions regarding:
- Economic issues regarding the devaluation of currency, public debt, etc.
- Issues on religion and churches.
- Issues regarding counties and towns, etc.
- Issues on court cases.
- Issues regarding hunting on private property, fishing, etc.
- Issues about roads, bridges, canals, ferries, etc.
- Issues relating to schools.
- Issues on slavery.
- Seeking new legislation or repealing existing laws.
- Issues about military and government affairs and officers.
- Seeking payment from the government.
- Expressing approval of the U.S. Constitution.
- Seeking resolution of property and land problems, etc.
- Issues about crimes, pardon, amnesty, etc.
- Resolution of tax issues.

Volume 1, A Through K, pages 462 $92.40
Volume 2, L Through Z, pages 470 $94.00

NJ-06 **NEW JERSEY PETITIONERS, ETC., 1800 [1795-1804]
Volumes 1-3**© Compiled by John Stemmons, 2021. All volumes of
this book contain 13,144 names. Unlike the tax ratables, these records
cover the entire state for the period just after the Revolutionary War
These records provide a place of residence which can lead to other
records to search. For information on how to obtain this book search
by the title or "Books by John Stemmons" at Amazon.com. This
comes automatically with a paperback binding. It includes but is not
limited to petitions regarding:
- Public buildings including poor house, taverns, banks, etc.
- Issues on religion and churches.
- Issues regarding counties and towns, etc.
- Issues on court cases.
- Concerning voting opportunities
- Issues about roads, bridges, canals, ferries, water rights, storage of gunpowder, etc.
- Issues relating to schools.
- Issues on slavery.
- Seeking new legislation or repealing existing laws.
- Issues about military and government affairs and officers.
- Seeking payment from the government.
- Seeking resolution of property and land problems, etc.
- Issues about crimes, pardon, amnesty, etc.
- Resolution of tax issues.

Volume 1, A Through E, pages 423 $84.60
Volume 2, F Through R, pages 529 $105.80
Volume 3, S Through Z, pages 358 $71.60

NJ-07 **NEW JERSEY TAX RATABLES, 1770 [1765-1774]** This
book contains 2373 names of those who are taxable. They do include
important details about the property they held and may provide clues
regarding relationship, etc. For information on how to obtain this book
search by the title or "Books by John Stemmons" at Amazon.com.
This comes automatically with a paperback binding.
250 pages $50.00

NJ-08 **NEW JERSEY TAX RATABLES, 1780 [1775-1784]** This
book contains 4358 names of those who are taxable. It includes
important details about the property they held and may provide clues
regarding relationship, etc. For information on how to obtain this book
search by the title or "Books by John Stemmons" at Amazon.com.
This comes automatically with a paperback binding.

440 pages $88.00

NJ-09 **NEW JERSEY TAX RATABLES, 1790 [1785-1794]** This
book contains 2307 names of those who are taxable. Unfortunately,
Burlington and Cape May counties are not covered by this period. We
are fortunate though in have the petitions that cover the same time. It
is interesting to compare the two sets of records. They were not
combined because that would make the books too large. The tax
ratables do include important details about the property they held and
may provide clues regarding relationship, etc. For information on how
to obtain this book search by the title or "Books by John Stemmons"
at Amazon.com. This comes automatically with a paperback binding.
268 pages $53.60

NJ-10 **NEW JERSEY TAX RATABLES, 1800 [1795-1804] ,
Volumes 1-2** This book contains 8396 names of those who are
taxable. It includes important details about the property they held and
may provide clues regarding relationship, etc. For information on how
to obtain this book search by the title or "Books by John Stemmons"
at Amazon.com. This comes automatically with a paperback binding.
Volume 1, A Through K, pages 456 $91.20
Volume 2, L Through Z, pages 449 $89.80

NC-01 **NORTH CAROLINA PETITIONERS, ETC. 1780 [1775-
1784]**© Compiled by John Stemmons, 2021. This book contains 4866
names and was assembled from records located at the North Carolina
State Archives. This was before the federal census was taken and is a
valuable resource for locating people in this early time. Included are
some names from what is now, Tennessee. For information on how to
obtain this book search by the title or "Books by John Stemmons" at
Amazon.com. This comes automatically with a paperback binding.
- Economic issues regarding the devaluation of currency, public debt, etc.
- Issues on religion and churches.
- Issues regarding counties and towns, etc.
- Issues regarding hunting on private property, fishing, etc.
- Issues about roads, bridges, canals, ferries, etc.
- Seeking new legislation or repealing existing laws.
- Issues about military and government affairs and officers.
- Seeking resolution of property and land problems, etc.
- Issues about crimes, pardon, amnesty, etc.

568 pages $113.60

1009-**ROWAN COUNTY, NORTH CAROLINA TAX LISTS
1758/1759, 1761, 1768, 1778, 1779**© Compiled by John D and E.
Diane Stemmons, 2004. This publication serves as a census for Rowan
County for about three decades which includes two major conflicts,
the French and Indian and Revolutionary wars. Thus, one may be able
to track individuals that stayed in the county over a significant period
of time. Sometimes sons and slaves are given plus other important
information. These tax lists are listed alphabetically in three separate
sections.
218 pages $43.60

OH-01 **TERRITORY NW OF OHIO RIVER, PETITIONERS,
ETC. 1790-1800 [1785-1804] (Now Ohio)**© Compiled by John D
Stemmons, 2021. It contains 217 names for 1790 and 3047 names for
1800. This book may include many heads of household at that time
and serves as a substitute for missing or no censuses. It even
incorporates the names of many native Americans. These records
provide an incredible amount of information about these early people.
While censuses help track people, the records this book contains are
even better in some respects than the census because it helps us
understand some of their personal information not recorded by a
census. Some additional biographical details may be included, plus
possible relationships with other family members. For information on
how to obtain this book search by the title or "Books by John
Stemmons" at Amazon.com. This comes automatically with a
paperback binding. It includes but is not limited to petitions regarding:

- Petition of the French inhabitants of Gallipolis regarding their purchase of lands from the Scioto Company.
- Inhabitants on the Muskingum to Governor St. Clair.
- Petitions about land and issues with John Cleves Symmes.
- 1800, Population Schedules, Washington County. Territory Northwest of the River Ohio.
- Petition by inhabitants telling of losses in the "Late Indian war" and their inability to obtain land in Kentucky.
- Petition by inhabitants of Hamilton County seeking approval to purchase reserved land in order to build a grist mill because it has a sufficient stream of water.
- List of Gallipolis proprietors and the amount of their land purchases.

285 pages $57.00

PA-01 PENNSYLVANIA CHESTER COUNTY TAX LIST 1771© Compiled by John D Stemmons, 2021. It contains 5621 names. This record lists all taxable people in the county, and as such, is a good census substitute. It is not known what is meant by the abbreviations or "inmate". Perhaps they were incarcerated in jail or were indentured in some way. Often an occupation is listed. Occasionally there will be information about family relationships. It is helpful that this book includes the information about the taxable property. For information on how to obtain this book search by the title or "Books by John Stemmons" at Amazon.com. This comes automatically with a paperback binding.
399 pages $79.80

South Carolina

South Carolina has a remarkable series of records that makes it unique for the Colonial period. These are the "Jury Lists" compiled by the government to function as a list of names from which members of a jury could be assigned. They cover the period 1720-1783 and, according to the act in 1731, were compiled from tax lists of the preceding year [which no longer exist], listing every person who paid a tax of twenty shillings or more. Those who paid five pounds or more were listed as grand jurors. The poorer class of people would not be listed. While not a complete list of the heads of household, they represent a sizeable proportion. They serve as a census during a period of growth, migration, and war. Usually only the name is given, but sometimes an occupation or name of the father is listed, etc. Many names are on more than one list for a particular year.

1010-SOUTH CAROLINA 1720 JURY LIST© Compiled by John D and E. Diane Stemmons, 2004. This publication has 840 entries covering a time when South Carolina was only 50 years old and the population was very small with only an estimated 885 heads of household. Unfortunately, it does not list a residence other than South Carolina. For information on how to obtain this book search by the title or "Books by John Stemmons" at Amazon.com. This comes automatically with a paperback binding.
48 pages $9.60

1017-SOUTH CAROLINA 1731 JURY LIST© Compiled by John D and E. Diane Stemmons, 2005. This book contains 2160 entries. It lists the locality of every person. For information on how to obtain this book search by the title or "Books by John Stemmons" at Amazon.com. This comes automatically with a paperback binding.
110 pages $22.00

1011-SOUTH CAROLINA 1740 JURY LIST© Compiled by John D and E. Diane Stemmons, 2004. This book contains 2160 entries. It lists the locality of every person. For information on how to obtain this book search by the title or "Books by John Stemmons" at Amazon.com. This comes automatically with a paperback binding.
111 pages $22.20

1012-SOUTH CAROLINA 1751 JURY LIST© Compiled by John D and E. Diane Stemmons, 2004. This book contains 2170 entries. It lists the locality of every person. For information on how to obtain this book search by the title or "Books by John Stemmons" at Amazon.com. This comes automatically with a paperback binding.
109 pages $21.80

1013-SOUTH CAROLINA 1757 JURY LIST© Compiled by John D and E. Diane Stemmons, 2004. This book contains 2624 entries. It lists the locality of every person. For information on how to obtain this book search by the title or "Books by John Stemmons" at Amazon.com. This comes automatically with a paperback binding.
135 pages $27.00

1014-SOUTH CAROLINA 1767 JURY LIST© Compiled by John D and E. Diane Stemmons, 2004. This book contains 2385 entries. It lists the locality of every person. For information on how to obtain this book search by the title or "Books by John Stemmons" at Amazon.com. This comes automatically with a paperback binding.
127 pages $25.40

SC-07 SOUTH CAROLINA 1780 [1775-1784], VOLUMES 1-2© Compiled by John D Stemmons, 2021. It contains 13,444 names. This record of jury lists consist of many people during the Colonial/Revolutionary War period and as such, is a good census substitute. Since Loyalists owned property that they paid taxes on, they may be included as well. These records provide a place of residence which can lead to other records to search. For information on how to obtain this book search by the title or "Books by John Stemmons" at Amazon.com. This comes automatically with a paperback binding.
Volume 1, 502 pages $100.40
Volume 2, 575 pages $115.00

TN-01 TENNESSEE PETITIONS, ETC., 1770-1790 [1765-1794]© Also known as Territory South of Ohio River. Compiled by John Stemmons, 2021. This book was assembled from *Territorial Papers of the United States* and contains 1 name for 1770, 12 names for 1780, and 1161 names for 1790. These people listed seem to be the more prominent persons, so, most of the less noteworthy individuals would not be listed. Still, the people listed clarify this early time before Tennessee became a state. The amount of biographical information is significant compared to the other books we have compiled from *Territorial Papers of the United States*. Many Native American names are included. For information on how to obtain this book search by the title or "Books by John Stemmons" at Amazon.com. This comes automatically with a paperback binding. It includes but is not limited to petitions regarding:

- "One of twelve men selected by the Cumberland people to govern the settlement, 1783; appointed by the Governor of North Carolina judge of the courts, Davidson County, 1783.
- Appointments about military and local officers, etc.
- Name on the "Treaty of Holston", 2 Jul 1791 between the President of the US and "Chiefs and Warriors of the Cherokee Nation of Indians."
- Memorial, 1 Aug 1791, to the President from the civil and military officers of Mero District explaining recent depredations of the Indians and seeking an "Act of Cession" from North Carolina.

95 pages $19.00

TN-02 TENNESSEE PETITIONERS, ETC. AND GRAINGER COUNTY TAX LISTS 1800 [1795-1804]© Compiled by John Stemmons, 2021. Also known as Territory South of Ohio River. This book was assembled from Grainger County Tax Lists 1800 and *Territorial Papers of the United States* and contains 182 names for the *Papers* and 247 names for the tax lists. From *Territorial Papers of the United States* the names mostly seem to be persons appointed to official or military positions or are members of the Knoxville Convention. Thus, they seem to be the more prominent persons, so, most of the less noteworthy individuals would not be listed. Still, the people listed clarify this early time before Tennessee became a state.

The tax lists record the names of those who are taxable and are much more inclusive. They do include important details about the property they held. For information on how to obtain this book search by the title or "Books by John Stemmons" at Amazon.com. This comes automatically with a paperback binding. It includes but is not limited to petitions regarding:
- List, 21 Dec 1795, of members of Knoxville Convention.
- Appointments of military and local officers, etc.

49 pages					$9.80

TN-03 **TENNESSEE GRAINGER COUNTY TAX LISTS 1810 [1805-1814]**© Compiled by John Stemmons, 2021. This book was assembled from Grainger County Tax Lists 1810 and contains 1242 names of those who are taxable. They do include important details about the property they held and may provide clues regarding relationship, etc. For information on how to obtain this book search by the title or "Books by John Stemmons" at Amazon.com. This comes automatically with a paperback binding.
146 pages					$29.20

TN-04 **TENNESSEE GRAINGER COUNTY TAX LISTS 1820 [1815-1824]**© Compiled by John Stemmons, 2021. This book was assembled from Grainger County Tax Lists 1820 and contains 1161 names of those who are taxable. They do include important details about the property they held and may provide clues regarding relationship, etc. The lists for 1800-1820 furnish an excellent opportunity to track the population growth of the county. For information on how to obtain this book search by the title or "Books by John Stemmons" at Amazon.com. This comes automatically with a paperback binding.
131 pages					$26.20

VA-01 **VIRGINIA PERSONAL PROPERTY TAX LISTS, 1780 [1775-1784]** (Accomack and Albemarle Counties)© Compiled by John Stemmons, 2021. This book was assembled from Accomack and Albemarle Counties Personal Property Tax Lists ca 1780 and contains 2553 names of those who are taxable. They do include important details about the property they held and may provide clues regarding relationship, etc. They even furnish the entry for, it is assumed, future president Thomas Jefferson! For information on how to obtain this

book search by the title or "Books by John Stemmons" at Amazon.com. This comes automatically with a paperback binding.
252 pages					$50.40

VA-02 **VIRGINIA PERSONAL PROPERTY TAX LISTS, 1790 [1785-1794]** (Accomack and Albemarle Counties)© Compiled by John Stemmons, 2021. This book was assembled from Accomack and Albemarle Counties Personal Property Tax Lists ca 1790 and contains 2679 names of those who are taxable, plus 3 from *Territorial Papers of the U.S.* They do include important details about the property they held and may provide clues regarding relationship, etc. They even furnish the entry for, it is assumed, future president Thomas Jefferson! Data on the age range of males is also included. For information on how to obtain this book search by the title or "Books by John Stemmons" at Amazon.com. This comes automatically with a paperback binding.
333 pages					$66.60

VA-03 **VIRGINIA PERSONAL PROPERTY TAX LISTS, ca 1800 [1795-1804]** (Accomack and Albemarle Counties)© Compiled by John Stemmons, 2021. This book was assembled from Accomack and Albemarle Counties Personal Property Tax Lists ca 1800 and contains 3788 names of those who are taxable. They do include important details about the property they held and may provide clues regarding relationship, etc. They even furnish the entry for, it is assumed, future president Thomas Jefferson! Data on the age range of males is also included. With the lists for 1780-1800 one can track population growth in these countries. An individual showing up for the first time may indicate potential age. For information on how to obtain this book search by the title or "Books by John Stemmons" at Amazon.com. This comes automatically with a paperback binding.
436 pages					$87.20

Population estimates were obtained from U.S. Bureau of the Census, *Historical Statistics of the United States, Colonial Times to 1957*, Washington, D.C., 1960, Library of Congress Card No. A 60-9150; and United States. Bureau of the Census, *A Century of Population Growth From the First Census of the United States to the Twelfth, 1790-1900* Washington: Government Printing Office, 1909. A household size of 5.7 persons was assumed.

Good morning.
We received the gift book of "Georgia Petitions 1785-1794". Fantastic book and a great tool in researching that time period. I like the format which is easy to read and puts in one place the petitions for research. I personally have searched many of the petitions and love this new tool. The introduction and the list of petitions gives much added information to understanding the petitions for the various individuals.
I look forward to ordering more books in July after our budget is in place. Thank you for contacting our library and making us aware of your fine publications. Have a great day.
Thanks,
Irene Godwin
Ellen Payne Odom Genealogy Library
204 5th St. S.E.
P.O. Box 2828
Moultrie, GA 31768

EXAMPLES OF THE KIND OF INFORMATION CONTAINED IN OUR BOOKS

Cicotte, J. Bte.,		Michigan Territory, District of Detroit, "Cote des Poux"

Cicotte, J. Bte.,	45-Over?	Male	**Color:**	White	
10-16		Male	**Color:**	White	
10-16		Male	**Color:**	White	
16-26		Male	**Color:**	White	
45-Over		Female	**Color:**	White	

1810 Census of the District of Detroit
MS/Witherell (B. F. H.) Collection, LMS, Burton Historical Collection, Detroit Public Library, Folder 2
Cicotte, Jacques,	Michigan Territory
	Cicotte, Jacques,		Male
Petition, 26 Oct 1807, to Congress from inhabitants of Michigan Ter. seeking time to file claims to their land, claims on 1+ parcels be confirmed, farms on Detroit River be extended to 80 arpents, & occupancy later than 1 Jul 1796 be allowed [pp. 138-49].
Territorial Papers of the US - volume: 10 page: 146

Holeday, Jas,   Territory NW of Ohio River   Knox County, Vincennes
          Holeday, Jas,   Male
Address to Colonel Josiah Harmar by American inhabitants of Post Vincennes dated 4 Aug 1787
Territorial Papers of US - volume: 2 page: 65
Holliday, Heirs of James,   Territory NW of Ohio River   Knox County, Vincennes
          Holliday, Heirs of James,   Male
Petition, 7 Aug 1797, to Congress by inhabitants of Knox County, who migrated to Vincennes around 1786 and received land, but never obtained a deed.
Territorial Papers of US - volume: 2 page: 621
Lajoye, Pierre ,   Spanish North America, St. Louis
          Lajoye, Pierre,   Male
          "Pierre Lajoye, formerly of Prairie du Rocher on the American side of the Mississippi".
Letter, 1790, by Governor St. Clair to Manuel Perez concerning an American boy in the possession of Pierre Lajoye [pages 237-238].
"Mr. Mayet has just complained to me that a Mr. La Joye, to whom he has entrusted an American boy, whom he took from the savages, to be returned to the parents of the latter, has not returned him, but is holding the boy as a slave and refuses to return the boy to them on the pretext of some debt. I am convinced that you will not find it proper that a free child should be held as a slave for the debts of another--and will order Mr. La Joye to return him to Mayet."
Letter, 26 May 1790, from St. Louis by Manuel Perez to Governor St. Clair concerning an American boy in the possession of Pierre Lajoye [pages 237-240]:
"MY DEAR SIR: In order to take cognizance of the subject of the claim in your favor of the 20th instant concerning the child who is today in the possession of Mr. Lajoye, I had the latter appear before me and from the questions which I put to him and the reasons which he advanced to me on this subject I have found in him only a disposition to render service to the Unhappy Father who lost him and who asks for him in a letter of which the said Mr. Lajoye is the bearer.
     After studying this matter carefully, I find that the above-mentioned child claimed by Mr. Mayet can leave the possession of Mr. Lajoye only to go to that of the Father now living at Natches. I think also that it is just for the said Mr. Mayet to be reimbursed for what he actually gave the savages in order to get him out of their barbarous hands; . . .
     When the young man arrived at Mr. Lajoye's house, he came and notified me of it at once and that he would write to the lower part of the Colony to learn in what district the Father of the said child lived. He learned later from the letter of which he is the bearer, that he resides at Natchez; accordingly he will send him down on the first opportunity."
Territorial Papers of the US - volume: 2 page: 237
Mayfield, Geddeon, Kentucky Barren County
          Mayfield, Geddeon,   Male
Acres of land: 200; Barren Co.; watercourse: Mill Creek; Entry: Geddeon Mayfield; Survey: same; Patent: 0; white males over 21: 0; white males 16-21: 0; blacks over 16: 0; total blacks: 0; horses: 0; stud horses: 0; retail stores: 0; tavern license: 0.
Barren County Tax Book, 1800, part 1 - page: 10 FAMILY HISTORY LIBRARY film 7865

LEGISLATIVE PETITIONS

Petitions to the governor, legislature, etc., were a particularly important way for individuals to communicate with their government regarding issues that were very essential to them. Their influence in making changes throughout our history has contributed to making our society what it is today. They are an important link in our legislative and judicial history. In these early petitions one can trace the growing desire for democracy. In fact, they are one of the most visible manifestations of democracy in practice. It is fascinating to view the changes in the reasons for submitting petitions over time (see the lists below.)

Because petitions represent the feelings of one or more individuals, they provide a window into the soul of the petitioners that illuminates the historical landscape. Most aspects of the human condition are addressed in some form by these important documents. The names listed with the petition can be used as a census of inhabitants for a particular locality. Often it is possible to determine useful information about individual persons from these records. They can help compensate for lost or destroyed county records. Petitions are original records that contain historical background about our culture and society.

Unfortunately, petitions are among the most inaccessible and underused records because there are so many, they are often difficult and time-consuming to read, and are usually housed only in the state archives or other repository in their un-microfilmed condition.

To help resolve this problem, we have abstracted the content of many petitions and indexed the names of the petitioners. A brief context of the petition is provided with each name. Generally, we have not included those petitions with fewer than 10-12 names.

GENEALOGY AND LOCAL HISTORY BOOKS IN PDF FORMAT ON A FLASH DRIVE

705 Local and Family History books for $75-or 11 cents a book!!! All 4 volumes of Savage's Genealogical Dictionary of New England would cost you about $0.44!*
You can have in your library/home more books of this type than most libraries have. They cover nearly all aspects of human experience including law, medicine, biography, history, etc., etc.

Concerns?
1. **Question:** I am uncomfortable in letting patrons use this small drive as it may become lost.
   Answer: Simply download the contents of the drive onto your computer(s) and keep the drive in a safe place. We will replace it at no charge if it becomes lost.
2. **Question:** Some of our books, including those on microfilm, that are also on your flash drive are in poor condition because of patron use through the years, especially when copies are made. Copies made from microfilm are not always the best quality. How can you help us with these problems?
   Answer: Once our books are on your computers, your originals can be kept in a secured area so that no more damage will occur because of hands-on use. The images on the computer can be easily printed, usually with better quality.
3. **Question:** We are only interested in items covering the locality our patrons live in.
   Answer: Many of your patrons were born outside of your area and/or have ancestry from all over the United States, etc.
4. **Question:** Are these books under copyright restrictions?
   Answer: They are in the public domain and so are not copyrightable.

Approximately how many pages do the 705 books add up to?
Total cost (from Stemmons Publishing) for hard copies: $7044 (not available now)
Approximated total pages of text on the flash drive: 221,307
Approximated total images on the flash drive: 58,272

A huge genealogical library of 705 books on your computer for only $75
A dealer's discount is available of $45 for 5 or more flash drives.
Imagine 705 books… 60,417 images… 230,642 pages on a small flash drive.

You may be able to find these books on Google, Ancestry, or FamilySearch. To make a hard copy from these sources may be expensive, especially if you were to copy all 705! I may be mistaken, but I'm not sure you can print just a single page from those services. You can with my books. You also have them immediately at your fingertips without needing to go to the effort to search these other services.
The downside to these books is that many are not indexed.
No problem: just check the index provided by these other sources before using our books.
"In 2016, popular genealogy blogger Dick Eastman surmised that perhaps ninety percent of the resources you may need to fill out your family tree are not yet available on the Internet." This statement was found on the Boston Public Library website. If that is true, some of the books on our flash drive may not be found on the Internet.

You may obtain a copy of the drive by sending check, money order, or cash to John Stemmons at 1078 Shields Lane, South Jordan, Utah, 801-254-2152 (Call between 9:00 a.m. and 5:00 p.m. Monday through Friday. If no one answers, please leave a message.), stemmonspublishing@gmail.com. We have been in this business since 1975! Check BBB if you need to.

The fee for shipping and handling is $10.00 unless you send a shipping container, deliverable to you, with sufficient postage to mail to you. Please allow 4-6 weeks for delivery.

The books on the drive are in the public domain and are not copyrighted. You may make as many copies of them as you would like. Please do not place the contents of the drive, in part or in full, on the Internet except for individual pages.

We do not do credit cards and PayPal. If you are unhappy with the drive, please return it for a refund of your money.

If you would like a list of questions and answers or a list of the books, please let us know.

*How are we able to do this? Simply by reducing each page so that 2-6 pages can be placed on a single 8½ by 11 sheet of paper and still be readable. With the computer, you can enlarge it as many times as needed.

Number of books by locality:

US-99, Regional-32, AL-1, CT-31, DE-1, GA-2, IL-1, IN-1, KY-1, ME-23, MD-15, MA-91, MI-1, MN-1, MO-2, NH-20, NJ-28, NY-81, NC-9, OH-9, PA-51, RI-6, SC-26, VT-2, VA-47, WV-1; Family History-62; CN-5; EN-39; IR-10; SCOT-7=705 books!